Canada's favourite ...sor

Tim Cestnick

Winning the Estate Planning Game

ESTATE PLANNING STRATEGIES FOR CANADIANS

Prentice Hall Canada

A Pearson Company
Toronto

Canadian Cataloguing in Publication Data

Cestnick, Timothy J., 1966–
Winning the estate planning game : estate planning strategies for Canadians

ISBN 0-13-028517-X

1. Estate planning – Canada. I. Title.
KE5974.C47 2000 332.024'01 C00-931460-1
KF750.C47 2000

ISBN 0-13-028517-X

Editorial Director, Trade Division: Andrea Crozier
Acquisitions Editor: Andrea Crozier
Managing Editor: Tracy Bordian
Copy Editor: Laurel Sparrow
Art Direction: Mary Opper
Cover and Interior Design: Gary Beelik
Cover Image: Kathleen Campbell/Tony Stone
Author Photograph: Kirk McGregor
Production Manager: Kathrine Pummell
Page Layout: Brian Taft/ArtPlus Limited

1 2 3 4 5 TC 05 04 03 02 01

Printed and bound in Canada.

Pearson Education Canada

A Pearson Company

Dedication

To my mom, dad, John, Grandma Preston, Grandma Cestnick, and my mother- and father-in-law, Burt and Margaret. Thank you for your love and support.

Acknowledgments

I know that this may sound presumptuous, but I'm expecting that this book will be a best-seller. The final product is something that I'm quite proud of, and I have a number of people to thank for this. First, I've got to thank my staff at The WaterStreet Group for their assistance with this book in so many ways. Specifically, I want to thank Karen Ellis, Leigh Vyn, CA, CFP, and Tim Purvis for their help. My friend and associate, Brian Quinlan, CA, at the firm Campbell Lawless is to be commended for his contributions to Chapter 7, and thanks to a number of my lawyer friends across Canada who assisted with different provincial issues. To Prentice Hall, I extend my warmest thanks for their patience as I finished this book—good things are worth waiting for (and wait they did!). Finally, thank you to my wife, Carolyn, and my children, Winston and Sarah, for their understanding every time I locked myself away to write.

Table of Contents

Estate Planning Tip Sheet

Let me make your life as easy as I can. I know that simply reading a book may not be enough to get you out of your seat and motivated to action. This *Estate Planning Tip Sheet* has been designed to make the design of your estate plan as easy as one, two, three. One: read each tip in the book. Two: flip back to this tip sheet and ask the question "Does this apply to me?", then answer "Yes," "No," or "Not Sure." Three: once you're done, revisit the "Yes" and "Not Sure" answers. These will form a list for further action. What type of action? It depends on the tip. Some tips will require a visit to a lawyer, some will require you to prepare lists, while others may simply require you to discuss issues with your family. If you're still confused about any particular strategy in the book, don't hesitate to take this tip sheet to a reputable financial advisor who can assist you in better understanding the concepts. Be careful out there—and remember, no one cares about your money as much as you do!

Tim's Tips	**Strategy**	**Does This Apply to Me?**		
		Yes	**No**	**Not Sure**
Chapter 1.	Preparing for the Final Lap: Estate Planning Basics			
1.	Understand what estate planning is.	○	○	○
2.	Identify your estate objectives before you go any further.	○	○	○
3.	Consider discussing your plans with your family, even though this may be uncomfortable.	○	○	○
4.	Be aware of family law issues that could impact your estate plan.	○	○	○
5.	Know which professionals should implement your estate plan.	○	○	○
Chapter 2.	Eyes on the Finish Line: Wills and Powers of Attorney			
6.	Understand the problems in dying without a will.	○	○	○
7.	Understand the basic format of most wills.	○	○	○

Tim's Tips	Strategy	Does This Apply to Me? Yes	No	Not Sure
8.	Recognize how and when to revise your will—then get a lawyer involved.	○	○	○
9.	Choose your executor with great care—it's the most important role to be filled once you're gone.	○	○	○
10.	Understand the variety of fees that could affect your estate after your death.	○	○	○
11.	Make sure that your will is prepared and signed properly, or you could die intestate.	○	○	○
12.	Take very seriously the drafting of clauses in your will—you could impact the lives of others.	○	○	○
13.	Know what it means to grant power of attorney over your affairs.	○	○	○
14.	Give careful consideration to who should be your attorney—it's an important responsibility.	○	○	○
15.	Understand the responsibilities and powers of the attorney you designate.	○	○	○
16.	Recognize that provinces can vary in their laws around powers of attorney.	○	○	○
Chapter 3.	Your Biggest Competitors: Death and Taxes			
17.	Be aware of the deemed disposition of your property immediately prior to your death.	○	○	○
18.	Recognize that your heirs will not pay tax on the inheritance you leave behind—just on the income afterwards.	○	○	○
19.	Learn to calculate capital gains and losses properly.	○	○	○
20.	Understand the exemptions available to shelter your capital gains on death from tax.	○	○	○
21.	Recognize the tax hit you'll face on death if you've got RRSP, RRIF, or other registered plan assets.	○	○	○
22.	Recognize the various other income and assets that can give rise to various taxes on your death.	○	○	○

Tim's Tips	Strategy	Does This Apply to Me? Yes	No	Not Sure
23.	Identify the tax returns which may be filed on your behalf after your death, and when they're due.	○	○	○
Chapter 4.	Winning the Race: Beating the Tax Collector at Death			
24.	Consider giving assets away today to reduce taxes at death.	○	○	○
25.	Understand how an estate freeze can cut, defer, and establish your tax bill on death, among other benefits.	○	○	○
26.	Reduce the tax hit on a second property by planning for its succession today.	○	○	○
27.	Designate the right person as the beneficiary of your RRSP or RRIF to minimize the tax hit.	○	○	○
28.	Arrange for a tax-free death benefit from your employer.	○	○	○
29.	Minimize the impact of U.S. estate taxes on your assets at the time of your death.			
30.	Leave it to your spouse to minimize a tax hit on death.	○	○	○
31.	Establish testamentary trusts in your will to save your heirs significant tax after you're gone.	○	○	○
32.	Consider donating assets to charity on death, and carefully choose how and which assets to donate.	○	○	○
33.	Recognize that an offshore inheritance trust can defer taxes for a significant time.	○	○	○
34.	Make note of the many elections that your executor should consider making after you're gone.	○	○	○
35.	Understand how any losses can be utilized after your death to save tax and provide a greater inheritance to your heirs.	○	○	○
36.	Utilize life insurance to provide the cash for taxes if you've got illiquid assets in your estate.	○	○	○

Tim's Tips	Strategy	Does This Apply to Me? Yes	No	Not Sure
Chapter 5.	Giving Your Best: The Art of Dying Broke Through Gifts			
37.	Beware of the deemed disposition at fair market value when giving assets away.	○	○	○
38.	Understand the impact of the attribution rules on any gifts that you make during your lifetime.	○	○	○
39.	Watch for the potential double-tax problem that can arise when selling assets at less than market value.	○	○	○
40.	Make tax-friendly gifts to your heirs during your lifetime to avoid an erosion of your estate.	○	○	○
41.	Consider changing the nature of the gift if you're concerned about continued control over the property.	○	○	○
42.	Consider taking advantage of the capital gains reserve when transferring assets to your heirs during your lifetime.	○	○	○
Chapter 6.	Ensuring First Place: Understanding the Life Insurance Maze			
43.	Identify the reasons you are buying life insurance before handing over any premiums.	○	○	○
44.	Understand the two broad types of insurance, then choose the type that suits your purposes.	○	○	○
45.	Determine how much insurance to purchase by first deciding the purpose and type of insurance.	○	○	○
46.	Consider an insured retirement plan as a top-up to your other retirement savings or pension plans.	○	○	○
47.	Consider investing in seg funds when the benefits outweigh the additional fees attached to them.	○	○	○
Chapter 7.	An Ally in the Race: Making the Most of Trusts			
48.	Recognize that a trust is not an entity—it's a relationship!	○	○	○
49.	Choose the right trustee for an inter vivos or testamentary trust.	○	○	○

Tim's Tips	Strategy	Does This Apply to Me? Yes	No	Not Sure
50.	Arrange for the terms of your trust to be drafted by a lawyer—not your brother-in-law.	○	○	○
51.	Understand how inter vivos and testamentary trusts are taxed.	○	○	○
52.	Be aware of the 21-year rule, which could trigger a huge tax hit down the road!	○	○	○
53.	Take advantage of an inter vivos trust to reduce taxes on death and protect your estate.	○	○	○
54.	Consider establishing an alter ego or joint spousal trust for a number of benefits.	○	○	○
55.	Take advantage of a testamentary trust to provide your heirs with tax savings and asset protection.	○	○	○
Chapter 8.	Passing the Baton: Solving the Business Succession Puzzle			
56.	Recognize the options that you have regarding the succession of your business.	○	○	○
57.	Consider the use of life insurance to fund a properly drafted buy–sell agreement.	○	○	○
58.	Understand the tax issues surrounding the succession of your business.	○	○	○
Chapter 9.	Helping Others in the Race: Planned Charitable Giving			
59.	Understand the tax relief that is available when you give, but make sure that your primary motivation is a desire to help.	○	○	○
60.	Structure gifts after your death properly in your will, or you may lose the donation credit in your final year.	○	○	○
61.	Recognize the various assets that can be given, then choose the ones that are best for you.	○	○	○
62.	Recognize the various vehicles through which gifts can be made.	○	○	○

Tim's Tips	Strategy	Does This Apply to Me? Yes	No	Not Sure
Chapter 10.	Bad News at the Finish Line: Handling Probate Fees			
63.	Understand the probate process and what it means to receive "letters probate."	○	○	○
64.	Recognize that probate fees are simply another type of tax, and can be minimized with proper planning.	○	○	○
Chapter 11.	Racing Down South: Canadians with U.S. Connections			
65.	Understand who is liable to pay tax in the U.S., and plan for those taxes if you're in this boat.	○	○	○
66.	Figure out whether you'll be liable for U.S. estate tax on death, then take steps to reduce the tax hit.	○	○	○
67.	Understand how the U.S. gift tax works, and how to avoid the tax where possible.	○	○	○
Chapter 12.	After the Race: Planning for Your Funeral			
68.	Provide clear instructions to your executor regarding your funeral plans—today.	○	○	○
69.	Understand the cost of various funeral options and don't pay more than you need to.	○	○	○
70.	Recognize the benefits of pre-planning your funeral.	○	○	○
71.	Consider donating your organs and carry a signed donor card.	○	○	○
72.	Pre-paying for your funeral could offer tax breaks among other benefits.	○	○	○

FOREWORD: BEATING THE BUZZER

In 1992, Jeremy Edge—an Owensboro, Kentucky, high-school basketball player—scored seven points in one second in a January game against Hancock County. Jeremy was fouled with one second left in the game and made both free throws. With the clock still stopped, a technical foul was called against Hancock County and Jeremy made both shots. When the ball was inbounded, he got off a three-point shot before the buzzer sounded. Seven points—and his team won by a point. How's that for coming up big before the final buzzer?

The problem is that most Canadians plan for their estates in the same way. Most simply delay and delay their planning until they figure that it just can't wait any longer—then they make a heroic effort just before the final buzzer, hoping that it will be enough. In many cases, it's not.

Call to Action

Waiting until the final buzzer to plan for your estate is a mistake! Take the situation, for example, where a friend of mine failed to make those changes to his will that he was meaning to make, or to establish powers of attorney, before suffering a mental incapacity. No, he didn't appear to be failing mentally, but it was happening ... slowly, subtlely. By the time that his family realized that he had failed to make the changes, it was too late. By law, he was not permitted to change his will.

Consider also the gentleman who passed his business to his son. He had wanted to protect the business from his son's wife in the event that the marriage didn't work out. This wasn't handled properly, and when divorce became a reality, she was entitled to nearly half of the value of the business.

Finally, think about the well-meaning woman who owned $100,000 worth of mutual funds and put her daughter's name on the account with her own. The woman did this to avoid probate fees on her death. You know what? She's going to avoid probate fees of $1,000 on her death, but she triggered a $10,000 tax bill in the process. Oops.

The point is, a little planning ahead of time can save you taxes during your lifetime, at the time of your death, and after you're gone. Proper planning can also ensure that your assets pass quickly and efficiently to your heirs.

So, this is a call to action. Act now, well ahead of the final buzzer!

Right Place at the Right Time

You're in the right place at the right time. The place I'm referring to is this book. The time? Today—before you're gone. I've designed this book to be very practical. There's no sense in filling your mind with useful information if it's just going to sit in a mental file folder. So, I've created the *Estate Planning Tip Sheet*. When you've finished each chapter, refer to the Tip Sheet at the front of the book where you'll find each of my tips listed. For each tip, ask the question: "Does this apply to me?" Then check the appropriate answer: "Yes," "No," or "Not sure." Each "Yes" or "Not Sure" response will form the basis for your complete estate plan once you've read the entire book. I recommend that you visit a reputable financial advisor once you've completed the *Estate Planning Tip Sheet*. Your advisor can assist you in properly implementing the ideas that apply to you.

Again, thanks for taking the time to read *Winning the Estate Planning Game*. I dare say that you, and your heirs, will be glad that you did!

Tim Cestnick, CA, CFP, TEP
February 2001

PREPARING FOR THE FINAL LAP: ESTATE PLANNING BASICS

Walk before you run, but then run to the finish—ahead of the tax collector.

1

You'll have to forgive me if you're not a sports fanatic. I am. It's sort of a Jekyll-and-Hyde syndrome with me. By day, I'm a mild-mannered bean counter, sitting at my desk reading tax stuff. By night, I'm a loud, boisterous, nervous wreck as I sit in front of the television, watching sports. Actually, not all sports can get me shouting at the television, demanding control over the TV remote, and generally insulting the competence of any pro athlete who makes a bad play. Basketball, for example, doesn't do it for me. Lawn bowling, on the other hand, can really get my blood boiling.

I must confess, I was thrilled to watch Donovan Bailey, Canada's foremost sprinter, race Michael Johnson—supposedly the fastest man in the U.S. at the time—over that 150-metre stretch at the Skydome in Toronto back on June 1, 1997. Watching Donovan take the prize made that 14.99-second race one of the most memorable sporting events of the decade.

Estate planning is all about the final lap of a very important race. A long-distance race—called life. Estate planning is all about finishing the race in the most efficient manner—ahead of the tax collector. The race takes planning. After all, you don't want to run out of steam, or financial resources, before you reach the finish line.

This chapter is about the basics. These are the things you should understand first, before plotting the estate planning strategy that is going to win you the race at the end of the day. So, lace up your shoes, and let's start this journey running.

Understanding Estate Planning

You've got to understand what estate planning is before you can put a proper estate plan into place.

Tim's Tip 1: Understand what estate planning is.

What is estate planning? It's simply the process of structuring your affairs to preserve your wealth and to transfer, in an orderly fashion, what's left at the time of your death to those of your choosing—whether family, friends, partners, or charities.

Let's look at this a little more closely.

It's simply the process of structuring your affairs...

That's right, estate planning is a proactive thing. It's going to take a little time (perhaps the time it takes to read this book) to identify how you should rearrange your current affairs, and then actually make those changes. For some, rearranging their affairs will be as simple as revising their will and adding a clause or two. For others, this rearrangement could mean setting up a family trust, completing an estate freeze, transferring ownership of assets today, or other measures—all of which I'll talk about in this book.

...to preserve your wealth and transfer, in an orderly fashion, what's left at the time of your death...

The idea here is to keep as much in your pocket as you can, and hand as little as possible to the tax collector. Why? It should be obvious. Whether you choose to spend more in retirement or pass it to your heirs, you—and not the tax collector—should be the one to decide whom your hard-earned money will ultimately benefit.

Keep in mind that anything you don't spend and you leave behind should transfer to your heirs in an orderly fashion. If you don't plan properly, things can get messy after you're gone. Your heirs will have enough emotional injury at the time of your death, so don't add insult by making it difficult or costly for a final distribution of your assets to take place. In the next chapter, when I talk about wills and powers of attorney, you'll come to understand some of the pitfalls to watch for.

...to those of your choosing—whether family, friends, partners, or charities.

Who is going to receive your assets after you're gone? I don't expect you'll include the tax collector in your list of heirs, but there's a particular comment that I hear once in a while. It's a comment that never ceases to amaze me. It goes something like this: "Tim, my kids have more than they need already. I'm quite content to let

Action Step

Regardless of your age, it's highly likely that you should prepare an estate plan. If you're a young family, there will be a need to provide for children in the event of a breadwinner's death and the need to appoint a guardian in the event that both parents die, among other things. Older folks are generally closer to that day when they won't be around anymore, so the need to do estate planning becomes more obvious. Take steps today to put a plan in place, and don't assume you're immortal just because you're young.

the government take its share of my estate when I'm gone, and the kids can have whatever is left over—and that will still be plenty for them."

Sorry, I can't buy that reasoning. It makes about as much sense as saying "Tim, I'm going to make sure that my kids inherit my entire estate, but I'm going to leave specific instructions in my will to ensure that they convert it to cash, shred a large portion of it, then burn it. After all, they don't need all of it."

You see, it may be true that your heirs will be just fine without that portion of your estate stolen by the tax collector. The question, however, is this: Why would you rather hand a large portion of your estate to someone you don't know personally, with no real idea where the money will end up, when reducing this tax collector's bite can be as simple as spending a couple of hours and a few bucks to plan your affairs? Give it to your heirs instead. Let them burn it if they don't need it.

TO MAKE A LONG STORY SHORT:

- Estate planning is the process of structuring your affairs to preserve your wealth and transfer, in an orderly fashion, what's left at the time of your death to those of your choosing. This is going to take some planning.
- Don't make the mistake of paying too much to the tax collector at the time of your death simply because your heirs will be fine without your money.

Tim's Tip 2: Identify your estate objectives before you go any further.

No two individuals are identical, and there's a good chance that your estate objectives are different from your neighbour's. Before you get too involved in the estate planning process, you've got to have a clear picture of what your estate objectives are. Why? Because any rearrangement of your affairs should accomplish your objectives—otherwise you've got to wonder why you're doing the rearranging.

This reminds me of a guy I knew in the past who stated, as one of his estate planning objectives, that he wanted to set up a testamentary trust on his death for the benefit of his children (I'll talk more about these trusts in Chapter 7). He then proceeded to put all his assets in joint names with his kids so that he could avoid probate fees at the time of his death (I'll talk more about probate fees in Chapter 10). The problem? Holding assets jointly will certainly avoid probate fees on death, but will also make it difficult, if not impossible, to leave those assets in a testamentary trust at the time of death. Oops.

What are your estate objectives? Let's identify them now. Below, you'll find a list that includes the most common objectives I've seen. In the left column, check off those that represent your objectives. Once you've done this, determine for each objective you've checked whether you want to accomplish this today (during your lifetime), on and/or after your death, or both, and check the appropriate boxes to the right. Finally, rank your objectives as best as you can. Number them in the right-most column, marking your most important objective as "1." Got it? Good.

	My Estate Planning Objectives	Today	On/After Death	Rank
❑	Minimize income tax bill	❑	❑	
❑	Pay off all debts	❑	❑	
❑	Simplify affairs	❑	❑	
❑	Donate money to charity	❑	❑	
❑	Provide for a disabled dependant	❑	❑	
❑	Reduce tax burden for heirs	❑	❑	
❑	Pay for education of a (grand)child	❑	❑	
❑	Split estate equally among heirs	❑	❑	
❑	Split estate fairly, but not equally	❑	❑	
❑	Minimize probate fees	N/A	❑	
❑	Minimize U.S. estate taxes	N/A	❑	
❑	Other:	❑	❑	
❑	Other:	❑	❑	
❑	Other:	❑	❑	
❑	Other:	❑	❑	

Great. This list of objectives will govern which of this book's strategies you'll want to include in your overall estate plan. By the way, there's a copy of this checklist at the back of the book in Appendix A. You can copy the above information there if you'd like to have it in an easily accessible place.

TO MAKE A LONG STORY SHORT:

- Everyone has different estate planning objectives.
- Using the checklist provided, you should identify your objectives so that you'll know which strategies will suit you best as you go through this book.
- This checklist is reproduced in Appendix A at the back.

Action Step

It's often a good idea to sit down with your kids to discuss your estate affairs at a time when everyone is home together—during the holiday season, for example. The meeting should be between you and your children only, with your lawyer present to answer any legal questions if you feel that this would be beneficial. Consider discussing with your kids: Whom you've appointed as executor and why, who is getting what and why, and your funeral wishes. You might also receive valuable input from them as to what they would each like to see happen.

Getting the Family Involved

Estate planning is not something that you should do in a vacuum. On the contrary, your family should be very aware of the planning you've done.

Tim's Tip 3: Consider discussing your plans with your family, even though this may be uncomfortable.

Sure, this task can be difficult. I'm talking about having a heart-to-heart with your kids or other heirs. You know, to fill them in on what your estate plan will accomplish. This will involve telling them what your will says, and sharing with them your intentions. The benefit of being open and honest about your affairs is that it can avoid misunderstandings and hard feelings once you're gone.

I can still remember one occasion when I was sitting at a table listening to a lawyer reading the will of a deceased client, Harold. Also around the table were Harold's son and his nephew Ronald. When the lawyer got to the last paragraph, it read: "To my nephew Ronald, who I always promised I would remember in my will: Hello Ronald." I had to laugh out loud. We all did. Except Ronald, of course. Turns out that Ronald received the square root of nothing (which is nothing) from his uncle. As it turns out, Ronald said that he would have felt much better about the whole thing if his uncle had talked to him earlier about the fact that he wasn't going to get anything. I have to admit, though, that the rest of us enjoyed the laugh.

To be sure, there will be situations where it may make sense not to discuss the provisions of a will with the family, but these situations should be the exception—not the rule.

By the way, if you plan to leave someone out of your will entirely, be sure to discuss the issue with a lawyer who is experienced in family law and estate issues. The reason? You could be opening the door to problems after you're gone. A family member might contest the will in an attempt to have it changed. Further, leaving your spouse out of your will entirely is a no-no in most provinces, and it could be that your spouse will have rights that might supercede your will.

TO MAKE A LONG STORY SHORT:

- Consider discussing your estate plans with your family and other heirs to avoid misunderstandings about your intentions.

- Situations where it may not be appropriate to discuss your affairs with your heirs should be the exception, not the rule.
- If you're going to leave someone out of your will entirely, be sure to discuss this with a lawyer who is experienced in family law and estate issues.

Tim's Tip 4: Be aware of family law issues that could impact your estate plan.

I know, I know. Your family drives you crazy sometimes. Sometimes you wonder why you should leave them anything at all when you pass away. Maybe you've decided you're not going to leave a particular child or other family member an inheritance. Or, could it be that your family situation is more complicated than the Jones' next door—perhaps you're remarried, in a common-law relationship, in a same-sex relationship, or have dependants with special needs?

In these cases, family law in your province may have something to say about your estate planning. You see, each province has its own legislation, designed to protect those in your family who may need it, and while the law varies from one province to the next, the intent of the legislation is pretty consistent wherever you go. Here's a primer on family law issues.

Caution!

You should be aware that the executor of your estate can be held personally liable for your spouse's financial loss where you have neglected to provide for your spouse in your will and where that executor has failed to consider the rights of your spouse to receive some of your assets on your death.

Marriage and Spouses

If you were thinking of excluding your spouse from your will, think again. Legislation in most provinces will ensure that your spouse's right to a fair share of your estate is protected. If you were to divorce your spouse, he or she would be entitled to a certain share of the family property. Why would you expect anything different in the event of your death? In short, your will can be overridden if you leave your spouse high and dry.

This assumes, of course, that you and your spouse have not signed a marriage or single-purpose contract restricting what your spouse is entitled to inherit once you're gone. These contracts can override the provincial legislation that requires you to leave your spouse with a defined portion of your estate. A contract can make sense, for example, where you are entering a second marriage with significant business or other assets and you want to ensure that those assets remain the property of specific individuals and do not go to your spouse on your death. Before signing any contract, make sure you obtain legal advice independent of your spouse's legal advice. Find a lawyer specializing in family law who doesn't know your spouse.

Ontario.

If you happen to die in Ontario, this province's family law legislation will apply to you—even if your will was written outside of Ontario. The laws of Ontario require that all property acquired during a marriage be split equally if your marriage breaks down—and the death of a spouse counts as a breakdown of your marriage. The bottom line? Your spouse is entitled to accept the terms of your will or, if you leave your spouse with less than 50 percent of the "net family property," to make an election to receive an equalization payment as a top-up. If your spouse doesn't make the election for the equalization payment, he or she is assumed to have accepted the terms of your will.

Kevin died last month and left his wife, Suzanne, a right to an annual income from his assets. He did not, however, leave any of his assets to her outright. On his death, the couple's net family property amounted to $500,000, consisting of $350,000 in Kevin's name, and $150,000 in Suzanne's name. The couple was living in Ontario at the time of Kevin's death. Under

Ontario's Family Law Act, Suzanne can accept the terms of Kevin's will, or she can make an election to ensure that she keeps 50 percent of the net family property. This would amount to $250,000 (50 percent of $500,000). Since Suzanne already owns $150,000 of this net family property, she would be entitled to $100,000 from Kevin's estate as a top-up if she elects. She'll have to compare this result to the value of the income stream she expects under Kevin's will to see which she'd prefer. A financial advisor can lend a hand with the calculations.

Keep in mind that it's the value of the net family property owned the day before your death that is used in the calculation. So, any life insurance proceeds paid as a result of your death are excluded from the calculation.

Action Step

If you live in Ontario, be sure to structure your affairs so that you leave your spouse with enough that he or she doesn't have to make an election to receive an equalization payment. This will avoid hurt feelings and unwanted disputes between family members. Imagine how your heirs could feel if you short-changed your spouse in your will and he or she had to obtain a court order to take a portion of what you left to those heirs.

Quebec.

If you live in Quebec, your spouse also has an entitlement to the family palimony, which consists of the following assets net of any debts, regardless of who holds legal title:

- family home and household effects
- family vehicles
- RRSP or other pension benefits accrued during marriage.

Alternative Relationships

The rights and benefits that accrue to married couples don't necessarily apply to those who are living in a common-law or same-sex relationship.

Common-law relationships.

I've got good news and bad news for you here.

If you're living common-law, you'll enjoy the same treatment as legally married spouses under our tax law. This is good news, for the most part. It means that you can leave any assets you'd like, including RRSPs and RRIFs, to your common-law spouse on your death and receive a tax-free rollover to that spouse. I'll talk more about the tax implications of death and your RRSPs and RRIFs in Chapter 3.

Now, for the bad news. Common-law relationships are not recognized in quite the same way as marriages under family law. Your common-law partner may have a claim for ongoing support after you're gone, but he or she does not have the same rights to property that a married spouse would have.

Same-sex relationships.

At the time of writing, same-sex couples, like common-law couples, do not hold the same status as married couples under family law. This means that provincial family law will not currently provide rights to property to a same-sex partner who survives the death of the other partner. Beginning in 2001, however, our tax law does recognize same-sex partners, like common-law partners, as being entitled to the same treatment provided to spouses. The bottom line? Tax-free rollovers on death, which I'll talk about in Chapter 4, are now available to same-sex partners.

Times, they are a changin'. As the result of a recent Supreme Court of Canada decision on May 20, 1999, known only as *M vs. H*, the federal government proposes to change a whole slew of legislation to recognize same-sex partners in various ways. Our tax law has been changed effective January 1, 2001, as I've mentioned. Provincial and municipal law will likely follow suit over time if it has not already changed. For example, it's likely that a surviving same-sex partner will soon be entitled to pension benefits after the death of the other partner where the survivor has been named as beneficiary.

Further, CPP benefits will likely accrue to a surviving same-sex partner. The *M vs. H* case dealt with the issue of spousal support, and the court ruled that M, a lesbian, was in fact entitled to support from H, her partner of 10 years.

The dust hasn't settled, however, around the issue of same-sex couples yet. In the *Toronto Star* today it was announced that the City of Toronto is seeking guidance from the court as to whether, in view of the recent Supreme Court decision, it should be issuing marriage licences to same-sex couples. Who knows what the result will be?

Until federal, provincial and municipal legislation is changed to account for same-sex relationships, it's likely that your same-sex partner may be entitled to support after you're gone, but is not likely to be entitled to any of your property. My best advice to you is that you should make your wishes very clear in your will and powers of attorney or other estate planning documents. This way, you'll be assured that your same-sex partner will be treated in accordance with your wishes.

Action Step

If you want your common-law or same-sex partner to get a fair share of your estate, don't expect provincial family law to provide this protection as it does with married spouses. Rather, be sure to do one or more of the following: (1) Own property jointly with that partner with right of survivorship, (2) name each other as beneficiaries in your wills and on your life insurance, RRSPs or RRIFs, (3) provide each other with powers of attorney in the relevant documentation, or (4) prepare a co-habitation agreement that deals with support and property in the event of break-up or death.

Support for Dependants

Who is a dependant? Someone who relied on you for financial support immediately before your death. *Dependant* is generally defined to include a spouse and dependent children, but in some provinces (Ontario and P.E.I., for example) the definition can extend to include a common-law partner, parents, and grandparents.

All of this matters because your obligations to support these dependants will continue beyond your death and will impact how you distribute your assets. In a nutshell, if you fail to provide adequate support and maintenance to your dependants, they can apply in court to obtain an order against your estate for the support that they need. Make no mistake: the wording in the relevant provincial legislation is likely to give the court broad powers to choose a level of support that it deems appropriate.

Don't forget too that, if you've signed a marriage, divorce, separation, co-habitation, or other agreement that requires you to provide a certain level of support after your death, your will should reflect these provisions. Otherwise, your will can be overridden to satisfy your obligations under those contracts. If you don't want your support obligations to continue after you're gone, make sure that your agreements specify this.

Province of Residence

If you pack up your things and move from one province to the next, or to a location outside of Canada, make sure that a lawyer familiar with family law in your new jurisdiction looks at your will and reviews your other estate plans. You'll want to make sure that your estate objectives are still accomplished. In most cases, simply moving from one province to another won't require a change to your overall estate planning, unless your situation is rather unusual.

TO MAKE A LONG STORY SHORT:

- Family law can impact the distribution of your assets after you're gone. Your spouse and certain dependants, for example, are generally entitled to a portion of your estate, or to support.

- Common-law and same-sex partners are treated differently than married spouses under family law, and are generally entitled to support, but not the property of a deceased partner unless this is clearly spelled out in a will or other relevant documentation.
- If you move to a new jurisdiction, have a lawyer review your estate planning to ensure that your objectives will still be met.

Getting the Right Advice

Designing and implementing a proper estate plan will likely require some professional help. Make sure you get advice from the right people!

Tim's Tip 5: Know which professionals should implement your estate plan.

If you're looking for help in designing and implementing your estate plan, whom should you turn to? I know, your brother-in-law seems to know a lot about money issues. After all, he's the one who gives you all those hot tips on which high-tech stocks to buy, and he talks as though he really knows his stuff. At the risk of insulting your brother-in-law, allow me to suggest that you look for another opinion—unless he's on the list of professionals I'm about to detail for you, of course. The point is, friends and family have the best intentions—we all know that. But what most friends and family don't have is a thorough understanding of tax, family, insurance, securities, and other relevant law.

Depending on the complexity of your estate, you're likely going to need the help of professionals with expertise in four skill sets:

- estate and related law (typically a lawyer)
- taxation (typically an accountant)
- insurance (typically an insurance broker)
- investments (typically an investment advisor).

If any one individual claims to have sufficient expertise in every one of these areas to completely design and implement an estate plan for you himself—run for the hills! You see, it's going to take the cooperation of a few professionals to implement your estate plan. A lawyer has to draft your will—no one else should be doing it (and I discourage you from doing it yourself for reasons I'll talk about in Chapter 2). Your estate plan should be reviewed by a tax specialist, and insurance and investments should only be sold to you by licensed individuals.

All you really need is for one of these professionals to act as a "quarterback" for your estate planning. This person can bring the others into the picture if and when needed. What you'll often find is that the insurance and investments are handled by one professional alone—which is usually just fine.

I won't go into more detail on how to choose your team of advisors—there are more than a few books written about this issue. I will say, however, that a referral from a friend or family member usually works best. When it comes to education credentials, look for the following:

- Lawyer. LL.B, or LL.M.
- Accountant. Chartered Accountant (CA), or Certified General Accountant (CGA).
- Insurance Broker. Chartered Life Underwriter (CLU) or Chartered Financial Consultant (CHFC).

Caution!

Make sure you understand how any professional advisors you deal with are paid, and what it's going to cost you for their services. Keep in mind, however, that I'm not suggesting you skimp on advice. If paying $3,000 for advice is going to save you many thousands of dollars in taxes or probate fees, this could be the best investment you've ever made (aside from buying this book, that is!). Too many Canadians refuse to pay for professional advice—and their heirs end up paying for it later, and then some, once they're gone.

- Investment Advisor. Certified Financial Planner (CFP), Registered Financial Planner (RFP), Certified Investment Manager (CIM), Fellow of the Canadian Securities Institute (FCSI), Chartered Financial Analyst (CFA), or a university degree.

TO MAKE A LONG STORY SHORT:

- No one individual is able to both design and implement an entire estate plan—particularly if your affairs are complex (if you own a private corporation, for example).
- The four areas of expertise most often required are: estate and related law (lawyer), taxation (accountant), insurance (insurance broker), and investments (investment advisor).
- Referrals from a friend or family member are usually best.

WINNING THE ESTATE PLANNING GAME

Before you move on to Chapter 2, turn to the *Estate Planning Tip Sheet* at the front of the book. You'll find a summary of the tips we've just covered in this chapter. For each tip, ask yourself the question: "Does this apply to me?" Then check the appropriate answer: "Yes," "No," or "Not sure." This tip sheet will form the basis for your complete estate plan once you've read the entire book. Now, let's move on to Chapter 2 and talk about wills and powers of attorney.

EYES ON THE FINISH LINE: WILLS AND POWERS OF ATTORNEY

Where there's a will there's been some planning—or an attempt at it.

2

Jack is a client of mine. He's a funeral director, and was at work one day when his daughter, Kelly, was in a bicycle accident. She had been riding on a busy road when she was knocked off her bike by a car that had nudged her back tire. She was dazed for a minute, and when she came to, she saw a lady hovering over her. "Is there anything I can do?" the woman asked. "Call Smith's Funeral Home," Kelly moaned. The lady looked surprised. "Oh, I don't think that's necessary, you'll be all right dear," she reassured her.

It's a funny story, and Kelly walked away that day, but the whole incident served to cause Jack and his wife to think again about how short life can be—and to remind them of their own mortality. Much to my surprise, Jack and his wife had not even prepared wills at the time of Kelly's mishap, and the scare of the event caused them to prepare wills the next day! I kept telling Jack that he's got to plan his finances as though he's going to live to age 100, but plan for his estate as though he's going to die tomorrow—and this means having a properly drafted will. Are you in good shape in this department?

Dying Without a Will

If you've been thinking that it's not a problem to die without a will—think again.

Tim's Tip 6: Understand the problems in dying without a will.

Next to eating a plateful of asparagus (I can't stand asparagus), I can't think of a more unpleasant task than trying to look after the affairs of someone who dies without a will. If you die without a will, you are said to die "intestate," and there are more than just a few problems with this. Let me share with you the top eight problems associated with dying intestate:

1. "Who gets what" may not be what you'd like.

Talk about inflexible. If you die intestate, your provincial intestacy laws will dictate who gets what. So, if you were hoping for your spouse to get everything on your death, and for your children to get everything only after your spouse dies—don't hold your breath. Sure, your spouse is going to be entitled to something, but it may not be the amount that you intended. This can be even more disastrous if you're living in a common-law or same-sex relationship because these partners are not entitled to any of your property on your death unless you specify your wishes in a will.

The big question, of course, is this: Exactly who gets what if you die without a will? The answer depends on your province. In a nutshell, your spouse is likely to receive a certain portion of your assets with the balance being split between your spouse and any kids that you have. Want the specifics? Check out Appendix B at the back for a complete table.

2. Assets may be unintentionally liquidated.

What a letdown it would be if your heirs were forced to sell some cherished family asset just because you didn't have a will. It could happen if provincial intestacy laws require a certain dollar amount to be handed to your spouse or kids but there is insufficient cash to split your assets in this way.

Picture a situation where you're in a second or subsequent marriage, and you have children from a previous marriage. Do you want your kids to inherit all your assets after you're gone? They might not if your new spouse outlives you, since some of your assets will end up in the hands of your new spouse if you die intestate (without a will), and who knows where those assets will end up on his or her death—perhaps in the hands of his or her own children. In short, second marriages require special attention to properly prepared wills!

Caution!

Shannon died last year without a will. At the time of her death, she owned a cottage worth $200,000 and cash of $50,000. Under the intestacy laws of Saskatchewan, where she lived, she's got to leave her husband, Kurt, $100,000 plus one-third of the balance of her assets (another $50,000). Their two kids are entitled to receive the remaining $100,000. If the family can't arrive at another solution, it may be necessary to sell the cottage to come up with the cash necessary to pay the kids their $100,000. Shannon could have avoided this problem simply by preparing a will.

---

3. Distribution of your estate can be delayed.

If you die without a will, the provincial court will appoint an administrator to distribute your stuff to your heirs in accordance with the intestacy laws of your province. The problem? It can be a slow process to appoint this administrator, especially if more than one person applies for the job. When appointing an administrator, the court will typically choose from among family members in the following order:

- husband or wife
- child or grandchild
- brothers and sisters.

The person appointed may not be your first choice. Heck, they may not even be any choice you would have made.

There's a big problem in waiting for the court to appoint an administrator: no one has the authority to deal with the assets of your estate until the administrator is appointed. If this happens to take a while, the potential consequences can be ugly. For example, investments that should be sold may not be sold on a timely basis. If you own a business, it may be that no one can make business decisions on a timely basis either.

4. Costs of administering your estate can be higher.

The fact is, court costs can be much higher when you die without a will. Why? Because the court has to issue directives in place of your will. This is going to require that someone provide the court with full information about your assets, debts, and beneficiaries—and this can be time consuming. Don't be fooled into thinking that the courts work for free. The more difficult it is to compile the required information, the higher the fees will be.

5. Taxes paid on your death could be much higher.

The fact that you'll likely pay more tax in your year of death without a will than if you prepare a will should not exactly surprise you. I've already mentioned that dying intestate means that your spouse will not automatically receive all your assets—your kids are going to get some of your property. The problem with this is that anything left to your kids is deemed to have been sold at fair market value immediately prior to your death. This could trigger a tax hit big enough to cause any of your heirs to cringe, curse, or cry.

Preparing a will allows you to manage any tax liability that might otherwise rear its ugly head on your demise. I'll talk more about tax strategies in Chapter 4.

Think about how messy things could get if you die with minor children and no will to appoint a guardian. This gets really ugly where you're separated, divorced, or living in a common-law relationship. Will custody of your child be obtained by your new spouse or partner, your previous spouse, or someone else? The answer may not be what you intended, and a knock-'em-down-drag-'em-out custody battle could ensue. This isn't fair to your child, or anyone else. Prepare a will.

Caution!

6. Guardians over your kids may not be appropriate.

Uncle Bill just got out of jail. He seems to be over his kleptomaniac tendencies. It even looks as though he has learned how to read. Not only that, but guess what? He's going to be the guardian of your kids.

Okay, so it's unlikely that you've got an Uncle Bill with this type of baggage. I'd bet, however, that you've got strong feelings about which of your family members should not look after your kids if you and your spouse happen to die. If you die without a will, the provincial child welfare service becomes their guardian. A family member or someone else can apply for an order appointing them as guardian, but it's the court that will ultimately decide who will look after your kids. You may not agree with the decision.

Do your kids a favour and name a guardian in a will.

7. Investment alternatives may stink.

If you happen to die without a will, an administrator will have to be appointed by the courts to look after the distribution of your estate assets. Once the administrator is appointed, he or she will still be limited to investing your assets in accordance with your province's Trustee Act. What does this mean? In some provinces, your administrator will have to invest your assets in accordance with a list of acceptable investments.

The problem with this is that the list, while conservative, may not allow your administrator to choose those investments that would best suit your heirs. Even worse, your administrator might be required to sell an investment when market conditions are not ideal, or to obtain the court's approval not to sell—which means more fees. Other provinces have adopted a "prudent investor" rule, which will generally allow your administrator to invest the assets you've left behind in a manner that a prudent investor would. This is better than the restrictive list under the Trustee Act in some provinces, but is still not ideal.

Your best bet is to prepare a will and to spell out the investment powers of the executor in the will. This way, you can rest assured that the needs of your heirs are met.

8. Conflicts over a family business can arise.

If you don't spell out in a will the details about what should be done with your business once you're gone, things could get ugly after your death. You may, for example, have two or more kids or other relatives in the business who want to take control over things when you're gone. Avoid problems; prepare a will and provide for the succession or sale of your business.

TO MAKE A LONG STORY SHORT:

- There are at least eight significant drawbacks to dying intestate—that is, dying without a will.
- In virtually every case, dying intestate will mean greater costs to your estate, in fees, taxes, or lost investment opportunities.
- Administering the estate of someone who has died intestate is worse than eating asparagus.

Basics About Wills

Now that you're convinced of the importance of having a will, let's talk about will basics. These are the things that every Canadian should know about preparing a will.

Tim's Tip 7: Understand the basic format of most wills.

Most wills look alike. Not in what they say specifically, but in their components—that is, the issues they cover. For the most part, six different components are commonly in a will. Here they are:

1. Identifying the testator.

If the will is yours, then you're known as the "testator." At the beginning of the will, the testator will generally identify himself, state his address, and make a declaration that the document is his last will and testament.

2. Revoking former wills and codicils.

Following the identification, the testator then usually revokes all previous wills and codicils. A codicil, by the way, is simply a document that supplements a will and changes the original wording of the will.

3. Naming the executor.

Next, the testator names an executor who is responsible for carrying out her wishes as specified in her will. I'll talk more about

Did You Know?

It is possible to have more than one will. This is common, for example, where you might have assets in two different jurisdictions, and a will in each jurisdiction to handle the distribution of those particular assets. Recently, an Ontario court case established that it's possible to have two wills in the same jurisdiction (Ontario in this case) for the purpose of minimizing probate fees (see Tip 64, point 7). Care will have to be taken when dealing with multiple wills so that one will does not revoke the other.

naming an executor in Tip 9. By the way, you should be sure to name an alternative executor in the event that your first choice is unable or unwilling to act in that capacity.

4. Authorizing the payment of debts.

The next issue typically covered in a will is the issue of final debts. The testator usually authorizes the executor to pay all debts, which can include income taxes, probate fees, legal or accounting fees, and funeral expenses (which could be quite low if you skip the casket and opt for a bag and a quick memorial service—but more on funeral costs in Chapter 12).

5. Distributing the assets.

Next is the distribution of your stuff. Distribution typically takes place in one of three ways:

- **Gift of cash.** A gift of cash from your estate can be made. This is often referred to as a "legacy."
- **Gift of property.** You might choose to give some asset other than cash to an heir. This gift of property is often referred to as a "bequest."
- **Gift of the residue.** No, this has nothing to do with that soap scum residue you'll find in your bathtub. The residue of your estate is what's left over after paying all debts, and making all specific gifts of cash and property. It's common to find a will addressing what should be done with the residue of the estate. In fact, if you don't have a clause dealing with the residue of your estate, then any assets not specifically mentioned as a gift of cash or property would fall under your provincial intestacy laws—as though you didn't have a will with respect to those assets.

I should mention that gifts of cash, property, or the residue can be made directly to certain individuals, or to one or more trusts for the benefit of those individuals (for example, where the beneficiaries are minors). I'll talk more about testamentary trusts in Tip 55.

6. Appointing a guardian.

Chances are pretty good that if you've got children under the age of majority, you've got strong feelings about who should (or should not) look after them if you and your spouse (or the other parent) don't survive until the kids are adults. It's critical that your will identify who the guardians should be in this event. I'll talk more about choosing a guardian in Tip 12.

Speaking of Tip 12, I'll talk more about specific clauses to include in your will in that tip a bit later in this chapter.

TO MAKE A LONG STORY SHORT:

- While the specific wording of each will can be different, there are generally six common components to any will: (1) identifying the testator, (2) revoking former wills and codicils, (3) naming the executor, (4) authorizing the payment of debts, (5) distributing the assets, and (6) appointing a guardian for minors.

Tim's Tip 8: Recognize how and when to revise your will—then get a lawyer involved.

Don't be surprised when I tell you that your will is going to change over time. This could be for any number of reasons. Keep in mind that, as long as you're of sound mind, you can change your existing will or create an entirely new will as often as you'd like. In fact, you should make it a habit to review your will often, especially if one of the following events has taken place:

Action Step

It's possible for you to change your will as often as you'd like, as long as you're still of sound mind. Changing your existing will just slightly is best done by way of a *codicil* to your will (a simple attachment to your will identifying the changes). If you're making big changes, your best bet may be to draft an entirely new will. If you've got a family member who may not be of sound mind for much longer, but is currently competent, it's time for him to revisit his will one last time!

- your marital status has changed
- the marital status of beneficiaries or others has changed
- beneficiaries, an executor, trustee, or guardian has died
- there's been a birth in the family of someone to include in your will
- the competence of an executor, beneficiary, or trustee has changed
- you have moved to a new jurisdiction
- your executor, trustee, or beneficiaries have moved to a new jurisdiction
- you have acquired real estate in another jurisdiction
- your net worth has changed significantly
- you have new dependants
- your executor or trustees are no longer willing to accept their roles
- you have changed your mind about who should get what
- you have changed your life insurance coverage
- tax laws have changed.

Whew, that's a long list! I'll bet some of these things have already taken place since you drafted your will—that is, if you've already got a will. If your will needs changing, I can't stress enough the importance of having a lawyer make the changes. You run the risk of making certain provisions, if not the entire will, invalid if you do it yourself.

Specific Circumstances

Now, let's take a closer look at specific circumstances that can require you to revisit your will.

1. Changes in the law.

Believe me, laws related to your estate planning are changing regularly, and there are different bodies of legislation that could affect your will: income tax law, trust law, and succession law, to name a few. Check with your lawyer, financial advisor, and tax accountant annually to determine if there's anything that you should be concerned about.

2. Marriage or remarriage.

Be aware that getting married or remarried will automatically revoke your will. So, if you have a will and then marry at some point in the future, you will die intestate (without a will) unless you create a new will after your marriage. There's an exception here. If your will is written in contemplation of an upcoming marriage and specifically names your future spouse, then the will won't be revoked. In addition, it may be possible in some provinces for a new spouse to elect to accept your will (and not to have it revoked), although don't count on this happening since your new spouse is not likely named as a beneficiary in that will.

Caution!

If you're going to revise your will in contemplation of getting married and you're going to name your future spouse in that will, make sure that the marriage takes place! In fact, the will should be worded so that any bequests to your future spouse are dependent upon the marriage happening. You'd hate to have your fiancé(e) back out of marriage at the last minute, only to have you die in a car crash the next day: your fiancé(e) could be left owning your assets in this case.

3. Separation.

Don't count on automatically excluding your estranged spouse from your will if you separate. The truth is, the provisions of your will remain effective as long as you're legally married, and separation won't change that. If, however, you sign a separation agreement with your spouse, the provisions of your will relating to that spouse will be overridden by that separation agreement. That is, you can exclude your estranged spouse from taking any part of your estate. My advice? If you separate, prepare a new will. If your separation agreement calls for continued support of your children or other dependants, don't forget to make sure that your new will provides this support to them.

4. Divorce.

In the event of divorce, your will is not automatically revoked as it is with a marriage or remarriage. Nor does the will remain completely in effect as it does with a separation (outside of a separation agreement). Here's what happens in divorce: certain provisions of your will become invalid. Specifically, those provisions that give any powers, property, or income to your ex-spouse are considered invalid. Your will is interpreted as though your ex-spouse has died. Who is considered a spouse here? Generally, *spouse* includes legally married spouses and common-law spouses as well, for the purposes of this provision.

Action Step

If you move, consider whether or not you should change your executor. Keep in mind that your executor should live close to where you live. Why? Because wrapping up your estate from a distance can be very difficult since it may mean trips to your bank, lawyer, accountant, and other advisors. In addition, an executor who lives outside of Canada may have to post a bond, and will have to deal with Canadian tax and other laws, which could be unfamiliar territory to him or her.

5. Moving your home.

What happens if you move from one province to another, from Canada to another country, or from another country to Canada? Is your will still valid? Generally, your will is still valid in your new jurisdiction when moving from one province to another, or between Canada and the U.S. I should mention, however, that it's important to visit a lawyer in your new jurisdiction to ensure that your wishes, as spelled out in your existing will, are still going to be carried out on your death. In many cases, it's going to make sense to create a new will in that new jurisdiction.

Glen and Linda moved from Alberta to Ontario this year. Glen's assets total $800,000. If Glen were to die tomorrow as a resident of Ontario, Linda would be entitled to at least *one-half of Glen's estate ($400,000) under Ontario legislation. Glen's will, however, only provides Linda with $300,000, leaving the residue of his estate to his son. Glen's wishes would have been carried out in Alberta, but not in Ontario, where Linda is entitled to one-half of all that he owns.*

This example makes one thing clear: rules vary from one province to the next. In some provinces, your spouse will have a right to the matrimonial home and to no less than if you had divorced. So, you've got to re-evaluate whether your spouse's share of your estate is still appropriate in the new jurisdiction.

Finally, if you move to a new jurisdiction, be careful if you decide to use multiple wills (one in each jurisdiction, for example). You see, a will generally revokes all other wills written in the past. This could become a problem if you have more than one will—particularly where a beneficiary or another person contests your will. If you're going to have more than one will, make sure that the lawyers in each jurisdiction work together to avoid any problems.

6. Destroying your will.

If you destroy your will by, for example, tearing it up or burning it, and your intention was to revoke the will, then the will is no longer valid. If you're no longer of sound mind, you won't be able to revoke the will in this manner.

7. Written intention to revoke.

You'll be able to revoke your will by making a written declaration that you intend to revoke it. To do this properly, the declaration must be in writing and be signed by you and at least two witnesses. Be careful! If you revoke your will in this way, you could die intestate unless you make a new will right away.

8. Creating a new will.

As I've mentioned before, most wills automatically revoke any previous wills. This is the case because the more recent will typically declares all previous wills to be invalid.

Take a look at the checklist that I've provided in Appendix C at the back. This should help you to determine whether or not it's time to revise your will.

How to Revise Your Will

If it's time to change your will, you've got two options. The first is simply to create and sign an amendment to your will—known as a codicil to your will. If you're only making minor changes to your will, such as naming a new executor or adding one or two short provisions, then a codicil can make sense. The codicil will actually refer to the original will, and will be signed by you and by at least two witnesses. For minor changes, opt for a codicil rather than, say, crossing out names or writing in new paragraphs yourself in the original will. This could make your will invalid. The bottom line? Visit a lawyer to draft the codicil to ensure that it's done properly.

If you're planning to make more significant changes to your will (to add, for example, a testamentary trust for your heirs) or if you've now got several codicils to your will already, it may make better sense to create a whole new will. You want to avoid any ambiguity or potential confusion for your executor as to what your wishes and intentions are. Having too many codicils, or a lengthy codicil, can lead to problems.

TO MAKE A LONG STORY SHORT:

- There are many circumstances that will require you to review and possibly revise your will, including marriage, separation or divorce, the death of certain people, or changing family circumstances.

- Your will can be revised by a simple codicil, or by creating a whole new will. Use a lawyer in either case.

Tim's Tip 9: Choose your executor with great care—it's the most important role to be filled once you're gone.

Once you're gone, your executor will act as your personal representative. The executor's responsibilities are many, and include everything from gathering and distributing your assets to filing tax returns. You should understand that there are really two types of executors: professional executors (including lawyers, accountants, and trust companies), and non-professional executors (typically family members or friends).

The executor has a lot of weight on his or her shoulders—and plenty of potential liability if he or she mishandles your assets once you're gone. Generally, you'll provide the non-professional executor with the power to seek professional advice if needed. This can ensure that the affairs of your estate are dealt with properly.

Action Step

Most people name a non-professional executor, such as a friend or family member, in their will. Perhaps it's because they like the familiarity of the friend or family member, or they are averse to paying the fees that some professional executors will charge. Often a non-professional executor works well, but sometimes this backfires. If you'd like a non-professional executor, try to find someone with a strong business or financial background.

Now, let's take a closer look at the responsibilities of your executor.

Executor's Responsibilities

Your executor is going to have a lot on his or her plate upon your death. There are five key responsibilities that your executor will have:

- **Making funeral arrangements.** This might come as a surprise, but your executor is not bound to follow your wishes for your funeral. Having said this, make your wishes known to your executor outside of your will (since the will may not be located or read before your funeral), preferably in writing. Chances are very good that your wishes will be respected. I have devoted Chapter 12 to the issue of funerals.

- **Managing your estate assets.** Your executor will be the one to locate your assets, liquidate some if necessary (perhaps to free up cash to pay taxes or other debts), and manage or invest the assets for the benefit of your beneficiaries until the assets are distributed to them. Make sure that your executor has a copy of your will today, or knows where to get it on your death.
- **Paying your final debts.** You're going to have some final bills to pay after your death. Your executor will look after paying these amounts, such as funeral expenses, income taxes, and legitimate claims of creditors.
- **Filing tax returns.** Did you know that in the year of your death, it's possible that your executor might file up to four different tax returns for you (see Tip 23)? Your executor will have to obtain a "clearance certificate" from the tax collector (Canada Customs and Revenue Agency, or CCRA for short). The clearance certificate simply provides the executor with assurance that, from CCRA's point of view, all taxes have been paid. Only after this certificate has been received is it safe for the executor to distribute the remaining assets of the estate to the beneficiaries.
- **Distributing your assets.** Here's where your beneficiaries come in. After the other responsibilities have been fulfilled, the executor can pass your assets to your beneficiaries in accordance with your will.

Action Step

If you're a beneficiary, it can be easy to get frustrated over delays in receiving your share of the deceased's estate. Be patient! The fact is that the executor has much to do, not the least of which is to pay all debts, including income taxes, and obtain a clearance certificate from CCRA before you can receive the balance of what's coming to you. Getting a clearance certificate can take as long as eight to twelve weeks from the time that Form TX19 is filed requesting the certificate.

Choosing More Than One Executor

Should you name more than one executor? You're permitted to name more than one. If you don't want the burden of settling your affairs to fall on the shoulders of one person alone, or where you think that two heads are better than one in making decisions related to your estate, then co-executors can make sense. Even if you don't name co-executors, you should be sure to name an alternative executor in the event that your first executor is unable or unwilling to act in that role. If, for example, you name your spouse as executor and you both die in a joint disaster (say, a car crash), the alternative executor can step in. It's particularly important to name an alternative executor where you've named an individual (as opposed to a trust company) as executor.

Qualities to Look For

What should your executor look like? How about short, bald, with glasses—you know, an accountant-type. Although your executor's appearance may not matter much, his or her personal abilities and willingness are crucial.

The role of executor should be filled by someone who is not afraid to deal with numbers—because there will be a lot of numbers to crunch (from adding up the value of your assets to signing tax returns). Someone with a good financial or business sense would do just fine. If you are a business owner, it should be someone who is familiar with the nature of your business.

The executor should ideally be someone who lives close by. I've mentioned this before. You see, there could be trips to the bank, lawyer, accountant, financial advisor, and the need to physically locate your assets, not to mention the responsibility of arranging your funeral, which will require being close in proximity to where your funeral is to be held (probably close to your home).

Finally, your executor should be someone who is highly likely to outlive you. For example, you wouldn't normally name your grandfather as your executor! Choosing someone who is the same age or younger makes sense.

Professionals vs. Non-professionals

Okay, now the important question of whether to name a professional executor (such as a lawyer, accountant or trust company), or a non-professional executor (such as your spouse, child, or sibling). If you're lucky, one of your close family members or friends will also be a lawyer or accountant who is willing to act as your executor.

My advice is this. You should consider a professional executor if one of three situations exists:

- Family members or friends would have difficulty handling the job, or handling it impartially.
- Your affairs are complex (for example, you're a business owner or partner in a business, or you own significant assets either inside or outside Canada).
- Your will creates one or more trusts that will exist for many years to come—perhaps beyond the lifetime of the non-professional executor or trustee whom you might otherwise name in your will.

If you're going to choose a professional executor, make sure that you first understand how that executor will be paid, what type of information will be provided to your beneficiaries, how often the executor will meet with beneficiaries, and how that executor would work with a family member or friend who might be named as a co-executor

Did You Know?

Your will may establish one or more trusts for your beneficiaries upon your death. This will be the case, for example, where you die while your children are still minors and you leave them some assets. In this event, it's going to be necessary to name a trustee for each trust in your will. You may simply name your executor as trustee over any trusts, or you may name someone different. In any case, recognize that the executor's job and the job of any trustee are really two different roles.

(a nice compromise to choosing a professional or non-professional executor exclusively).

TO MAKE A LONG STORY SHORT:

- There are five key responsibilities for any executor related to locating, managing and distributing your assets, and filing tax returns.
- There are two types of executors: professional and non-professional. Most people opt for non-professionals, but this may not make sense in some cases.
- The executor that you name should have good financial or business sense, live close by, and be likely to outlive you.

Tim's Tip 10: **Understand the variety of fees that could affect your estate after your death.**

Your will can give rise to, or have an impact on, several different types of fees. Some are avoidable, others won't be—it just depends on your circumstances. Here are the five fees that come to mind:

- **Legal fees.** In most cases, it's going to be necessary to get a lawyer involved after you've passed away. A lawyer will help with things like making any necessary applications to court, filing for letters probate, and transferring assets into the name of the estate. The fees? They will vary by lawyer, but you can generally expect to pay a rate of $150 to $300 per hour, or more if the lawyer is quite experienced.
- **Accounting fees.** Your executor may also have to fork over fees to an accountant (not that there's anything wrong with accounting fees!). As an accountant, I can share with you the kinds of things that I have done for executors after a loved one has died: locating assets, performing valuations of company shares, assisting the executor in deciding which tax elections to make on the deceased's final tax return, and preparing final tax returns and tax returns for the estate. The fees? Typically $150 to $300 per hour, or more.

- **Executor fees.** The executor of your estate will be permitted, in many cases, to take a fee for the work involved. The fee can range from three to five percent of the value of your estate. This is not an annual fee—it's a total fee, regardless of how long your estate takes to wind up. If the executor also happens to be a beneficiary, he or she could be denied a fee unless the will specifies that the executor is entitled to an amount over and above the inheritance. If the beneficiary feels that the fee taken by the executor is too high, he or she can ask the executor to "pass accounts" (not to be confused with passing the caviar, or passing the puck) in court. The executor will have to present an account in court of all work done, and a judge will then set the fees to be paid to the executor—which could be higher or lower than the fees actually taken.
- **Probate fees.** Think of these fees as a tax, if you want. Most provinces levy probate fees in order to validate the will. You see, some third parties (banks or other financial institutions, for example) may not be willing to hand your assets to your heirs until they know that the will is valid. The fees vary by province (see Appendix D for a schedule of probate fees). I'll talk more about how to minimize these fees in Tip 64.
- **Income taxes.** Call these fees if you'd like. Income taxes can certainly be the largest of all the amounts paid by your executor after you're gone.

TO MAKE A LONG STORY SHORT:

- Your will could give rise to, or have an impact on, a number of different fees.
- The fees to watch for include: legal, accounting, executor, and probate fees, and income taxes.

Tim's Tip 11: **Make sure that your will is prepared and signed properly, or you could die intestate.**

If you were on an airplane that was about to crash, and you pulled out a piece of paper—perhaps the back of a napkin—to scribble down your wishes, and then signed the thing, this paper could qualify as your will. Trust me, however: you don't want to write your will in this manner if you can avoid it. After all, you'd hate for that spot of gravy on the napkin to be mistaken for a "do" instead of a "don't," or "$100,000" instead of "$10,000."

A handwritten will is called a "holograph will." Actually, there are three types of wills: (1) a holograph will, (2) a pre-written will, and (3) a formal will.

Be careful if you plan to prepare a holograph will (a handwritten will). Typing up a will and then signing it without proper witnesses is not the same thing as a holograph will, which must be entirely in your own handwriting. There are many drawbacks to preparing your own will—even using those will kits. My advice to clients is always the same: get a lawyer involved in preparing your will. The fees are worth it to ensure that the will is valid and clearly written.

Caution!

Holograph Wills

Avoid these like the plague. A holograph will is a will written entirely in your handwriting. It does not require the usual signatures of witnesses; your signature alone will suffice. The pitfalls of this type of will can't be ignored, however. Want a list of drawbacks? Consider these:

- there's no guarantee that the will wasn't prepared under duress; that is, that the writer of the will wasn't influenced by someone else at the time of writing
- the writer's intentions and wishes might be lacking in clarity since the usual legal jargon won't be used

- the handwriting might be difficult to read
- the will could be altered by an unscrupulous person
- since there may not be witnesses to the will, it could be contested on the grounds that the writer was not mentally competent to write a will
- the executor may have to prove that it was really the handwriting of the deceased
- some provinces don't allow holograph wills.

When should you choose a holograph will? When you're on that plane I was referring to, and you're about to meet your demise without a formal will. Otherwise, you've got time to prepare a will in a better way.

Pre-written Wills

A pre-written will is one of those "fill-in-the-blank" wills that you can buy at a book, stationery, or computer software store. These wills come with brief instructions on how to fill in the blanks to create a valid will. While a pre-printed will is better than no will at all, it's still a bad choice. As with a holograph will, there could be confusion about what your true intentions were since the wording is largely left up to you, with the exception of the sentences that are already pre-written. A pre-written will must be signed by you and witnessed by two others.

Formal Wills

Now, here's the way to go. A formal will is drafted by a lawyer who has experience in preparing wills in your province. The lawyer is there to do more than simply put words on a page. He or she will provide advice on matters such as executors, trustees, guardians, and the legality of splitting your assets in certain ways among your beneficiaries. A formal will should ensure that your intentions are clear, leaving no guesswork for your executor or the courts.

In my view, the cost associated with having a lawyer prepare a formal will is very low when compared to the benefits. You can expect to pay between $150 and $300 for a very basic will (double this for two wills—one for each spouse or partner).

Keep in mind, however, that every lawyer has different degrees of experience in different matters. You should ensure that a tax professional (a Chartered Accountant or Certified General Accountant specializing in tax) has a chance to review your will before you sign it. Most lawyers have a basic understanding of tax, but may not have an in-depth knowledge on the topic.

Aron thought he could save money by preparing his own will, and one for his wife Vonnie. After contemplating whom he wanted to be his executor, deciding what to leave his wife and kids, and discussing with Vonnie an appropriate guardian for the kids, Aron turned on his computer and started creating his will—and Vonnie's. The wills were signed by each of them, and stored in a safety deposit box at the bank. Aron may not realize it, but if he or Vonnie were to die tomorrow, they would die intestate. The wills created by Aron and signed by each of them were not properly witnessed. Their wills are not considered acceptable holograph wills because they weren't completely handwritten. Further, neither will deals with the residue of the estates of each of them, leaving certain assets subject to their province's intestacy laws—even if the wills had been properly witnessed.

Aron and Vonnie's example reveals just a couple of the problems that can be encountered if you prepare your own will. Do yourself and your heirs a favour—have a lawyer prepare a formal will.

Did You Know?

If a person is in a position where he or she may not be able to sign a will—perhaps because of blindness or an inability to read—then it's possible for a lawyer or notary to sign a statement declaring the limitations of the individual, and that the individual appears to have understood all provisions of the will. There really is no excuse for not preparing and signing a valid will!

Signing Your Will

If your will isn't properly signed, all of the provisions of the will can be meaningless. Generally, a formal or pre-written will must be signed by two adults of sound mind, and be sure to keep beneficiaries away from this task. If a beneficiary signs a will as a witness, the beneficiary might receive nothing under the will since it's possible that the beneficiary may have influenced the provisions of the will.

TO MAKE A LONG STORY SHORT:

- There are generally three types of wills: a holograph will, a pre-written will, and a formal will.
- A formal will can help you to avoid a number of pitfalls, and will virtually always be worth the cost.

Clauses to Consider

They say it is probably the most difficult clause to live up to, ever written in a will. I'm referring to the Santa Clause. When Kris Kringle passed away, he left the task of making a worldwide tour each Christmas eve to his son, also named Kris. If you believe that, I've got some land in Florida that I'd like to sell you.

The fact is, however, that the clauses you write into your will can have a significant impact on the work your executor must undertake (excuse the terminology) after you're gone, the priorities of any guardian of your children, peace and harmony in the family, and how you're thought of once you're gone.

Tim's Tip 12: **Take very seriously the drafting of clauses in your will—you could impact the lives of others.**

I have already dealt with the basic components, or clauses, of any will. Refer back to Tip 7 for that discussion. At this point, I want to talk about a variety of other clauses that you'll find in many wills.

1. Common disasters.

While it may seem farfetched that you and your spouse might die together, or within thirty days of each other, it can happen and you've got to be ready for it. I recently sat in a meeting with a client who understood this all too well: his parents had died in a plane crash together. Things can happen.

Your will should provide for alternative beneficiaries in the event that you and your spouse die together, or within a certain number of days of each other—normally 30 days. That is, your will should specify that, in order for a beneficiary to inherit the assets you've left—he or she must survive you by at least 30 days. Imagine a situation where you and your spouse have left everything to each other in your wills, and then both die at the same time without alternative beneficiaries being named. This would be equivalent to both of you dying intestate, without a will.

Unless your will provides differently, the distribution of your estate will be based on the will of the spouse who actually dies last when there's a joint disaster. If you both died at the same time, it's presumed that the younger spouse died last for purposes of distributing your estate.

2. Executor's powers.

In most cases, wills are drafted to provide the executor with a broad range of powers. This enables the executor to do what is best for the beneficiaries in every situation. Consider explicitly giving your executor, in your will, the power to:

- make any tax elections necessary to reduce the tax burden arising from your death (see Tip 34)
- invest the assets of the estate in any investments he or she sees fit to invest in

- encroach on capital to provide certain beneficiaries with access to money as it is needed.

3. Guardian for children.

When my wife, Carolyn, and I prepared our wills, we had to contemplate who would be named guardians of our children if we were to die. Carolyn was pretty adamant about the issue: "Tim, I want someone loving, caring, responsible, with a strong moral character and who shares our beliefs."

"Carolyn," I replied, "if we knew someone like that, we should give the kids away today."

We finally agreed on Carolyn's sister and her husband. "How do we ask them to do this?" Carolyn wondered.

"No problem," I said. "We tell them: 'Look, when we die and you come to our funeral, bring the mini-van.'"

All kidding aside, you need to appoint a guardian for your children if you are a single parent, or if you're married, in the event that you and your spouse die in a joint disaster—you know, a car or plane crash, for example—as unlikely as that may seem.

The guardian of your kids is responsible for looking after them until they reach age of majority. Now, your will only provides temporary custody over your kids, and the guardian must apply to the courts to take permanent custody. Generally, the courts will grant custody to the guardian named in your will, but this is not automatic. The court will look

Action Step

Personally, I like to separate the role of guardian and trustee over the kids' inheritance. You don't want to put your guardian in a situation of being tempted to use for his or her own purposes some of the money that you leave behind for your kids. Don't tempt fate. Even the best-intentioned people can do crazy things when money is at stake. Your best bet is to name a different person as trustee over your kids' inheritance, or at least name a co-trustee along with the guardian.

at a number of things, including the wishes of your children, if they're old enough to voice their opinions. It's a very good idea to express in your will the reasons why you have chosen a particular guardian, and if there is someone in particular that you do not want as a guardian, don't be afraid to spell this out in your will too—it can only help the courts in providing the guardian you've named with permanent custody.

Before signing your will, be sure to discuss the issue with the guardian whom you are appointing. After all, you want to make sure that he or she is willing to do the job. In addition, please, leave some money in trust for your kids if possible. That is, be sure you are leaving some money behind to help with the support of your children. In young families, the money you leave behind is likely to come from an insurance policy or two. A joint second-to-die policy pays out its death benefit when both you and your spouse are gone. It's cheaper than buying insurance on your life, or your spouse's life, alone. Look into this type of policy if you've got young children.

Ask yourself a few questions before finalizing your choice of a guardian:

- Is he or she willing to take on this role?
- Does he or she share your values and beliefs?
- Would your children want to live with the person?
- Will the person be able to financially support the raising of your children, either with his or her own resources or money that you leave in trust for your children?
- Have you made arrangements to leave money behind—perhaps through a life insurance policy?
- Does your spouse agree with you on your choice of guardian?

Any "no" answers to these questions could spell trouble if steps aren't taken to rectify the situation today.

4. Testamentary trusts.

A testamentary trust is created after your death, in your will. The trust can be thought of as another taxpayer in the family. The benefit? Your heirs can split income with the trust so that the total tax bill paid by the trust and your heirs each year is less than what would be paid if your heirs alone paid all of the tax on the income generated by your inheritance after you're gone. I'll talk more about testamentary trusts in Tip 55.

5. Insurance trusts.

An insurance trust is really a form of testamentary trust that is created on your death in your will, but it's designed to hold insurance proceeds that are paid out after your death. The benefit of the trust is that your heirs can split income with the trust. Further, the insurance proceeds, which would normally be subject to probate fees if you leave the proceeds to your estate (normally a necessary maneuvre to place the insurance proceeds in a testamentary trust) will now avoid probate fees with an insurance trust. I'll talk more about this idea in Tip 55.

6. Registered plans.

You have the option of naming the beneficiaries of your RRSP or RRIF in your will. Generally, I recommend that you designate these beneficiaries in the RRSP or RRIF documentation itself, since this will allow you to avoid probate fees on the plan assets. If, however, your financial institution won't allow more than one beneficiary and you'd like to name more than one, you can do this in your will. Just recognize that a designation in your will may subject those plan assets to probate fees.

7. Protecting the inheritance.

In most provinces, inheritances do not form part of your child's net family property where he or she is married. As a result, the inheritance is generally protected from the claims of your child's spouse in the event of divorce. In some provinces, it's also possible to specify in your will that the income and growth on the inheritance is also excluded from your child's family property. Another method of protecting an inheritance for your child is to place the inheritance in a testamentary trust.

8. Disinheriting a child.

If you hope to leave one or more family members, or your spouse, out of your will, or to give them a reduced inheritance, you could have some difficulty here. The courts will look at each case on its own merits, but you should be aware that the courts can and have changed, or "varied," wills where the distribution of assets left a child or spouse with less than his or her fair share. A better way to accomplish an uneven distribution of assets may be an inter vivos trust (a trust created during your lifetime) or gifting assets during your lifetime. Speak to a lawyer if your intention is to disinherit anyone.

9. Life interests.

Rather than leaving someone a particular asset outright, it's possible for you to leave the person with a right to use the asset during his or her lifetime—called a "life interest." You could, for example, leave certain investments in a trust and provide that your spouse is entitled to all of the income each year, but not the capital. The capital may, for example, transfer to your kids on your spouse's death. This can work well where your surviving spouse is likely to remarry, and you want to guarantee that your kids (and not the new spouse) will get the assets when your surviving spouse dies.

TO MAKE A LONG STORY SHORT:

- There are a number of clauses to consider adding to your will, including clauses related to common disasters, executor powers, guardians, testamentary trusts, insurance trusts, registered plans, protecting the inheritance, disinheriting family, and life interests.

Powers of Attorney

There's nothing I want more than to be sane for the rest of my life, and to be able to handle all of my own financial affairs, and medical decisions. The truth is, it may not happen this way. Canadians are getting older. In fact, by the year 2030, a full 25 percent of the Canadian population will be over age 65. We could see a growing number of situations where our own relatives are not able to handle their own affairs any longer.

Enter: the power of attorney. A power of attorney enables a person or company of your choosing to handle your affairs in the event that you can't do this yourself. It's an important document. You see, if you become unable to handle your own affairs and you haven't granted power of attorney to anyone, don't assume that your immediate family will be able to step in and fill your shoes. It doesn't work this way. In this case, the Public Trustee office in your province will step in and manage your affairs—and the decisions made by the Public Trustee may not suit you well.

Before anyone else (perhaps a family member or spouse) could manage your affairs, he or she may have to apply to the court for approval. The person may even have to submit a plan as to how your assets will be managed. This is time consuming and unnecessary when a power of attorney has been granted by you.

Keep in mind, however, that a power of attorney is different than a will. It only has effect during your lifetime. Once you're gone, your will applies and any powers of attorney cease to have effect.

Tim's Tip 13: Know what it means to grant power of attorney over your affairs.

A power of attorney is a legal document that empowers someone of your choosing to act on your behalf in certain situations. Most commonly, you probably think of powers of attorney that come into effect in the event that you become unable to manage your own financial affairs or medical decisions, due to mental incapacity.

Types of Powers of Attorney

Actually, there are four common types of powers of attorney. Let's take a brief look at each.

1. Enduring power of attorney for property.

A power of attorney for property gives the "attorney" the ability to make decisions on your behalf related to your financial affairs. The designated individual is typically able to sign cheques, make deposits, withdraw funds, choose investments, sell your home, and generally handle any financial transactions you'd handle on your own if you could. Your attorney is, however, not able to revise or write a will on your behalf. Only you can do this while you're still mentally competent.

Caution!

When you grant a general power of attorney over your financial affairs, you should be aware that your attorney can generally write cheques on your account, withdraw cash, or complete similar transactions effective immediately—even if you're not mentally incapacitated. You can protect yourself by not giving that attorney a copy of the document, or by drafting the power of attorney so that it only takes effect in the case of a certain event coming to pass.

A power of attorney for property should be "enduring," which simply means that it remains in force after you suffer a mental incapacity. If the document is not worded properly, it may not be enduring, and the power of attorney would cease to have any force once you become mentally incapacitated.

2. Enduring power of attorney for personal care.

A power of attorney for personal care works in much the same way as for property, but your attorney is granted the power to make medical decisions on your behalf if you become unable to act for yourself.

This type of power of attorney goes by other names, depending on your province of residence. It can also be called: a living will, advance medical directive, healthcare directive, representation agreement, mandate, authorization, or personal directive. A rose by any other name is still a rose, however, and so is a power of attorney for personal care.

Again, the power of attorney should be written so that it is "enduring," otherwise it will have no effect once you're mentally incapacitated—just when you need it most.

3. Limited powers of attorney.

It's possible to grant another person authority to act on your behalf for a specific situation, or for a limited time. Consider the situation, for example, where you'll be travelling the world at a time when your home is being sold, or you should be selling certain investments. In these cases, a limited power of attorney can give someone else the ability to act on your behalf and complete these transactions.

Tibor was unexpectedly called away to Europe on a business trip. The date was April 20, and he hadn't yet filed his tax return for that tax season. Prior to leaving, he signed a limited power of attorney giving his son the authority to sign his tax return on his behalf. Canada Customs and Revenue Agency (formerly Revenue Canada) accepted the tax return as being filed appropriately by Tibor. The limited power of attorney made it clear that the only authority being granted to Tibor's son was the ability to sign any tax forms, and to deal with CCRA on Tibor's behalf while he was away.

---

4. Bank powers of attorney.

Your local bank has its own forms for granting powers to another individual to deal with your bank accounts. In fact, some banks will insist that you sign their forms, in their presence, rather than accepting your general, or limited, power of attorney for your property. They do this to protect themselves. Check with your local bank about their requirements to ensure that the attorney named by you in your power of attorney for property will be able to handle your bank accounts in the event of your mental incapacity. Be careful here; signing a power of attorney at your bank could revoke your more general enduring power of attorney for property unless there is a provision that specifically says that you are not revoking your other powers of attorney. Check the fine print.

Preparing and Revoking Powers of Attorney

What's it going to cost to prepare your powers of attorney? Maybe less than you think. I had mine prepared for $75 at the same time I had my will prepared. Sure, you can buy those pre-printed forms at the book, stationery, or computer store to save yourself some money, but I don't recommend it for the same reasons I discourage people from preparing a will this way. The wording of the powers of attorney is too important to do it yourself. For example, powers of attorney in your province may have to be worded so that they make reference to other pieces of legislation, such as the *Homestead Act* in Manitoba, or the *Mental Health Act* in Ontario. A lawyer can make sure you've covered all the bases.

You've got to be of the age of majority to be able to designate a power of attorney, and don't forget the importance of being mentally competent. Your power of attorney must generally be signed by two witnesses (similar to your will), and your province may place some restrictions on who can and cannot be a witness. In Ontario, for example, your spouse, child, and certain other individuals cannot witness your power of attorney.

If you spend time or own property in more than one jurisdiction, it's likely that you should prepare a separate power of attorney in each jurisdiction. Speak to a lawyer in each locale to get the details.

There are a number of situations in which your power of attorney may be revoked. Specifically, your power of attorney will be revoked by:

- your death

- your mental incapacity (unless you have created an "enduring" power of attorney through proper wording in the document)
- your bankruptcy (in this case, you'll lose control over your assets, so you won't need an attorney)
- a written revocation signed by you and properly witnessed
- delivery of a letter to your attorney announcing revocation of his powers (make sure you contact any financial institutions or other parties that the attorney may have had dealings with to inform them of the same thing)
- the death of your attorney (unless you've named an alternative attorney in the document)
- expiration of a time period (where the power is granted for a specific time only)
- intervention of the Public Trustee in the event that your attorney is improperly managing your affairs.

Caution!

You may find it best to name your spouse as your attorney for your property. If you don't do this, or if you name your spouse as a co-attorney with someone else, he or she might find it very inconvenient to do simple tasks like paying the bills. Your spouse may be stuck having to get third-party approval to write a cheque for the groceries. Unless your spouse is unable to handle the job of attorney appropriately, I would caution against choosing someone else where your spouse would be inconvenienced.

TO MAKE A LONG STORY SHORT:

- A power of attorney simply gives authority to someone else to handle your financial and medical decisions if you're not able to.
- There are really four types of powers of attorney: enduring powers of attorney for property or personal care, limited powers of attorney, and bank powers of attorney.
- It's important to properly prepare a power of attorney, and you should visit a lawyer to have this done.
- Your power of attorney can be revoked in several situations.

Tim's Tip 14: Give careful consideration to who should be your attorney—it's an important responsibility.

When I use the term "attorney," I'm not referring to a lawyer. I'm talking about that person to whom you've granted power to handle your affairs under your power of attorney documents. Whom should you designate as your attorney? Well, we've got to talk about the attorney for your property and for personal care separately.

Attorney for Property

You can name just about anyone as your attorney for your property: your spouse, a family member, a friend, or a professional (including a trust company). The person that you name must have reached the age of majority. It's important to speak to the potential attorney before naming him or her. You want to make sure that the person is willing to take on the job. Ideally, the attorney should be business-minded, and should be someone you know well, and can trust without question.

There's nothing wrong with naming co-attorneys so that you've got two people sharing the responsibilities. In this event, however, there could be problems if the two attorneys can't agree on how to handle certain assets. If you don't identify in the power of attorney document how co-attorneys are to resolve differences, there could be problems down the line. You could simply say that, in the event of a difference, one of the attorneys (name him), has final say.

Finally, make sure you name an alternative attorney. If the attorney that you name in your document dies or becomes mentally incompetent, the alternative attorney will step in to handle things.

Attorney for Personal Care

The person whom you designate as your attorney for your property may not necessarily be the same person whom you name as your attorney for your personal care. Consider my family, for example. My parents have named each other and me as co-attorneys over their property—because I'm the geeky bean-counter in the family—but they have named each other, my sisters and me together as co-attorneys over their personal care. Why? Well, if a decision had to be made about when to "pull the plug" for either of them, they both wanted it to be a family decision.

Again, make sure you speak to your potential attorney to find out if he or she is willing to take on the responsibility of acting on your behalf if necessary. Naming an alternative attorney also makes sense.

Paying Your Attorney

In many cases, your attorney will not expect any fees for managing your affairs. This is particularly true in the case of family members. If you hire a professional as your attorney, there will be a fee associated with the services provided—so check these out first. In any event, even if a family member who acts as your attorney doesn't expect payment, it may be reasonable to include a fee in your documentation in case the task ends up being much more time consuming than expected.

TO MAKE A LONG STORY SHORT:

- You've got to decide who will be your attorney to look after your financial and medical affairs if you're not able. Your spouse, family members, friends, or a professional are all common choices.
- Make sure your attorney agrees to take on the role, and consider naming co-attorneys where appropriate, and an alternative attorney.
- Your attorney may expect fees for the services provided.

Tim's Tip 15: **Understand the responsibilities and powers of the attorney you designate.**

There are a number of things that your attorney is responsible to do, and his or her powers can be broad, or limited. Let's take a look at both the responsibilities and powers of your attorney.

Responsibilities of the Attorney

Your attorney is responsible to:

- understand his or her duties and powers as attorney
- act for your benefit, not his own, in good faith
- consult with you whenever possible about issues related to your property
- avoid conflicts of interest
- consult with your family and with those looking after your personal care
- look after your financial needs, then those of your dependants
- exercise good judgment
- keep records of all transactions
- meet specific guidelines, if any, on how your money is to be spent.

Powers of the Attorney

The powers that your attorney has are generally narrow under provincial legislation, unless you provide for broader powers in the power of attorney document. Those powers that you give your attorney can be broad, or narrow—it's up to you. You might want to consider restricting the powers of your attorney, but keep in mind that this could limit his or her ability to act in a timely manner when necessary.

Peter had a lawyer prepare an enduring power of attorney for property for him. He designated his brother Simon as the attorney. Peter was concerned, however, about granting his brother powers over all his financial affairs immediately, so he included a provision in the document that required Peter to become mentally incapacitated before Simon could act on his behalf. A few years later, Peter started showing signs of Alzheimer's, and Simon felt that he should step in to manage Peter's affairs. The problem? It took quite a long time to obtain confirmation from a doctor that Peter was unable to handle his own affairs. In the meantime, Peter lost significant amounts in the stock market because he was unable to make prudent decisions.

See the problem here? Simon couldn't act on Peter's behalf until it was certain that Peter was mentally incapable of handling things himself. Sometimes, determining mental incapacity can be difficult and time consuming.

Nevertheless, you may feel strongly about limiting your attorney's powers. Consider these ideas to accomplish this:

- do not provide a copy of the power of attorney document to the attorney until certain conditions are met (i.e., you become mentally incompetent), at which time your lawyer can provide a copy to the attorney
- create a limited power of attorney that only allows powers over certain property
- include a provision that makes the powers effective only when certain conditions are met (your incapacity, for example)
- name co-attorneys so that two people must act together before making any decisions
- require the attorney to provide an accounting of your property on a quarterly or annual basis to family members, or to a professional that you trust.

Caution!

A problem can arise where you've become physically incapacitated and would like your attorney to handle your affairs, but your power of attorney requires that you be mentally incompetent first. That's the danger of restricting the powers of your attorney until you are mentally incompetent. You may be better off giving your attorney broader powers, then instructing your lawyer to hold onto the power of attorney document, and to give it to the attorney only once you've been diagnosed as mentally incompetent.

TO MAKE A LONG STORY SHORT:

- Your attorney has specific responsibilities under provincial law that he or she must adhere to.

- The powers of your attorney can be broad, or narrow, depending on your own preference.
- There are a number of practical ways to limit the powers of your attorney if you'd like, but be careful not to restrict your attorney so much that he or she can't act in your best interest when needed.

Tim's Tip 16: Recognize that provinces can vary in their laws around powers of attorney.

In this tip, I'm going to take a look at some specifics related to powers of attorney in different provinces. Don't be offended if I don't talk about your province or territory. Generally, the rules work similarly across the country, but there are certain exceptions to note.

British Columbia.

Effective September 5, 2000, residents of B.C. will need to prepare a Representation Agreement in accordance with the *B.C. Representation Agreement Act* in order to accomplish the same thing as an enduring power of attorney for property or personal care. The agreement will appoint a representative to look after your financial, medical, and other personal affairs. Your representative is required to act in accordance with your own beliefs and values if these are known to the representative. Speak to a lawyer in B.C. if you've got questions about this agreement.

Ontario.

In Ontario, the *Substitute Decisions Act* will allow any person to apply to the Office of the Public Trustee to manage your property in the event that you become incapable of this and you haven't prepared an enduring power of attorney. This application can be made without the applicant even going to court. While this applicant must provide a management plan for your property, and may be required to post a bond, even this requirement can be waived by the court, particularly where the applicant is a family member. This doesn't sound very appealing to me. Anyone could end up managing your affairs in some cases. Preparing a power of attorney ahead of time will avoid any problems.

Quebec.

Quebec does not refer to a power of attorney. Rather, you'll hear the term "mandate" instead. Specifically, a *Mandate Given in Anticipation of Incapacity* is prepared. If you're the one establishing the mandate, you're considered to be the "mandator," and the person you name who is granted power over your affairs is the "mandatary." Before your mandatary can act on your behalf, he or she must apply to the courts to certify your incapacity, which might require certain tests on your part. A mandate generally covers both financial and medical issues.

TO MAKE A LONG STORY SHORT:

- Laws surrounding powers of attorney are generally similar from one province or territory to the next.
- British Columbia, Ontario, and Quebec have differences worth noting.

WINNING THE ESTATE PLANNING GAME

That's a lot of information about wills and powers of attorney. Keep in mind that things can differ from one province to the next, so be sure to visit a lawyer in your province if you have any specific questions after reading this chapter. Now, turn to the *Estate Planning Tip Sheet* at the front of the book and revisit the tips you've read about in this chapter. For each tip, ask yourself "Does this apply to me?" Then check the appropriate answer: "Yes," "No," or "Not sure." Each "Yes" and "Not sure" answer could mean an opportunity for you to take action.

YOUR BIGGEST COMPETITORS: DEATH AND TAXES

Tax loopholes are like parking meters. As soon as you see one, it's gone.

3

There's one surefire way to avoid income taxes at the time of your death—don't die. You'd be surprised at what immortality could do to reduce your tax bill over the long run. The problem, of course, is that we're all going to face that inevitable appointment with the undertaker at some point.

The purpose of this chapter is to shed some light on what exactly happens from a tax point of view at the time of your death. That's right, I'm going to talk about both death *and* taxes—your two favourite subjects, no doubt. I know you'll be tempted to skip over this chapter if you don't want to face your own mortality, but let me encourage you to stay the course—you'll be glad you did.

Taxed to Death and After

It's no secret that the undertaker and tax collector are friends. When the undertaker comes knocking at your door, you can count on the tax collector to be there by his side. I don't mean to scare you, but the amount of tax you pay in the year of your death could be greater than the total of all the tax you paid during your lifetime if you don't plan your affairs properly. Let's take a look at how this can happen.

Tim's Tip 17: Be aware of the deemed disposition of your property immediately prior to your death.

The fact is, Canada doesn't levy a death tax per se, when you die, and unlike our friends south of the border, we haven't got an estate tax either—not since 1971, that is. We do, however, have a set of tax rules that will deem you to have sold all of your capital property at fair market value, immediately prior to your death. What property am I talking about? Everything from your home, car, vacation properties, business assets, personal effects, investments, and more. The result? Where anything you own has appreciated in value since you acquired it, you could end up paying tax on those gains in value in the year of your death. That's right, Canada's tax on death is really a capital gains tax for the most part. There are some exceptions, like your RRSPs and RRIFs, which I'll talk more about later.

Ramesh died two months ago. At the time of his death, Ramesh owned, among other things, a $30,000 Guaranteed Investment Certificate (GIC), a principal residence worth

$200,000 that had originally cost him $110,000, and mutual funds worth $100,000 that he had purchased for $40,000 a few years ago. The tax collector deems Ramesh to have sold, immediately prior to his death, all of these assets at fair market value. The GIC worth $30,000 also had an original cost of $30,000, so there is no taxable gain that results from this deemed disposition. There is a $90,000 gain on the principal residence upon Ramesh's death, but he won't face tax on this gain since he can take advantage of his principal residence exemption, which will shelter the gain from tax. As for the mutual funds, the gain of $60,000 will be reported on his final tax return, and he'll have to pay tax on that gain, which will cost his heirs $15,000 in tax at a marginal tax rate of 50 percent.

How can you avoid the tax on this deemed disposition on death? There are a number of things to consider—most notably, leaving assets to your spouse. You see, if you leave assets to your spouse on death, that ugly deemed disposition at fair market value that I was telling you about now takes place at your cost—otherwise known as your adjusted cost base, but more on this in the next chapter, which I have devoted to sharing tax strategies that will save you taxes on death, and after. For now, let's continue talking about those taxes that arise on your death.

Did You Know?

At the time of your death, you're deemed to have sold all of your capital property (stuff that could give rise to capital gains or losses). There are two points to note here. First, cash and near-cash investments like GICs, term deposits, and Canada Savings Bonds will not generally give rise to income taxes upon death because, while they do generate income, they don't appreciate in value. Second, your principal residence won't generally face tax upon death because the *principal residence exemption* typically will offset any gain triggered by the deemed disposition on death.

TO MAKE A LONG STORY SHORT:

- You are deemed to have sold, immediately prior to your death, all of your capital property at its fair market value. This could result in taxable capital gains on your death.
- Cash and near-cash investments do not generally give rise to income taxes on death; nor does a principal residence.
- I'll talk more about tax strategies to reduce this tax hit in the next chapter.

Tim's Tip 18: **Recognize that your heirs will not pay tax on the inheritance you leave behind—just on the income afterwards.**

It's a common myth. I'm referring to the claim that those who inherit money in Canada somehow end up paying significant amounts of tax in the year they inherit their money. You should be aware that anyone who inherits non-registered assets (assets outside of an RRSP or RRIF) in Canada is not taxed on the original capital inherited. Rather, your heirs will instead pay tax on any interest, dividends, capital gains, or other income earned on that inheritance after it's received.

Todd's father passed away earlier this year. Todd inherited a stock portfolio that was worth $200,000 at the time of his father's death. His father's adjusted cost base of the stocks was just $50,000. On his father's final tax return, a capital gain of $150,000 ($200,000 less $50,000) was reported, and this led to a tax hit of $37,500 on his father's final return. Todd did not have to pay any additional tax on the $200,000 portfolio inherited, however. Todd expects to generate some dividend income and to realize capital gains this year on that portfolio. Todd's adjusted cost base is $200,000—the fair market value on the day he inherited the portfolio. The bottom line? Todd is only taxed on income and growth of the portfolio from the day he inherited it onward.

You'll notice that Todd's adjusted cost base is simply the fair market value of his father's property at the time of his father's death. There's an exception to this rule: where you leave property to your spouse, you're deemed to have sold that property at your original cost—not at fair market value, so the adjusted cost base to your spouse of property that he or she inherits from you is generally your original adjusted cost base (unless you elect otherwise). In other words, your spouse simply steps into your shoes from a tax point of view. Make sense? I'll talk more about this later.

By the way, there are measures that you can take to minimize the tax that will be paid by your heirs on the growth and income your inheritance generates. I'm thinking of a testamentary trust, which I'll deal with in Chapter 7.

TO MAKE A LONG STORY SHORT:

- Your heirs will not generally pay tax on the capital that they inherit from you. Rather, they will only be taxed on the income and growth from the day they inherited the property. This tax can be minimized with a testamentary trust, which I'll talk about in Chapter 7.
- The adjusted cost base to your heirs of the property you leave behind is generally the fair market value on the day they inherited it from you (your date of death), unless the heir is your spouse, who generally inherits your original adjusted cost base.

Taxing Capital Gains

Okay, so now you know that the deemed disposition that takes place just prior to your death could trigger significant capital gains in the year of your death. This deserves a primer on how capital gains are taxed.

Action Step

The amount of your capital gains that are taxable (the inclusion rate) was reduced from 75 percent before the 2000 federal budget, to two-thirds for capital gains realized after the budget, to just 50 percent for gains realized after Paul Martin's mini-budget of October 18, 2000. For the year 2000, you've got to calculate your net gains or losses for three separate periods in the year: the pre-budget period (January 1 to February 27), the pre-mini budget period (February 28 to October 17), and the post-mini budget period (October 18 to December 31). Want examples of how the calculation is done? Grab a copy of my book, *Winning the Tax Game 2001* (page 151), or visit the Department of Finance Web site at **www.fin.gc.ca** and read their year 2000 budget material.

Tim's Tip 19: Learn to calculate capital gains and losses properly.

The formula for calculating capital gains and losses seems simple enough:

	Proceeds of Disposition
Less:	Adjusted Cost Base
Equals:	Capital Gain/Loss

Get the picture? On the date of your death, you're deemed to have sold your property for its fair market value, which is the proceeds of disposition in the formula above. The adjusted cost base is typically the amount you paid for the property. Things aren't always as simple as they seem, however. Here's what I mean: the fair market value of your property on your death might be easy to determine, or very complex, depending on the asset. The adjusted cost base may be much different than simply the amount you paid for the asset.

Proceeds of Disposition

Your proceeds of disposition on death will be the fair market value of the property deemed to have been sold, but how do you determine that fair market value? In the case of marketable securities such as stocks, bonds, and mutual funds, it's easy: just look in the paper or online for the daily values. For assets like real estate, private company shares, machinery, or equipment, you might need to hire a valuator or appraiser to come up with an accurate value.

Adjusted Cost Base

Depending on the assets you own, your adjusted cost base (ACB) may not simply be the amount that you paid for the asset back when you acquired it. There are a number of things that can affect your ACB, most notably:

- any capital improvements (an addition to your cottage, or renovating a rental property, for example)
- a capital gains election from 1994 (you may have used up all or a portion of your $100,000 capital gains exemption in 1994 when it was available for the last time. If so, the amount of the exemption claimed will have increased the ACB of the assets on which you made the election)
- reinvested distributions (where you own mutual funds, any taxable distributions that were reinvested in more units of the fund will increase your ACB of the fund)
- a V-day valuation (capital gains taxation was introduced in 1972, and any gains prior to 1972 are not generally taxable. A valuation at December 31, 1971, known as V-day, could be your ACB for tax purposes)
- other, less common, items that I would bore you with if I went into detail on them here.

Inclusion Rate

The 2000 federal budget announced a decrease in the capital gains inclusion rate from 75 percent to two-thirds for any capital gains realized after February 27, 2000. This inclusion rate was reduced again in the government's mini-budget of October 18, 2000, to just 50 percent, for gains realized after October 17, 2000. That is, just 50 percent of capital gains are taxable today.

What's the most tax you'll pay on your capital gains under the new rules? About 25 percent (50 percent of gains are included in income, and if your marginal tax rate is about 50 percent, then one-half of that, or 25 percent, will be your tax bill).

Mollie was a successful entrepreneur. She owned some real estate and mutual funds at the time of her death. She had acquired the real estate for $600,000 and had paid $150,000 to make capital improvements. The real estate was worth $850,000 at the time of her death. She also owned mutual funds worth $275,000 that she had paid $200,000 for. The total value included $100,000 of income that had been reinvested over the years. What is Mollie's capital gain, if any, on her death?

Here's the solution to Mollie's question:

ACB of Real Estate

Original purchase price	$600,000
Add: Capital improvements	$150,000
Adjusted cost base	$750,000

Gain/loss on Real Estate

Proceeds of disposition	$850,000
Less: Adjusted cost base	$750,000
Gain on death	$100,000
Taxable capital gain (50%)	$ 50,000

ACB of Mutual Funds

Original purchase price	$200,000
Add: Reinvested distributions	$100,000
Adjusted cost base	$300,000

Gain/loss on Mutual Funds

Proceeds of disposition	$275,000
Less: Adjusted cost base	$300,000
Loss on death	$ 25,000
Allowable capital loss (50%)	$ 12,500

Mollie's total taxable capital gains in the year of her death were $37,500 ($50,000 on the real estate, less the $12,500 capital loss on the mutual funds). This will give rise to a tax hit of $18,750 at a marginal tax rate of 50 percent.

Now that you're an expert in calculating capital gains and losses, take steps to estimate how much tax you're likely to pay on your demise.

TO MAKE A LONG STORY SHORT:

- Understanding how to calculate capital gains and losses in the year of death is important. You can now forecast what your expected tax liability on death will be.
- Your proceeds of disposition and adjusted cost base for each asset on death must be calculated carefully to ensure that you're not going to pay more in tax than you should.

Tim's Tip 20: **Understand the exemptions available to shelter your capital gains on death from tax.**

The tax collector isn't all bad. In fact, he'll let you get away with capital gains on certain property without having to pay any tax. I'm thinking specifically of your principal residence, and qualified small business corporation shares or qualified farm property.

Principal Residence

There's no place like home. There's no place like home. Dorothy from "The Wizard of Oz" wasn't just dreaming when she spoke these words. She was quite likely closing a home sale here in Canada. It's no secret that Canadian residents are entitled to sell their homes tax-free, but what makes this possible? It's the principal residence exemption.

Did You Know?

Your principal residence can be sheltered from tax on your death by use of the principal residence exemption. Interestingly, your principal residence can be more than simply your city home. The definition of a principal residence is a dwelling that you ordinarily inhabited, and can include a house, condominium, cottage, mobile home, trailer, live-aboard boat, or a foreign property. Sorry, but vacant land or a rental property that you've never lived in won't qualify as your principal residence.

You see, every family (which includes you, your spouse, and any unmarried kids under age 18) is entitled to one principal residence exemption. The exemption will shelter any gains on your home from tax. The key point to note here is that the principal residence exemption can also shelter any gains on your property from tax in the year of your death. Now, where you've got more than one property, your executor will have to choose which one to designate as your principal residence. Let me advise that if you own more than one property, your executor needs to visit a tax pro. It can be very difficult without professional help to determine which property to designate.

QSBC Shares or Farm Property

If you own shares in a small business, and those shares increase in value over time, there's a strong possibility that you'll be able to shelter up to $500,000 of that increase from tax through the $500,000 enhanced capital gains exemption. This exemption is available on your death to shelter gains that may arise from the deemed disposition of those shares on death.

To be eligible, your small company shares will have to be qualified small business corporation (QSBC) shares. Using the full $500,000 exemption could save you $125,000 in taxes if your marginal tax rate is 50 percent.

What in the world are QSBC shares? In general, these are shares that you (or a related person) must have owned for a two-year period.

In addition, the company must be a Canadian-controlled private corporation. The company must be using 90 percent or more of its assets to carry on an active business primarily in Canada, and the same must hold true for 50 percent or more of its assets throughout the two-year period you've owned the stock. Sound complex? The truth is, the definition has been simplified here. Be sure to have a tax pro review the company's financial statements to determine whether it qualifies for the $500,000 exemption.

Finally, you should be aware that shares of a family farm corporation and certain other farm property (farm quotas, for example) may also be eligible for some protection from capital gains taxes. The $500,000 enhanced capital gains exemption can be used to shelter gains on qualifying farm property. Again, you should visit a tax pro to determine whether or not the farm property that you own will qualify.

TO MAKE A LONG STORY SHORT:

- There are two key exemptions available that can be claimed in the year of your death to minimize the tax on capital gains that might arise: the principal residence exemption, and the enhanced $500,000 capital gains exemption.

Taxing Registered Plans

Capital gains taxes on your death are not the only taxes you may face. If you've got an RRSP or RRIF, those assets could also be subject to tax in the year of your death unless proper planning is done.

Tim's Tip 21: **Recognize the tax hit you'll face on death if you've got RRSP, RRIF, or other registered plan assets.**

Some people think it's a crime that the government would tax your RRSP or RRIF assets at the time of your death. Failing any kind of planning, the full value of your registered plan assets will be included in your income in your year of death. The rationale? Since you received a tax deduction when you contributed your money to the plan, you'll face tax on 100 percent of any withdrawals, and at the time of your death, you're deemed to have received the full value of the plan assets. Do the math. Where your marginal tax rate is 50 percent, you could hand one-half of your plan to the tax collector in the year of your death.

If you want some specifics here, your death will result in the following events taking place as far as your RRSP or RRIF is concerned:

1. You're deemed to have received, immediately prior to death, the full fair market value of your plan assets. This is taxable.
2. If you leave the plan assets to an eligible person, namely your spouse or a dependent child or grandchild, then they receive these assets as a "refund of premiums." In this event, you'll receive a deduction for the amount that was included in your income under the first step above. Result? No tax on your final tax return.
3. The eligible person (spouse, child or grandchild) receiving the refund of premiums will now be taxable on the refund of premiums received unless proper steps are taken to avoid the tax, which brings me to the last point:
4. If the eligible person transfers the plan assets received as a refund of premiums to their own RRSP, RRIF, or an annuity (in the case of minor children), they'll be entitled to a deduction for the amount transferred to their own plan or annuity. The result? Tax is deferred until withdrawn by the eligible person, at which time he or she will have to pay the piper.

Following me so far? I'll talk more about avoiding the tax hit on death on your RRSP and RRIF assets in the next chapter.

TO MAKE A LONG STORY SHORT:

- The full fair market value of your RRSP and RRIF assets could be taxable in the year of your death.
- This tax can be deferred by leaving the assets to your spouse or a dependent child or grandchild, which I'll talk more about in the next chapter.

Taxes of Other Sorts

While we're on the subject of taxes that arise on your death, we've got to talk about a few other types of taxes that can hit you.

Tim's Tip 22: Recognize the various other income and assets that can give rise to various taxes on your death.

As if the capital gains tax resulting from the deemed disposition of your property on death, or the tax on your registered plans weren't enough, here are three other taxes that you should be aware of:

1. Tax on unrealized income.

Picture this. On the date of your death you're still owed some salary from your employer, a bit of vacation pay, some dividends declared on some stocks you own, some interest income that had accrued on certain investments up to your death, and maybe even some Canada Pension Plan payments, or Old Age Security payments.

The fact is, these amounts must be reported in the year of your death as part of your income. There are some special rules that may allow you to report some of these types of income on more than one tax return in your year of death, which could save you tax, and I'll talk more about this idea in Tip 23.

2. Foreign estate tax.

It doesn't take much for a Canadian resident to face a requirement to pay U.S. estate taxes—or estate taxes in other countries. If you happen to own a few shares of Microsoft, Gillette, Walt Disney, or any other U.S. company, even if these are held in your Canadian brokerage account, and your worldwide estate is greater than $1.2 million (U.S.), you may have a U.S. estate tax issue. I'll talk more about U.S. estate taxes in Chapter 11.

3. Probate fees.

We might as well call these fees a tax. That's really what they are, and they're here to stay in most provinces, although residents of Quebec and Alberta have it pretty good—see Appendix D at the back for more information. Probate fees are levied by your province to effectively validate your will. Once letters probate have been received, third parties (such as banks, mutual fund companies, and the like) will then have a comfort level about distributing to your beneficiaries your assets held by the third parties. I'll talk more about probate fees in Chapter 10.

Caution!

If you're not careful, you could end up paying double-tax in the year of your death. You see, our tax law will generally allow a tax credit in the year of death for any estate taxes that you pay to a foreign government. Typically, these foreign taxes can be applied to reduce the Canadian tax on capital gains triggered in the year of death. The problem? It may happen that there are little or no capital gains taxes to pay in Canada on death because the assets have not appreciated much in value, but will still be subject to foreign estate tax. You could be left without any tax relief for those foreign taxes. Visit a tax pro if you're likely to pay foreign estate taxes.

TO MAKE A LONG STORY SHORT:

- In addition to capital gains taxes and tax on your registered assets on death, you may face taxes on unrealized income, U.S. or other foreign estate taxes, and probate fees.
- I'll talk more about U.S. estate taxes in Chapter 11, and probate fees in Chapter 10.

Tax Filings on Death

You think your tax filings are complicated now! Just wait until you're gone, then imagine the look on your executor's face upon finding out that he or she will have to file up to four tax returns for your year of death. The good news? Filing more than one tax return will generally mean tax savings for you, and more money to pass on to your heirs.

Tim's Tip 23: **Identify the tax returns which may be filed on your behalf after your death, and when they're due.**

Have you ever made your way to the post office at 11:30 p.m. on April 30 to file your tax return at the last minute? If so, chances are pretty good we passed each other in the line-up. You'll be glad to know that, after your death, the tax collector gives your executor a little more time to file your final tax return(s) than you might normally be allowed if you were still alive. So, your executor may not have to worry about standing in a line-up to file a tax return on April 30 for your final year.

The filing deadline for your last tax return(s) is the later of April 30 (the usual filing deadline) and six months after the date of your death. So, if you die after October in a given year, and before the filing deadline of April 30, your filing deadline will be extended.

William died on November 15, 2000. As a result, his tax return for 2000, which normally would have been due on April 30, 2001, was not actually due until May 15, 2001—a full six months after his death. If William had instead died on February 15, 2001, his tax return for 2000 (which would normally have been due on April 30, 2001) would not be due until August 15, 2001 (six months after his death). In this latter case, William's executor would file his tax return for 2000 by August 15, 2001, as well as a tax return for 2001 (his year of death) which would cover only the period January 1 to February 15 (up to the date of death). This tax return for 2001 would be due April 30, 2002.

Now, let's talk about the four types of tax returns that may potentially be filed for your year of death. I should mention that the real benefit of reporting different types of income on different tax returns in the year of your death is that, on each tax return filed, you'll be entitled to the same basic personal credits all over again, and the low rates of tax all over again on the first $30,000 of income. Think of this as an income splitting tactic.

Tax Return 1: Your Terminal Return

This tax return is simply your normal tax return for the year of your death. It covers the period from January 1 of the year you die, to your date of death. Generally, all your income received for the year to the date of death will be reported on this return and can include employment income (as reported on a T4 slip for your year of death), interest income, dividend income received, and other types of income and deductions.

Tax Return 2: Rights or Things Return

What in the world is a "right or thing"? Good question. These are amounts that were owing to you at the time of your death, and can include:

- dividends declared but not yet received
- salary, vacation pay, and certain unpaid bonuses not yet received
- unmatured bond coupon interest
- debts receivable (i.e. amounts due from the sale of business inventory)
- a herd of livestock where a farmer reports on a cash basis
- CPP and OAS owing for the month of death but not yet received.

Tax Return 3: Testamentary Trust Income Return

If a family member or friend has passed away and made you a beneficiary of a trust set up by way of their will, you could be receiving income from that trust each year. If you receive income from a testamentary trust in the year of your death, and the trust's year-end is not December 31, then that income can be reported on a separate tax return.

Tax Return 4: Sole Proprietor or Partner Return

If you happen to be a business owner and operate as a sole proprietorship or a partnership, and your business year-end is not December 31, you'll be able to report certain business income on a separate tax return for the year of your death. For example, consider someone who passed away on June 30 last year. If he had owned a business with, say, a January 31 year-end, then the business income earned from the date of his last year-end (January 31) to the date of his death (June 30) can be reported on a separate tax return.

Harold died on June 30, 2000. Between January 1, 2000 and June 30, 2000, Harold's income was as follows: $35,000 of salary and $20,000 of interest income from a trust that had been *set up on his wife's death. In addition, he was owed the following amounts on the date of his death: $6,000 of vacation pay, $15,000 in commissions, $6,250 in taxable Canadian dividends that had been declared but not yet paid, and $2,000 from matured bond coupons that he had not yet cashed.*

Did You Know?

While it's possible that your executor could file up to four tax returns for the year of your death, including one for proprietorship or partnership income, I should mention that the likelihood of filing a separate tax return for a deceased sole proprietor or partner is not very high anymore. Why? Well, changes were introduced in 1995 that caused many proprietors and partners to change to a December 31 business year-end for tax purposes. This special tax return on death only applies if you have a non-calendar year-end. Check out CCRA's interpretation bulletin IT-278R2, available on their Web site at **www.ccra-adrc.gc.ca**, for more information on this.

If Harold's executor had filed just one tax return for Harold in the year of his death, reporting all of this income, the total tax liability on Harold's final tax return would have been $26,240.

Let's see what would've happened if Harold's executor had filed more than one tax return for his year of death. His executor could have filed three different returns for Harold: (1) a terminal return to report the salary that Harold had received, (2) a rights or things return to report the vacation pay, commissions, dividends, and bond coupon interest, and (3) a return for the testamentary trust interest income. Filing three tax returns instead of one would mean a total tax bill of $15,885.

What a difference! The total taxes paid dropped by $10,355 ($26,240 less $15,885) just by filing more than one tax return. The reason for the savings is simple: each tax return offers a basic personal credit. By filing more than one return, the number of credits is multiplied. In addition, once income is over $30,004 you jump into the second federal tax bracket, which will result in a higher tax bill. In Harold's case, we managed to have more dollars taxed in the first tax bracket by dividing the income among more tax returns. The moral of the story is this: the more tax returns filed by your executor, the more money passed to the pockets of your heirs.

TO MAKE A LONG STORY SHORT:

- The filing deadline for the tax returns of a deceased taxpayer is the later of April 30 following the year of death (the usual deadline) and six months following the date of death.
- There are potentially four tax returns that could be filed by your executor for you in the year of your death. More tax returns can mean more tax savings and a greater inheritance for your heirs.

WINNING THE ESTATE PLANNING GAME

There you have it—a summary of what happens on your death from a tax point of view. All of this begs the question that I've introduced to you: how do you reduce these taxes on death? I've devoted the next chapter to answering that question. Before we move on, however, please turn back to the *Estate Planning Tip Sheet* at the front of the book and ask yourself this question for each tip I've written: "Does this apply to me?" Answer "Yes," "No," or "Not Sure." Don't forget that any "Yes" or "Not Sure" answers could form an important part of your overall estate plan. Now, let's move on to the next chapter and greater tax savings.

WINNING THE RACE: BEATING THE TAX COLLECTOR AT DEATH

Life without death is not realistic, but death without taxes is entirely possible.

4

No doubt about it. People who complain about paying their income taxes can be divided into two types: men and women. The tax collector knows, however, that once you're dead and gone, it's not exactly easy for you to object to a hefty tax hit, and the tax hit on death can be significant. You'll recall from Chapter 3 that there are many ways in which the tax collector can attack your estate once you're gone: capital gains tax on assets that are deemed to have been disposed of immediately prior to your death, full taxation of the amounts in your RRSPs or

RRIFs, taxation of other amounts received in the year of your death, and taxation of amounts owing to you on the date of your death, among others.

In Chapter 3, I answered the question: "What happens on my death from a tax point of view?". In this chapter, I'm going to take this discussion a step further and answer the question: "What can I do to minimize the tax hit on my death, and after?"

It could be that you're like many Canadians who hold the opinion that, for every tax problem, there is a solution that is straightforward, uncomplicated and wrong. In fact, some of the ideas I'm going to share today are quite simple—and effective to boot. Now, I've divided the tax strategies into three categories: (1) those that should be implemented during your lifetime, (2) those that must be addressed in your will, and (3) special elections that can be made by your executor after you're gone. Here we go.

Strategies During Your Lifetime

There are steps that you can take even today to ensure that you'll pay less tax in the year of your death. Consider the following ideas.

Tim's Tip 24: **Consider giving assets away today to reduce taxes at death.**

There's nothing like dying broke to avoid a tax hit on death. Now, I'm not going to suggest that you should give absolutely everything away during your lifetime. After all, I wouldn't want you living on a park bench if that could be avoided. You should recognize, though, that giving assets away today is the simplest (and a very effective) method of reducing taxes and probate fees at the time of your death. Let's talk briefly about gifts to family, friends, and to charity.

Gifts to Family and Friends

I've devoted the whole next chapter, Chapter 5, to giving assets away to family and friends during your lifetime, so I won't cover all the nitty gritty details here. Let me say, however, that there are right ways and wrong ways to give assets away during your lifetime. Most notably, you'll avoid a tax hit by giving assets to your spouse. You see, normally you're deemed to have sold, at fair market value, those assets that you've given away. This could trigger taxable capital gains when you've made the gift to a child, other family member, or friend. The exception is a gift to your spouse. In Chapter 5, I will talk more about giving away assets during your lifetime.

Action Step

Giving assets away during your lifetime is a very effective estate planning strategy. By giving assets away today, you'll no longer own them at the time of your death. The result? There can't be any deemed disposition of those assets on your death, and those assets will avoid probate since they will fall outside of your estate. One caution: you don't want to trigger a huge tax hit today to save a tax hit on death. Giving assets away could trigger some tax. There will be more on this issue in Chapter 5.

Gifts to Charity

Giving assets away to charity during your lifetime can accomplish the same thing as making a gift to a family member or friend. The name of the game is getting assets out of your hands and into someone else's. This will save you tax and probate fees on death. Keep in mind, however, that when you give to charity, you will never get back in tax savings more than you've donated. That is, while the charity will be grateful to you, don't forget that you may be leaving less to your other heirs as a result. The bottom line, then, is that your charitable giving should be motivated not solely by the tax benefits, but primarily by a desire to help others or as an act of service.

You've also got to recognize that donating assets, rather than cash, to charity will result in a disposition of those assets, which could give rise to taxable capital gains and reduce the benefit of the donation tax credit. Not to worry though; the donation credit will virtually always outweigh the taxable capital gain.

I have devoted all of Chapter 9 to planned charitable giving—so I'll refer you there for more information on this tactic to save tax on death.

TO MAKE A LONG STORY SHORT:

- Giving assets away during your lifetime will mean that you will die with less in your hands. This will minimize the tax from the deemed disposition on your death, and will also minimize probate fees.
- Gifts are generally made to one or more of three groups: family members, friends, and charities.

Tim's Tip 25: Understand how an estate freeze can cut, defer, and establish your tax bill on death, among other benefits.

What is this thing called an "estate freeze"? No, it has nothing to do with selling your possessions and moving to Nunavut—as cold as that might be. An estate freeze is simply the process of taking certain assets that you own today, and freezing them at their current value in your hands. An estate freeze allows you to freeze the value of an asset today, and to pass the future growth, or appreciation in value, to your heirs. There are ten potential benefits of an estate freeze:

1. ***Cutting the tax bill on death.*** When a freeze is completed, all future growth between the date of the freeze and your death will accrue in the hands of your heirs. That future growth would have been taxed in your hands at the time of your death, if not sooner, if the freeze hadn't been done. Those dollars will never be taxed in your hands after a freeze.

2. ***Deferring the ultimate tax bill.*** By passing the future growth in the asset's value to your heirs, you can defer income tax on that growth until a much later time. Although your heirs will eventually pay tax, these taxes may not be due, for example, until your heirs pass away.
3. ***Establishing the tax bill on death.*** By freezing the value of an asset today, you'll be able to establish, pretty accurately, what your tax bill will be upon death since you'll know the value at which those assets will be deemed to be sold on your death. This makes planning for those taxes much easier.
4. ***Utilizing the capital gains exemption.*** A freeze may allow you to take advantage of the *enhanced capital gains exemption* (see Tip 58 for more) where you own shares of a qualified small business corporation or qualified farm property. This exemption is available to all Canadian residents and can shelter up to $500,000 of capital gains on this type of property.
5. ***Splitting income with family members.*** In the process of completing a freeze, you will be placing certain assets (usually private company shares) in the hands of your heirs. These assets can provide an income to your heirs that will be taxed in their hands—not yours.
6. ***Protecting assets from creditors.*** It may be possible to protect certain assets from creditors by transferring their ownership to your heirs or, better still, a family trust, as part of a freeze.
7. ***Protecting assets from spouses.*** If your kids (or you) own valuable and growing assets prior to marriage, it may be possible to use a freeze to minimize the claims of future spouses or ex-spouses.
8. ***Reducing probate fees.*** A freeze will restrict the growth of the frozen assets in your hands. This means that you'll generally own less at the time of your death than you would have without the freeze, which will minimize probate fees.
9. ***Minimizing annual taxes.*** Freezing assets typically requires a corporation to be set up. Corporations that carry on an active

business are entitled to very low rates of tax (about 20 percent) on the first $200,000 of active business income. It may be possible to take advantage of these rates, depending on the assets that you're freezing.

10. ***Maintaining control over the property.*** You can enjoy the first nine benefits without having to give up control over or use of the assets during your lifetime.

Freezing private company shares makes sense when you're happy with the growth you've already achieved, and expect significant growth in the future between the date of the freeze and the time of your death, or the time you sell the shares, whichever comes first. On the other hand, be careful about freezing your shares where you expect the company to drop in value in the future, where you're simply going to wind-up the business when you retire, or where you're likely to sell the business to a non-related party in the very near future.

Caution!

Jack owned shares in a small private company at the time of his death. They had a value of $1,000,000, and an adjusted cost base (ACB) of just $100. He didn't complete a freeze during his lifetime, and he left his shares to his son. Jack faced a taxable capital gain of $999,900 ($1 million less the ACB of $100) on his death, and a tax bill of $249,975. He could have completed an estate freeze earlier, and it could have worked this way: Jack could have transferred (sold) the shares in his own business to a new holding company set up by him. In return for selling his shares to his new holding company, Jack would have taken back shares in the new company as payment. These new shares could have been special "freeze" shares that would not appreciate in value over time (hence the "freeze" is accomplished). In addition, Jack would be issued an entirely different class of shares that would possess plenty of votes, so that Jack will always control the company—

even if he redeems (cashes in) his freeze shares as a source of income in retirement. Finally, common shares in the new company would have been issued to Jack's children, and all future growth in the business would accrue to those shares. Jack will be able to maintain an income from the new holding company by taking dividends on his shares, or by redeeming some of his frozen shares over time, for cash.

Let's take Jack's example a step further. Jack could have completed a freeze earlier in his life at a time when his shares were worth, say, $500,000. If he had done this, the growth between $500,000 and the $1 million that the shares were worth at the time of his death would not have been taxed in his hands. Rather, that growth could have been placed in his son's hands. Further, if Jack had done a freeze earlier, he could have chosen the selling price at which he transferred his shares to the new holding company. This would have allowed him to take advantage of the $500,000 enhanced capital gains exemption, assuming that his shares would qualify. His story would have sounded much better.

Jack completed an estate freeze at a time when the shares of his small private company were worth $500,000. He completed the freeze by selling his shares to a holding company that he set up, and since he completed the freeze under Section 85 of our tax law, he was able to choose his selling price at any amount between his adjusted cost base (ACB) of $100 and the fair market value of his shares ($500,000). He chose a price (called the "elected amount") of $500,000. This triggered a $499,900 capital gain in Jack's hands ($500,000 proceeds less ACB of $100). The full gain was sheltered using Jack's enhanced capital gains exemption. The holding company paid Jack by issuing shares to him. The company also issued common shares to Jack's son so that all future growth accrues to him. The shares received by

Jack were special shares that were frozen in value at $500,000, and had an ACB of $500,000 (the elected amount chosen by Jack). At the time of Jack's death, he was deemed to have sold those holding company shares at their fair market value of $500,000 (they were frozen at that value), and his ACB was $500,000, so he had no tax to pay on these shares on his death.

Methods of Freezing

There's more than one way to skin a cat, and there's more than one way to complete an estate freeze. In Jack's example above, I've introduced what is known as a "holding company freeze." Not surprisingly, it involves setting up a holding company. It's also possible to complete what is known as an "internal freeze." An internal freeze works where the assets you're freezing are shares in a private company (as in Jack's example). With an internal freeze, there's no need to set up a new holding company. All you need to do is swap your existing shares in the company for new special shares (in that same company) that will be frozen in value. If you're freezing assets other than private company shares (perhaps you want to freeze the value of investments, antiques, a rental property, or other assets) then you'll generally have to use a holding company.

It is possible to use a trust to accomplish a freeze. You would simply transfer the assets that you want to freeze into a trust for the benefit of your heirs. The drawback to this is, however, that the transfer will have to take place at fair market value (you can't choose the selling price as you can with a holding company freeze), so you might trigger a sizeable tax hit where the assets have appreciated in value.

An estate freeze is not a stunt that you should be doing at home in your living room. You're going to need professional tax help!

Caution!

There are three things to measure before freezing real estate that you own: (1) the amount of land transfer taxes that may be payable, (2) the capital taxes that may be owed by the company on an annual basis as a result of the real estate (these are annual taxes levied by some provinces on certain assets owned by corporations), and (3) the additional tax that might be paid, if any, as a result of being unable to designate the real estate as your principal residence once it's in the company.

TO MAKE A LONG STORY SHORT:

- An estate freeze is the process of freezing certain assets at today's value, and passing the future growth in those assets to your heirs.
- There are five key benefits to a freeze: cutting your tax bill on death, deferring taxes far into the future, establishing the amount of your tax bill on death, utilizing the enhanced capital gains exemption, and maintaining control over and use of those assets during your lifetime.
- The most common methods to freeze an estate are: a holding company freeze, an internal freeze, or a trust freeze.
- Visit a tax pro to implement a freeze—don't try this stunt at home!

Tim's Tip 26: Reduce the tax hit on a second property by planning for its succession today.

Let's talk about second properties for a minute. This can include a vacation property, otherwise known as a "personal use property" (like a cottage, condo down south, and even a mobile home) or an income-producing property. We've got to talk about personal use properties and income properties separately since the tax collector treats them differently.

Personal Use Properties

I'll call personal use properties "PUP" for short. Any PUP is owned primarily for your own use and enjoyment. A cottage is a prime example, so let me refer to this property as your cottage, although it might include any other second property that is a PUP.

Here are three strategies that you should be aware of to minimize the family's tax bill on the cottage.

1. Transfer the cottage to your spouse.

You'll manage to defer a tax hit this way. When you transfer any property to your spouse, either during your lifetime or upon death, the transfer is deemed to take place at your adjusted cost base—not fair market value. This is true despite the "deemed disposition" on death that I talked about in Chapter 3, and regardless of whether the transfer to your spouse is a sale (even a sale at fair market value; although in this case, you can elect for the transfer to take place for tax purposes at fair market value), or a gift during your lifetime or upon death. If you transfer the property to your spouse on your death, you'll defer the tax hit until your spouse disposes of the property or dies.

2. Call the cottage your principal residence.

You see, each "family unit" (married spouses, common-law and same-sex partners, and unmarried children under age 18) is entitled to call one property their principal residence each year, which will effectively shelter all or a portion of any capital gains on that property from tax due to the "principal residence exemption." Typically, your cottage will qualify to be called your principal residence upon your death (and during your lifetime, of course). Your executor can elect after your death to call the cottage your principal residence to minimize any tax hit on the property. Finally, consider that things were different prior to 1982. Back then, it was possible for each spouse to claim his or her own exemption where each spouse owned his or her own property. Today, it's still possible to shelter pre-1982 capital gains from tax using two exemptions. So, at the

Action Step

Your adult children are entitled to their own principal residence exemptions. You may want to transfer the cottage to an adult child during your lifetime, which could multiply the number of principal residence exemptions that the family can use. If you don't want to give up control over the property, consider transferring the cottage to a trust with your children as beneficiaries—their exemptions will still be available on the property. Before you do this, however, count the cost of any tax bill that you might trigger by making a transfer—remember, it's a deemed sale.

time of your death, taxes on pre-1982 gains could be avoided on two properties.This is going to involve ensuring, however, that the properties are not owned jointly by you and your spouse, but that one property is in each name. There's a bit more to it than even this, so visit a tax pro for more information about this tactic!

3. Maximize your adjusted cost base (ACB).

The higher the ACB of your cottage, the smaller the capital gain and tax bill will be on death (or on a sale during your lifetime for that matter). For example, assume that you renovated your cottage three years ago, spending about $50,000. Capital improvements like this are added to your ACB. In addition, assume that the cottage was owned prior to 1972, when capital gains weren't taxed in Canada. In this case, special tax rules will ensure that only capital gains after 1971 are taxed. This fact could boost the ACB of your family's cottage significantly. Finally, you may have made an election with your 1994 tax return to use up the $100,000 capital gains exemption at that time. If so, that election will have resulted in an increase to the ACB of the cottage. The end result of all this is a revised ACB that could be much higher than you thought. A higher ACB will spell tax relief in the form of a lower capital gain on death. Do your executor a favour and document the ACB of your cottage or other property today, and leave this information with your will. It will save you tax on your death.

4. Buy life insurance.

The nice thing about life insurance is that it's paid out after your death completely tax-free and can provide the cash necessary to cover any tax bill that might arise from the deemed disposition of your cottage. Let's face it, without that supply of cash on your death, it may be necessary to sell the cottage to raise the cash to pay the taxes, unless you've got enough other liquid assets in your estate to pay the tax collector. Selling the cottage could be heart-breaking for your family if they're attached to it. By the way, if you're going to leave the cottage to your spouse after your death, there won't be any tax to pay on the cottage until your spouse dies (or otherwise sells it). So, consider buying a joint, second-to-die policy, which only pays out its benefits after the surviving spouse dies. It's a cheaper way to buy insurance, and besides, your heirs won't need the cash to pay the taxes until the death of the second spouse anyway.

Transferring the Property Today

Are you going to transfer ownership during your lifetime, or upon death as part of your estate? If the cottage is going to pass to the children or grandchildren at some point anyway, you might consider making this an inter vivos transfer—that is, a transfer during your lifetime. This, of course, is going to take some talking between you, your spouse, and the kids. The two obvious benefits of an inter vivos transfer are: (1) You'll pass the tax bill on any future capital gains on the property to the kids, and (2) you'll avoid probate fees on the cottage upon your death.

Keep in mind that transferring the cottage to the kids today doesn't have to mean giving up use or control over the property. You can always enter into an agreement guaranteeing you access to the cottage and specifying other conditions. By the way, an inter vivos transfer is usually a great way to ensure that you'll get the help from your kids that you need to maintain the property.

Transferring the Property After Death

All right, I can hear the rumblings already. The cottage is a sensitive issue in your family, and you don't really want to discuss it. Or perhaps you simply want complete ownership and control over the cottage during your lifetime without incurring professional fees. In this case, dealing with the cottage by way of your will—as part of your estate—may be your best option.

Remember, though, that the tax collector always comes knocking upon death. The cottage will be deemed sold at its fair market value when you die. In this Tip, I've already talked about how to handle that tax hit on death. Aside from the tax issue, you should understand the three most common ways to deal with the cottage in your will.

1. ***Leave it directly to the kids.*** This is certainly a hands-off option for you. Your kids will be left to figure out ownership, access, control, and cost-sharing issues on their own. You could make your thoughts known by way of a "letter of wishes."
2. ***Sell the cottage.*** Sometimes, the only way to avoid hard feelings once you're gone is to sell the cottage and distribute the proceeds, but why not give your kids the right of first refusal? This way, those who are interested can purchase the cottage before it's sold to a third party.
3. ***Set up a testamentary trust.*** A trust created upon your death by your will is a great way to avoid conflicts between siblings since the trustee acts as an arbitrator. A trust can also protect the cottage from a child's ex-spouse or creditors.

Action Step

Be sure to visit a tax pro if you're planning to convert your principal residence to a rental property, or your rental property to a personal use property. The reason? You'll generally be deemed to have sold the property at fair market value just prior to changing its use, and to have reacquired the property at that same fair market value. The result? You could face a tax hit in the year you change the use of your property.

Income Properties

Rental or other income-producing properties are treated a bit differently than your personal use properties. The big differences are these:

- an income property will not generally qualify as a principal residence, so any capital gains realized on death (or during your lifetime) cannot be sheltered from tax using your principal residence exemption
- income properties can be depreciated for tax purposes so that depreciation costs (called "capital cost allowance" or CCA) can offset the income earned on the property. Where CCA has been claimed in the past, a sale—including a deemed disposition on death—could result in "recapture." Recapture is simply an amount that may be included in your income where the value of the property has gone up, and the tax collector determines that you shouldn't have been entitled to claim as much depreciation as you did since the property didn't actually depreciate in value. I won't get into how recapture is calculated here
- where the tax collector determines that you didn't claim enough depreciation on your income property, you may be entitled to a "terminal loss," which is really the opposite of recapture and can be deducted against any source of income in your year of death.

How do you minimize the tax hit on an income property at the time of death? The strategies I referred to early in this Tip for your cottage will also work here, with the exception of the principal residence exemption. Namely, consider leaving it to your spouse, maximizing your ACB, and buying life insurance to cover the tax hit.

TO MAKE A LONG STORY SHORT:

- A second property can give rise to a tax hit on death due to rules that will deem you to have sold the property on death.
- There are two types of properties: personal use properties and income-producing properties.

- Consider leaving the property to your spouse, calling it your principal residence (personal use properties only), maximizing your ACB, and buying life insurance to cover a tax hit on death.
- Give consideration to whether you'll transfer the property to your heirs today, or after you're gone, and how that transfer will take place.

Tim's Tip 27: Designate the right person as the beneficiary of your RRSP or RRIF to minimize the tax hit.

It's a common question: "How can I avoid tax on my RRSP or RRIF assets when I die?" There may not be much magic here, but there are some things to consider. Your first line of defense is always to name your spouse as the beneficiary of your plan. Beyond this, the opportunities to avoid tax become slim, but if you have certain dependants—or have charitable intentions—there may be other opportunities.

Your Spouse as Beneficiary

If you name your spouse as the beneficiary of your RRSP or RRIF, then your plan assets will transfer directly to your spouse's plan upon your death on a tax-free basis. If your surviving spouse is age 69 or younger in the year of your death, those assets can be transferred to his or her RRSP, otherwise they'll be transferred to your spouse's RRIF. Your spouse generally has 60 days following the year of your death to make the deposit to his or her own plan. For example, if you were to die at any time in 2001, your spouse would have until 60 days following the end of the year—March 1, 2002—to contribute the balance of your RRSP or RRIF to his or her own plan.

Your Dependants as Beneficiaries

If you're not able to leave your RRSP or RRIF assets to a spouse, chances are good that you're going to leave the assets to your kids or grandchildren. In the vast majority of cases, this is going to mean a tax bill. Typically, you'll face tax on these plan assets on your final tax return; then the balance is distributed to the children or grandchildren. Like many rules in tax, however, there are always exceptions. In this case, there are two:

1. ***Infirm Dependants.*** You'll manage to avoid the tax collector if you leave your RRSP or RRIF assets to a child or grandchild, of any age, who was financially dependent on you at the time of your death due to a physical or mental infirmity. Your dependant will be eligible to transfer your plan assets tax-free to his or her own RRSP, RRIF, or annuity.
2. ***Minor Dependants.*** If a minor child was financially dependent on you at the time of your death, the child will be eligible to buy an annuity that pays amounts up to age 18 using your RRSP or RRIF assets. This won't defer tax for very long in most cases, but it beats paying tax on the plan assets in one year. If the minor is infirm, then the rules for infirm dependants apply in point 1 above.

Prior to the 1999 federal budget, you could take advantage of this tax-free rollover to your dependants only where you did not have a surviving spouse. Today, you can transfer your RRSP or RRIF assets to those dependants under these rules even if you have a surviving spouse (generally, however, your simplest bet will be to leave the assets to your spouse first). This change is effective for 1999 and later years, although the measure will be available for deaths after 1995 and before 1999 if the recipient of the RRSP or RRIF assets and the deceased's estate make a joint election for the new rules to apply.

Did You Know?

A child must be financially dependent on you at the time of your death to entitle you to a tax-free rollover of your RRSP or RRIF to that child. You'll be shocked at the tax collector's definition of "financially dependent." Are you sitting down? Where your dependant has income equal to the basic personal amount or more ($7,231 in 2000), he or she will not be considered financially dependent on you. No wonder it's a rare occurrence to find this tax-free rollover to dependants taking place. Shame on our government.

Your Favourite Charity as Beneficiary

As recently as 1999, this option was not widely used. You see, prior to the 2000 federal budget, naming a charity as the beneficiary of your RRSP or RRIF was great for the charity, but would not have provided you with any tax relief in the year of your death. That's changed now. Beginning in 2000, you'll be entitled to a donation tax credit on your final tax return when you name a charity as the beneficiary of your RRSP or RRIF. You'll be glad to know that, in the year of your death, you're entitled to claim a credit for donations totalling up to 100 percent of your income in the year of death, plus 100 percent of income in the year prior to your death. The bottom line is that all of the tax that would have otherwise been owing on your RRSP or RRIF at the time of your death will be completely offset by a donation credit if you name a registered charity as the beneficiary. Further, you'll also avoid probate fees on your plan assets if you designate the charity as beneficiary in the plan documentation.

Designating the Beneficiary

It's always best to name, or designate, the appropriate person or charity as beneficiary of your RRSP or RRIF on the plan application form itself. One reason for this is that you'll avoid probate fees on the amount of your RRSP or RRIF this way. Designating the appropriate person in your will as beneficiary of your plan can accomplish the same tax-free rollover to your spouse or dependent child, or provide a donation credit for leaving the plan to a charity, but probate fees will apply if your province levies these fees. I should also mention that, where you've neglected to designate your spouse or dependent child (but not a charity) as beneficiary of your RRSP or RRIF, either in the plan documentation or your will, your executor can make a special election under subsection 146(8.1) of our tax law to have this tax-free rollover take place (more on this when I talk about elections later in this chapter).

TO MAKE A LONG STORY SHORT:

- You'll always manage to avoid tax on your RRSP or RRIF assets upon death by naming your spouse as the beneficiary of your plan.
- You may also manage to defer tax on your plan assets by transferring your RRSP or RRIF to a person who is financially dependent on you at the time of your death.
- You can now name a charity as the beneficiary of your RRSP or RRIF and receive a donation credit in the year of death that will offset the tax otherwise owing from the RRSP or RRIF.

Tim's Tip 28: Arrange for a tax-free death benefit from your employer.

You may not realize this, but you can make arrangements today for your employer to pay a full $10,000 to your heirs upon your death as a death benefit. A death benefit is simply an amount paid, after your death, in recognition of your service to your employer. In actual fact, death benefits are taxable, but the first $10,000 paid out is exempt from tax. The surviving spouse of the deceased employee is the one who gets the exemption but, to the extent that the spouse receives less than $10,000 in death benefits, any remaining recipients can split the balance of the exemption. So, next time you're reviewing your salary with your employer, or you start a new position,

Action Step

If you happen to be a business owner who operates an incorporated business, you can arrange today for your business to pay a death benefit of $10,000 to your spouse or children in the event of your death. Further, it could make sense for your company to buy life insurance on your life rather than you buying it personally since it's usually cheaper to buy insurance with corporate dollars. These are just two of the ways in which the company you own can play a role in your estate planning. I'll talk more about insurance in Chapter 6.

negotiate a death benefit. Think of this as $10,000 of life insurance with no premiums to pay. Hey, if nothing else, it'll cover the cost of your funeral.

TO MAKE A LONG STORY SHORT:

- Your employer can pay a $10,000 death benefit to your spouse or other beneficiaries on a tax-free basis after you're gone.
- At your next salary review or before taking a new position, negotiate to have such a payment made. It's like life insurance without any premiums.

Tim's Tip 29: **Minimize the impact of U.S. estate taxes on your assets at the time of your death.**

So you thought you were exempt from tax south of the border? Maybe not. There are more Canadians than you likely realize who will have U.S. estate taxes to pay on death. Now, I'm going to spend Chapter 11 dealing with U.S. tax issues, but let me talk briefly about U.S. estate taxes here.

Who is subject to U.S. estate tax? Anyone who owns "U.S. situs property" including: real estate (a vacation property, rental property, private home, or business property), shares of a U.S. corporation (public and private companies), debt obligations issued by U.S. residents (individuals or government), and personal property located in the U.S. (cars, boats, jewelry, furnishings, club memberships, and more). The tax is levied on the fair market value of these assets on the date of your death, and the tax rate for U.S. estate taxes ranges from 18 to 55 percent of your U.S. assets, with most people facing a tax bill between 25 and 35 percent of U.S. assets (see Appendix F).

How can you minimize the impact of U.S. estate taxes? Consider the following:

- claim the unified credit to offset U.S. estate taxes owing
- leave your U.S. assets to your spouse and claim a marital credit
- consider holding your U.S. assets inside a Canadian corporation
- gift property to your spouse and children over time since each person is entitled to his or her own unified credit
- purchase life insurance to cover any U.S. estate tax liability
- restructure your debt so that non-recourse loans are secured by your U.S. assets since this debt will reduce the value of your taxable estate
- move your U.S. assets back to Canada.

Okay, enough said here about U.S. estate tax. I'll talk more thoroughly about this issue in Chapter 11.

TO MAKE A LONG STORY SHORT:

- Canadian citizens and residents can be subject to U.S. estate tax on U.S. property.
- The tax will generally cost between 25 and 35 percent of the value of those U.S. assets at the time of your death (see Appendix F).
- There are several methods to reduce U.S. estate taxes, and I'll deal with this issue more in Chapter 11.

Strategies for Your Will

I've talked at length about wills in general in Chapter 2, but it's time to look at some specific items that, if dealt with properly in your will, can save you a bundle of tax at the time of your death.

Tim's Tip 30: Leave it to your spouse to minimize a tax hit on death.

It's a recurring theme, but it's important to understand. The most effective way to get around a tax hit on death is to leave your assets to your surviving spouse. When you do this, the assets are inherited by your spouse at your original cost. The result? There will be no tax to pay until your spouse dies, chooses to sell the assets, or is deemed to have sold the assets (there are a number of situations that can give rise to a deemed disposition: death, giving up Canadian residency, and gifting the assets, for example).

If you choose to leave any assets to someone other than your spouse, realize that there could be some tax to pay. There are three ways to leave assets to your spouse:

1. ***Designate your spouse as beneficiary of your RRSP or RRIF.*** As discussed in Tip 27, you should always name your spouse as the beneficiary of your RRSP or RRIF. The assets of those plans can then be rolled directly to an RRSP or RRIF in your spouse's name with no tax consequences.

Did You Know?

Your "spouse" under tax law includes someone you're legally married to, or a person (same sex or not) with whom you've been living in a conjugal relationship for twelve months or more, or with whom you've had a child. Believe it or not, it's possible under our tax law for you to have more than one spouse. How? Consider a situation where you're separated from the spouse you're legally married to, but you've been living with someone else. You see, any tax rules (good or bad) that apply to your spouse will apply to both of them!

If you leave these plans to your children, or to anyone other than your spouse, the tax collector will take his share before the beneficiaries get anything. There's an exception where a child or grandchild was financially dependent on you at the time of your death. See Tip 27 for more details.

2. ***Leave assets outright through your will.*** By simply leaving assets to your spouse by way of your will, you'll manage to avoid the deemed disposition at fair market value that could result in taxable capital gains. I talked about this deemed disposition in Tip 17.
3. ***Set up a spousal trust through your will.*** Where you give instructions in your will to do so, you can have all or a portion of your assets transferred to a spousal trust. A spousal trust is one in which your spouse alone has access to the income and, where provided in your will, the capital of the trust during his or her lifetime. Nobody else can touch the income or capital while your spouse is alive. Leaving assets to a spousal trust is the same, for tax purposes, as leaving them directly to your spouse. That is, there will be a tax-free rollover to the trust.

I should mention that there may be situations where it makes sense to trigger capital gains upon death. For example, if you have losses earned in the year of death or in a previous year, you might actually appreciate the deemed disposition rules that could give rise to a capital gain. After all, the losses would offset that gain, and you'd have no tax to pay. Where you've left assets to your spouse to avoid the deemed disposition rules, the executor of your estate can make a special election to trigger a capital gain if it makes sense to do so—but only where your will provides your executor the power to make elections for tax purposes. I'll talk more about this and other elections in Tip 34.

TO MAKE A LONG STORY SHORT:

- Leaving assets to your spouse will result in a tax-free rollover of those assets to your spouse. Your spouse will inherit your adjusted cost base on those assets.
- There are three ways to leave assets to your spouse: designate your spouse as beneficiary under your RRSP or RRIF, leave assets to your spouse outright, or leave your assets to a spousal trust for your spouse.
- Your executor can elect to bypass the tax-free rollover to your spouse if this makes sense.

Tim's Tip 31: **Establish testamentary trusts in your will to save your heirs significant tax after you're gone.**

A testamentary trust is a terrific tool for splitting income. It works this way: a trust can be created upon your death through instructions in your will, with all or a portion of your assets being transferred to the trust upon your death, and your intended heirs being the beneficiaries of the trust.

Any income earned on the inheritance that you leave behind may now be taxed in the trust each year, rather than in the hands of your beneficiaries. You see, the trust is considered to be a separate person for tax purposes, and will be taxed at the same graduated tax rates as any individual. Rather than adding any investment income directly to the beneficiary's income where it will be taxed at his or her marginal tax rate—very likely between 39 and 50 percent—simply split income with the trust by having the trust pay tax on the income instead, at graduated rates.

Spousal Trusts

There are different types of testamentary trusts, and spousal trusts are just one type. I introduced spousal trusts in Tip 30. A spousal trust is set up solely for the benefit of your spouse while your spouse is alive. If you're thinking of a testamentary trust for your spouse to split income, the trust should be set up as a spousal trust in most cases. Why? Because this allows a tax-free rollover of the assets to the trust.

Did You Know?

A testamentary trust will not generally help you to avoid that deemed disposition on your death that will trigger a tax hit. Rather, it will allow your heirs to minimize their own taxes after they've received your inheritance. The inheritance that goes into the trust will be net of any tax you had to pay in your year of death. The exception to this is a spousal trust, to which assets can transfer on a tax-free basis, just as though you had left the assets directly to your spouse.

Dual Trusts

Here's a tactic that can make a lot of sense. It involves setting up two trusts in your will. The first trust will be a spousal trust. Any assets that have appreciated in value and would otherwise result in a tax hit on death can be left to the spousal trust. A tax-free rollover to the trust will result. Your spouse can then enjoy tax savings since the trust can pay the tax on any income earned on those assets annually. The second trust will be a family trust, with your spouse and children as income and capital beneficiaries. Any assets that will not give rise to a tax hit but that will produce income annually can be placed in this trust. I'm thinking of cash, GICs, Canada Savings Bonds, money market mutual funds, and other income-producing assets that have not appreciated in value. There will be no tax to pay on these assets on your death since they have not appreciated in value, but the income of the trust can be taxed in the trust's hands, saving your heirs tax. Your spouse can be named as sole trustee if you'd like, giving him or her control over the property in the trust. As trustee and a beneficiary, your spouse would have the ability to use those assets exclusively for him or herself for a lifetime, would be able to pass income or capital of the trust to the kids if desired, and probate fees will be avoided on the surviving spouse's death, among other benefits. I'll talk more about trusts in general in Chapter 7.

TO MAKE A LONG STORY SHORT:

- A testamentary trust will not necessarily save you tax in the year of your death, but can save your heirs tax after you're gone.
- A testamentary trust can be set up as a spousal trust, which will allow your spouse to split income with the trust after you're gone.
- Establishing dual testamentary trusts in your will can make sense. I'll talk more about trusts in Chapter 7.

Tim's Tip 32: **Consider donating assets to charity on death, and carefully choose how and which assets to donate.**

If your intentions are to leave something to a favourite charity, the gift could go a long way to saving you taxes that might be due on filing your final tax return, but be sure to include a clause in your will detailing your charitable wishes, and make sure your gifts are to a registered charity. Only registered charities are entitled to issue a donation receipt that you can use to claim a tax credit.

Donating Securities

If you're planning to give to charity on your death, carefully consider which assets you donate! You see, if you've got publicly traded securities in your portfolio, including stocks, bonds and mutual funds, among other things, then donating these investments to charity rather than, say, cash, could save you 50 percent of the tax you might otherwise pay on those investments in the year of your death. Here's the deal: on your death, you'll be deemed to have disposed of your assets at fair market value, and one-half of any capital gains will be taxable (if you don't leave the assets to your spouse). If you leave any public securities to charity, however, half of the capital gains arising on those assets will no longer be taxable, but just one-quarter will be taxable. That's right, the capital gains inclusion rate of 50 percent is cut in half. More on this in Chapter 9.

Donating Life Insurance

Life insurance can be an effective tool to donate to charity. If I had been writing this book prior to the 2000 federal budget, I would have advised you to leave the proceeds of your insurance policy to your estate after your death, then leave instructions in your will to donate the cash proceeds to charity. In doing this, you'd be entitled to a donation tax credit on your final tax return. Thanks to the 2000 federal budget, there's now a better way to donate life insurance proceeds after your death: simply designate your favourite charity as the beneficiary of your life insurance policy. This will now entitle you to a donation credit on your final tax return where it wouldn't have previously. By designating the charity as the beneficiary of the policy, you'll sidestep probate fees on the amount of the benefit paid out.

Other Charitable Strategies

There are other methods of giving to charity that fall outside of your will,

If you don't properly word your donations in your will, it could be that a gift after your death will result in tax relief for your estate, but not for you on your final tax return. You've got to specifically identify the charity which you'd like to benefit, and detail a specific amount or method of calculating an amount (such as a percentage of the residue of your estate), in order to entitle yourself to a donation credit on your final tax return. If you don't provide this detail, the gift could be deemed to be that of your estate instead. I'll talk more about this in Tip 60.

Caution!

including charitable remainder trusts, charitable annuities, and more. The focus here has been on the things to keep in mind as you consider donating to charity on your death. I'll spend more time on this issue of charitable giving in Chapter 9. See you there.

TO MAKE A LONG STORY SHORT:

- Charitable donations made on your death can save you significant tax dollars if done correctly.
- If done incorrectly, the donation could be deemed that of the estate, and not a donation by you.
- Consider donating publicly traded securities or life insurance.
- Other charitable giving strategies will be covered in Chapter 9.

Tim's Tip 33: Recognize that an offshore inheritance trust can defer taxes for a significant time.

Okay, I admit it: this idea can be sensitive to implement, but the tax savings can be so significant that I've just got to share the idea with you. Picture this: you have a relative who lives in another country and for Canadian tax purposes is definitely a non-resident of Canada. This relative of yours also plans on leaving an inheritance to you. You're now in a prime circumstance to save tax by using an offshore trust.

Here's how it works: rather than leaving assets directly to you upon death, your relative should consider leaving them in a trust, with you as beneficiary. That trust should, however, be resident in a low or no-tax jurisdiction—not in Canada. Any income earned in the trust annually will not be taxed in the trust if there are no income taxes where the trust resides. The benefit is obvious: the funds in the trust can accumulate tax-free—much like they would in your RRSP. Under new rules that were introduced in 1999, you'll now face tax on any distributions made from this type of trust, to the extent that the growth in the trust was not taxed elsewhere, and this includes tax on distributions of capital made from the trust. Nevertheless, the growth of the assets in the trust can be significant over time since taxes won't be levied annually. All you need is a cooperative non-resident relative who sets this strategy up before he or she dies.

TO MAKE A LONG STORY SHORT:

- If you're expecting a non-resident relative to leave you an inheritance, arrange for the inheritance to be placed in an offshore trust with you as beneficiary.
- Arrangements must be made before your relative dies.
- Assets in the trust can grow on a tax-efficient basis if the trust resides in a no- or low-taxed jurisdiction.

Strategies After You're Gone

There are a number of things that your executor should consider doing, after you're gone, in order to save tax and leave more to your heirs. Pass this handy list to your own executor today to ensure that he or she is aware of the possibilities.

Tim's Tip 34: **Make note of the many elections that your executor should consider making after you're gone.**

The fact is, there are a number of "elections" that your executor can make in the year of your death that could minimize the tax hit you'll face in that final year. Consider these:

1. Property transfers at fair market value.

By now you know that, upon your death, you'll defer a tax hit by leaving assets to your spouse. The deemed disposition of your assets that takes place at fair market value on your death will simply take place at your adjusted cost base (ACB) instead, when you leave the assets to your spouse. The result? No tax to pay in the year of your death. There are situations, however, where your executor may want to trigger a capital gain on your death rather than allowing certain assets to transfer to your spouse at your ACB. This can be the case where:

- you've got losses in your year of death to be used up
- you're in the lowest tax bracket in your year of death and very little tax will be paid on any capital gains. I had a client who died on January 2; as a result, he had virtually no income in the year of his death. So, we elected to trigger some capital gains to take advantage of his personal tax credits for that year.

Caution!

It's critical that your will provide your executor with the power to make any tax elections that he or she sees fit to make. Without specifically providing this power to your executor, he or she may be unable to make some of these elections that could save you thousands of dollars in tax in your year of death. You don't have to name every potential election in your will, but rather include a clause that allows your executor to make any elections that he or she considers to be beneficial.

2. RRSP contributions.

You'd figure that once you're gone, the tax collector would not allow any more contributions to an RRSP. Not true. The executor of your estate will be able to make contributions to a spousal RRSP provided your spouse is still eligible to have an RRSP (i.e., aged 69 or younger at the end of the year) and you had some contribution room available on the date of your death. The contributions can be made in the year of your death, or in the first 60 days of the following year. A deduction will be available to you on your final tax return for the contributions made. This deduction will help to offset any taxes due upon death.

3. The enhanced capital gains exemption.

While the $100,000 lifetime capital gains exemption disappeared in 1994, a $500,000 enhanced exemption is still available to shelter capital gains on qualifying small business corporation (QSBC) shares or on qualifying farm property. For shares to be QSBC shares, a complex set of criteria must be met, although many small private companies operating an active business will qualify. Upon your death, the shares in your QSBC are deemed to have been disposed of, along with your other assets. If those shares have increased in value, the enhanced capital gains exemption could save you up to $125,000 in taxes! Visit a tax pro to ensure that your shares qualify. The exemption can also be claimed to shelter gains on qualified farm property, which normally includes most family farms or farm quotas. There are some conditions that the farm property must meet in order to be eligible, so visit a tax pro to determine for sure whether you'll be entitled to the exemption. If you qualify, the exemption can save you a big tax hit on death (or during your lifetime).

4. Estate loss carryback.

Subsection 164(6) of our tax law could save you a bundle in taxes in the year of your death. This provision of our tax law will allow your executor to take any losses realized by your estate after your death, and carry those losses back to your final tax return to offset any gains that might have been realized in your final year. The losses must be realized, and this election made, within the first taxation year of the estate (typically the first year following the date of death).

At the time of George's death, he owned shares of ABC Ltd. that had gone up in value by $100,000. He left the shares to his son. His executor filed a tax return for his final year, and had to report the $100,000 capital gain, which cost him $25,000 in taxes *in his final year. In the first year after George's death, and before distributing the shares to George's son, the shares of ABC Ltd. dropped in value by $50,000. George's executor looked at this as an opportunity to recover some taxes paid by George in the year of his death. His executor sold the ABC shares and realized a loss of $50,000, which he carried back under subsection 164(6) to George's final tax return. This loss offset half the gain that was originally reported on George's final tax return, and allowed the estate to recover over $12,000 in tax!*

Action Step

If you fail to designate your spouse or dependent child as beneficiary of your RRSP or RRIF in the plan documentation, or in your will, your executor can still make an election under subsection 146(8.1) of our tax law by filing form T2019. This election is made jointly by your executor and beneficiaries, and will cause there to be a tax-free rollover to your surviving spouse or a dependent child. This is not, however, an invitation to neglect to designate the right beneficiaries! Look after this designation today.

5. Refund of premiums.

You'll recall that you can minimize the tax hit on your RRSP and RRIF assets by leaving those assets to your spouse or a dependent child at the time of your death (see Tip 27). You can accomplish this tax-free rollover by designating your spouse or dependent child as beneficiary in the plan documentation itself, or by naming them as beneficiary in your will.

6. Paying taxes over 10 years.

Subsection 159(5) is what I call the *election of last resort*. If your death triggers a significant tax liability, and the tax owing as a result of your death simply cannot be paid by the proper due date, then your executor can elect to pay that tax bill over a period not exceeding ten years. Sure, interest will apply to the outstanding balance annually, but this election can prevent a situation where certain assets in your estate might otherwise have to be liquidated in a hurry. Your executor may have to put up acceptable security in order to make this election.

TO MAKE A LONG STORY SHORT:

- There are a number of elections that your executor may make after your death that could save taxes in your final year.
- Your executor must have the power to make these elections as provided in your will.
- The elections include: transferring property to your spouse at fair market value upon your death, making one last RRSP contribution with your assets, utilizing the enhanced capital gains exemption, triggering losses in your estate and carrying them back to your final tax return, rolling your RRSP or RRIF assets to an eligible person on a tax-free basis, and paying your final tax bill over a period of up to ten years.

Tim's Tip 35: **Understand how any losses can be utilized after your death to save tax and provide a greater inheritance to your heirs.**

I don't want to add insult to injury by suggesting that you're going to die one day, and that you could wind up with losses at that time, or shortly thereafter, but it's true. If losses are going to be realized, you might as well understand how your executor can best make use of them.

Capital Losses on Death

Capital losses are not much fun. During your lifetime, any capital losses that you realize can be claimed only to offset capital gains you also realize. Now, those losses can be carried back three years, or forward indefinitely until they are used. Suppose that, at the time of your death, you still have unused capital losses. There's some good news for you. You'll generally be able to claim those capital losses in the year of your death to offset any type of income—not just capital gains! Like anything else in tax, there are always exceptions. Where, for example, you claimed all or a portion of your capital gains exemption, or claimed an allowable business investment loss in the past, you could be restricted in applying those losses against income other than capital gains. Do your executor a favour: if you've got unused capital losses, make sure you're keeping track of the balance remaining to be used. Keep a running schedule annually and leave it with your will. This way, there will be no mistake in claiming losses to save you tax in your final year.

Estate Loss Carryback

In Tip 34, I spoke about this concept. Where your estate realizes a loss within its first taxation year, the loss can be carried back and applied to reduce any taxable capital gains you might have reported on your final tax return—subsection 164(6) says so. Refer back to Tip 34 for more.

TO MAKE A LONG STORY SHORT:

- Any unused capital losses at the time of your death can generally be used to offset any type of income in your final year—not just capital gains.
- Any losses realized in the first taxation year of your estate can generally be carried back to offset gains reported on your final tax return. I covered this in Tip 34.

Tim's Tip 36: **Utilize life insurance to provide the cash for taxes if you've got illiquid assets in your estate.**

If you're not keen on the idea of paying income tax due to the ugly deemed disposition on your death, you might want to consider purchasing life insurance to cover any tax liability. There are ways of establishing today what your tax liability is going to be upon your death (an estate freeze can play a significant role in this—see Tip 25), giving you the opportunity to buy the needed life insurance. Further, where you've got few liquid assets in your estate (for example, where your estate is made up largely of real estate or private company shares), it may be tough to pay the tax bill arising on your death without the cash infusion that life insurance can offer. In many cases, the premiums paid on the life insurance will be much less than the taxes owing at death, making this a great idea.

Finally, where you're the owner of an active business operated through a corporation, it may make sense to have the company purchase the insurance on your life rather than you paying for it yourself. The reason? Using corporate dollars to buy the insurance is often a cheaper way to purchase the insurance than with personal dollars. I'll talk more about this in Chapter 6, when I deal with life insurance.

TO MAKE A LONG STORY SHORT:

- Life insurance may be the most practical way to deal with a tax bill at the time of your death.
- A joint, second-to-die, policy is cheaper than buying a policy on your life alone, and may serve your purpose better.

Action Step

If you plan to leave most of your assets (particularly the ones that can give rise to taxable capital gains on death) to your spouse, you'll generally be able to defer the tax on those assets until the death of your spouse. So, there may not be a need for life insurance until the death of the surviving spouse. In this case, consider buying a joint, second-to-die, life insurance policy. It's a cheaper policy to buy since two events have to happen before benefits are paid out: both you and your spouse must die.

- It may make sense to have your corporation purchase insurance on your life rather than paying for it personally.

WINNING THE ESTATE PLANNING GAME

Whew, that's a lot of information to absorb. Who said there are very few ways to minimize taxes on your death—and after? Now, give your estate planning a push in the right direction by referring to the *Estate Planning Tip Sheet* at the front of the book. For each tip, ask yourself the question: "Does this apply to me?" Then check the appropriate answer: "Yes," "No," or "Not sure." This tip sheet will form the basis for your complete estate plan once you've read the entire book. Now, let's move on to Chapter 5, where we'll take a look at giving assets away today.

GIVING YOUR BEST: THE ART OF DYING BROKE THROUGH GIFTS

A stitch in time may save nine, but a gift in time saves tax.

5

George lives next door to my parents. If there's one thing about George that stands out, it's that he's cheap. Thrifty to the core. This isn't such a bad thing, mind you: George has managed to accumulate more than just about anyone else I know. You know the phrase "reduce, reuse, and recycle"? Well, George is so cheap that he's taken the middle part of that phrase, "reuse," and has practised it daily for the last forty years. Take his tea bags, for example. When he's done with them, he hangs them up to dry just so he can use them again the next day.

I had a conversation with George the other day about his estate planning. Since he's accumulated so much, he's concerned about the potential tax hit on his death. I shared with George a number of ideas, some of which required a visit to a lawyer. Being thrifty, he wanted other ideas that wouldn't cost him a penny. "I've got just the thing for you, George," I said. "Give your assets away today, before you're gone." He liked this idea.

You see, giving assets away during your lifetime is probably the least complex, least expensive, estate planning technique. It doesn't have to involve drafting agreements, visits to an accountant or lawyer, or much else. The benefits of giving assets away today can't be underestimated. Think about it. If you were to give away everything you own, what would be the implication at the time of your death? No income tax (since there would be no assets to face the deemed disposition rules I spoke of in Tip 17), and no probate fees. Your estate would be very simple for your executor to administer, and your heirs would have the opportunity to enjoy the assets that you gave them while you're still around. You might just enjoy watching them enjoy the gifts. The fact is, however, that giving assets away must be done properly if you're going to do this.

In this chapter, I'm going to talk about the challenges you'll face when giving your assets away today, and some solutions to consider. I won't deal with charitable giving here, since I've reserved that discussion for Chapter 9.

Challenges to Gifting Assets

Giving assets away during your lifetime can be as easy as writing a cheque to your kids, or as complex as completing a corporate reorganization to pass your business to your successors. In any event, you should be aware of the potential challenges you'll face in gifting assets during your lifetime.

Tim's Tip 37: **Beware of the deemed disposition at fair market value when giving assets away.**

There are a number of situations in the life of any Canadian taxpayer that can give rise to a "deemed" disposition at fair market value. At the time of your death, you're deemed to have sold your property at fair market value (see Tip 17). Likewise, giving up Canadian residency for tax purposes will mean a disposition of much of your property at fair market value on the day you leave. Transferring assets to someone else (including a trust, partnership, or corporation) generally gives rise to a disposition that is deemed to take place at fair market value. This transfer of assets I'm talking about includes gifts to just about anyone.

Be aware that when you put a friend or family member other than your spouse on title to an asset, so that it's now owned jointly (this is commonly done with investments and real estate), this will count as a disposition at fair market value of a portion of the asset. If the asset has gone up in value since you acquired it, you could trigger a taxable capital gain by simply changing ownership in this way. Many people put assets in joint names to avoid probate fees, but trigger a large tax hit in the process!

Caution!

Jasmine has $500,000 worth of mutual funds in her name. In addition, she has $400,000 in her RRSPs, and a rental property worth $200,000. Jasmine has more than she needs to live comfortably, and has decided to give her daughter, Rachel, a significant gift. Jasmine has decided to give the rental property to Rachel. The rental property has an adjusted cost base (ACB) of $150,000, and a gift of the property to Rachel will trigger a deemed disposition at fair market value. The capital gain realized by Jasmine on the transfer is $50,000

($200,000 market value less the $150,000 ACB). One-half of capital gains are taxable in Canada, so Jasmine will have to report a taxable capital gain of $25,000 in her income in the year she gifts the property to Rachel. This will result in a tax bill of approximately $12,500 for Jasmine since her marginal tax rate is 50 percent.

You should be aware of a couple of things here. First, even if you sell your assets to your heirs at an amount below fair market value (as opposed to making a gift to them), you'll still be deemed to have sold the assets at fair market value. Second, if you give (or sell) assets to your spouse, you'll avoid the deemed disposition at fair market value. A gift (or sale) to your spouse automatically takes place at your adjusted cost base. The result? No tax to pay on the transfer to a spouse.

By the way, it is possible to elect out of this provision of our tax law so that a transfer to your spouse does take place at fair market value instead. In order to make this election, you've got to do a couple of things: (1) you must receive fair market value payment from your spouse (so a gift to your spouse won't work), and (2) you must file an election with your tax return detailing that you wish to have the transfer take place at fair market value, not cost. Why would you want to transfer an asset to your spouse at fair market value? You might want to trigger a capital gain in order to use up losses you've accumulated, or perhaps you'd like to avoid the attribution rules and have your spouse pay the tax on any investment income generated after the transfer. I'll talk more about the attribution rules in the next Tip.

TO MAKE A LONG STORY SHORT:

- Gifting assets to another person is just one of the situations that will give rise to a deemed disposition at fair market value.
- Making a gift to a spouse will not result in a disposition at fair market value, but at your adjusted cost base instead.

- Selling assets to a family member at less than fair market value will also result in a disposition deemed to take place at market value.

Tim's Tip 38: Understand the impact of the attribution rules on any gifts that you make during your lifetime.

Let's face it. If you make a gift to your spouse, child, or other heir in order to minimize your taxes on death, you might as well structure the gift so that you avoid taxes on the assets during your lifetime as well. You see, our tax law contains a set of provisions known as the "attribution rules" that are designed to tax certain income in your hands where you've transferred assets to your spouse or certain minors related to you.

Here's what I mean: suppose you were to give, say, $10,000 in cash, to your spouse, and your spouse invested the money. If he or she earned, say, $700 of interest income on that $10,000 in the first year, who do you suppose will pay the tax on the $700? You will. The attribution rules will tax you on any investment income earned by your spouse where you gave your spouse the assets that generated the income.

You can run into the same problem when you've given money or investments to a minor who is your child, niece, or

Action Step

If your spouse or child has any money of his or her own, make sure they use that money for investment purposes. The investment income then won't be attributed back to you. You are then free to give them money for other non-income-producing purposes such as paying a tax bill, household expenses, an education, or whatever else they might have spent their own money on. Further, giving money to a family member to generate income from a business will not result in attribution back to you!

nephew. In the case of minors, capital gains are an exception and do manage to sidestep the attribution rules. So, if you were to give your child $10,000 and he or she invested it and realized $1,000 in capital gains from selling the investment, those capital gains would be taxed in your child's hands and would not be attributed back to you. Consider the table, which highlights the impact of the attribution rules on a gift.

IMPACT OF ATTRIBUTION RULES	
Gift to spouse	Attribution of all income and capital gains back to the transferor.
Gift to minor child	Attribution of all income from property (interest, dividends, rents, royalties), but not capital gains, back to the transferor.
Gift to adult child	No attribution back to the transferor.

You should also be aware that the attribution rules can have an impact on more than just gifts. The rules can attribute income back to you in cases where you have also sold or lent property to your spouse or related minors. As for a sale, any sale at fair market value can avoid the attribution rules, but sales at less than fair market value will result in some attribution. What about loans? If you lend property to a spouse or related minor at an interest rate less than Canada Customs and Revenue Agency's (CCRA's) prescribed rate for the quarter, the attribution rules will apply. If you charge the prescribed rate (or commercial rates, if these are less), then you'll avoid the attribution rules. I should mention that loans to adult children, like gifts or sales, will not generally cause an attribution problem, even if the interest rate is lower than the prescribed rate (the exception, however, is where the loan was made to the adult child specifically for the purpose of shifting income and the related tax bill to the adult child, in which case the income earned on the loaned property can be attributed back to you).

To avoid the attribution rules, consider the following if you're going to make gifts to family members:

- wait until your kids are adults, then make the gift
- when making gifts to minors, ensure that the money is either spent, or invested to generate capital gains (but not income from property such as interest, dividends, rents, or royalties)
- when making gifts to your spouse, consider gifting property that will not produce much income annually, if any (a cottage or growth stocks come to mind), since all income will be attributed back to you.

TO MAKE A LONG STORY SHORT:

- The attribution rules could come into play when you've made a gift to a spouse or related minor. The rules will cause any income earned on the gifted property to be taxed in your hands instead.
- Certain sales and loans of property to family members can also cause an attribution of income back to you.
- Gifts to adults, gifts to minors that generate capital gains, and gifts to a spouse that do not generate income will not cause a problem under the attribution rules.

Tim's Tip 39: Watch for the potential double-tax problem that can arise when selling assets at less than market value.

If you're not careful, you could transfer property to a family member in such a way that there will be double tax to pay. There's nothing uglier, and more unfair, than paying tax twice on the same income or capital gains. Let's avoid this double-tax hit! You'll run into the problem where, rather than making an outright gift to a related person, you sell property to them at less than fair market value.

Eric owns a cottage worth $220,000 with an adjusted cost base of just $100,000. He has decided to sell it to his son, Eddie, at a very favourable price—just $150,000. Bad move. Here's what happens from a tax perspective: Eric is deemed to have sold his cottage to Eddie at fair market value of $220,000, so he'll have a $120,000 capital gain to report on his tax return in the year of the sale. Eddie, on the other hand, acquires the cottage worth $220,000 for just $150,000, so his adjusted cost base is just $150,000. If Eddie were to sell the cottage for its true value of $220,000 after acquiring it, he would pay tax on a gain of $70,000 ($220,000 proceeds less his adjusted cost base of $150,000). Eddie will pay tax on gains his father has already paid tax on.

Caution!

If you're going to make a gift (or sale) of real estate to a family member, be sure to first add up the provincial land transfer taxes that might apply! Generally, transfers between spouses are exempt from land transfer taxes, but transfers from a parent to a child can attract the tax to the extent that the child pays the parent (which can also include mortgages assumed by the child) for the property. Gifts made for love and affection generally do not result in land transfer taxes—but check your provincial rules first!

Did you catch the double-tax hit in the example? Eric sold the cottage to Eddie and paid tax on the value between $100,000 and $220,000. If Eddie sells the cottage (or faces a deemed disposition on death), he'll pay tax on the value between $150,000 and $220,000. The $70,000 gain between $150,000 and $220,000 is effectively taxed twice. Oops.

How can you avoid this double-tax problem? Consider these ideas:

- make a gift of the property to your heirs rather than selling it to them
- if you want to sell the property to your heirs for any reason, then set the selling price at the full fair market value, and

simply ask for the price to be paid partly in cash (if you don't want to take the full amount in cash), and partly as a loan owing to you. You can always forgive the loan on your death in your will, with no negative tax implications.

TO MAKE A LONG STORY SHORT:

- A double-tax hit can arise when you sell assets to your heirs at an amount less than fair market value.
- The problem arises because our tax law will not provide your heirs with an adjusted cost base equal to your deemed sale proceeds.
- Consider gifting the assets instead, or making the sale at full fair market value with part of the consideration being a loan to you.

Solutions to Gifting Assets

I hope you haven't been scared off by some of the challenges to making gifts that I've been talking about. Perhaps you've even thought of a few reasons of your own for not making gifts during your lifetime. Let's look at some tactics to make gifting an easy process.

Tim's Tip 40: Make tax-friendly gifts to your heirs during your lifetime to avoid an erosion of your estate.

A tax-friendly gift is simply a gift that will completely or largely sidestep the tax hit that can arise from a deemed disposition at fair market value (see Tip 37). Let's look at the five types of gifts worth talking about:

1. ***Cash and near-cash investments.*** Cash doesn't appreciate in value like stocks and equity mutual funds can. As a result, there will never be a taxable capital gain resulting from any deemed

disposition. Near-cash investments such as GICs and Canada Savings Bonds are in the same boat. The bottom line? Give as much cash and near-cash investments to your heirs as you'd like during your lifetime—there won't be a tax hit to face.

2. ***Assets with no or low accrued gains.*** If an asset has not appreciated in value much, if at all, or has dropped in value, then the deemed disposition at fair market value is not likely to trigger much, if any, tax. If this is the case, then you shouldn't be afraid to gift these types of assets to your heirs during your lifetime. I should let you know that if you transfer assets that have dropped in value to someone who is "affiliated" with you, the loss realized could be denied under certain "stop-loss" rules in our tax law. The good news? Your kids are not considered to be affiliated with you, although your spouse is, and certain corporations or partnerships can be too. Generally, if a loss is denied under these stop-loss rules, the loss is added to the adjusted cost base of the property in the hands of the affiliated person, so that when the asset is ultimately disposed of to a third party, any gain will be reduced or loss increased at that time.

3. ***Gifts made over time.*** So, you've decided to give assets away during your lifetime, including assets that have increased in value, and there's going to be some tax to pay. Consider, then, giving those assets away over a number of years. This way, you'll manage to defer some taxable

Action Step

Pushing a tax bill to a future year is virtually always better than paying the tax today. The only exception is where you expect your marginal tax rate to be much higher in the next few years. When it comes to capital gains, it is particularly true that pushing the taxable gain to the future likely makes sense. The reason? There has been downward pressure on the capital gains inclusion rate (the amount of any gain that is taxable—currently one-half) in recent years. We could see the rate drop again, but it's not likely to rise any time soon.

capital gains to future years. In addition, triggering sizeable capital gains in a single year can, in some cases, push you into a higher marginal tax bracket, which will cost you even more tax.

4. ***Gift of a principal residence.*** Giving a principal residence to a child or other heir won't generally create a tax hit. Why? Because any taxable capital gain arising on a deemed disposition can usually be sheltered with the principal residence exemption. Before you jump to giving away your home, however, there are some compelling non-tax reasons to avoid this gift. You see, if you give your home fully or partially to a child who ends up having problems with creditors, or a spouse, there's the risk that the home may have to be sold to make payments to these other parties. There's also the risk that you could be out on your ear if you're still living in the home and your relationship with your child turns sour. Think carefully and consult with a lawyer before giving away your home.
5. ***Gifts to your spouse.*** I've mentioned this before, but gifts made to your spouse will bypass the deemed disposition at fair market value. The result is that there will be no tax to pay on any accrued gains when transferring assets to your spouse. The fact is, however, that you could accomplish the same tax-free transfer to your spouse after your death by way of your will. So, what's the real advantage of making a gift to your spouse today? You'll save probate fees on your death, if you die first. Holding assets jointly with your spouse will allow probate fees to be avoided, regardless of who dies first. Transferring assets into joint names with your spouse, however, should not be automatic. You see, you throw away the option of transferring those assets to a testamentary trust on your death if they're held jointly (see Tip 55). Remember, the attribution rules will tax any income earned by your spouse in your hands where there has been a tax-free transfer of property to your spouse.

TO MAKE A LONG STORY SHORT:

- If you're going to make a gift of property during your lifetime—make it a tax-efficient gift.
- There are five types of tax-efficient gifts to consider: gifts of cash or near-cash investments, gifts of assets with no or low accrued gains, gifts made over time, the gift of a principal residence, and gifts to your spouse.

Tim's Tip 41: Consider changing the nature of the gift if you're concerned about continued control over the property.

I hear you loud and clear: you want the benefits of giving assets away today (namely, tax and probate savings on death), but you don't want to give up control over the property today. Maybe you don't completely trust your heirs to handle the assets appropriately, or perhaps you want the option of taking the property back again in the future. No problem—you can accomplish this—in four key ways.

Transfers to a Trust

A family trust can work wonders when your intention is to give up ownership of an asset but you still want control. You can, for example, transfer property to a trust, and as long as you're a trustee, you may have control over the property. The trust must be structured properly to avoid the various attribution rules in our tax law and, where this is done, you'll manage to split income during your lifetime, minimize income taxes and probate fees on death, and still control the assets while you're alive. You may even be able to arrange for the creation of the trust in such a manner that you are also named a capital beneficiary, which may allow you to take back ownership of the property again at a later date.

Making it a Loan

If you lend property to your heirs rather than make an outright gift to them, you'll have the ability to take the property back as you see fit. That is, you can simply demand that the loan be repaid. This will give you a measure of control over the property, even after it's been transferred. If you've transferred income-producing property to your heirs and have called it a loan, you'll have to watch out for the attribution rules (see Tip 38). In a worst-case scenario, you may have to charge interest at CCRA's prescribed interest rate (or commercial rates if these are less) on the amount of the loan to avoid attribution of the income back to you. A loan to a family member will remove a potentially growing asset from your hands, which may save you taxes on death, but the loan owing to you at your death is an asset of yours and will be subject to probate fees.

Enter an Agreement

A client of mine recently transferred ownership of the family cottage to his son. It was an estate planning maneuvre, to be sure. Any growth in the value of the cottage today will eventually be taxed in the hands of his son—not in his hands, and my client will avoid probate fees as well. There was no tax to pay on the transfer to his son even though the cottage has appreciated in value significantly since he used his principal residence exemption to shelter the gain from tax. My client wanted to maintain use of the cottage, however, and he wanted a say in what is done with the property. To this end, he entered

Did You Know?

You'll be glad to know that it's always possible to forgive a loan owing to you at the time of your death, and there will be no negative tax consequences to you or to the person who owes you the money. Forgiving a loan during your lifetime, however, could have disastrous tax implications. In a worst-case scenario, forgiving certain loans during your lifetime will cause the forgiven amount to be taxable in the hands of the person who owes you the money.

into a written agreement with his son that gives him the right to use the cottage for a certain period of time each year, and the cottage can't be sold without my client's consent. In this case, a written agreement provided my client with the necessary control he was looking for. An agreement might suit you too.

Transfer Property to a Corporation

If you refer back to Tip 25, I discussed the concept of an estate freeze at length. The most common method of completing a freeze is to transfer assets to a corporation. A freeze can be accomplished while providing you with continuing control and use of the assets you've given up. While this is a more complex method of gifting assets to your heirs, it may be a good option if you're intent on maintaining use and control of the property.

TO MAKE A LONG STORY SHORT:

- Maintaining control over and use of property that you've transferred to your heirs during your lifetime is possible.
- It may even be possible to take back the property at some point in the future.
- The four tools used most often to maintain control and use of the property you've given up are: transferring the property to a trust, making it a loan instead, entering into a written agreement, or transferring the property to a corporation as part of an estate freeze.

Tim's Tip 42: **Consider taking advantage of the capital gains reserve when transferring assets to your heirs during your lifetime.**

Picture this. You've got certain assets that have appreciated in value, and you'd like to gift the assets to your heirs, but you're concerned about a large tax hit in a given year. It may be possible to structure a transfer of the property to your heirs such that the taxable capital gain you trigger will be taxed over a five-year period. You see, our tax law will permit you to claim what is known as a "capital gains reserve," which is simply a tax deduction available to those who sell property but take payment in a future year, or over a number of years.

R*ajneesh owns shares in ABC Corp., for which he paid $100,000, but which are now worth $500,000. He wants to give these shares to his daughter, Chandar, but he'll trigger a tax bill of approximately $100,000 if he simply gives her the shares this year. Here's what he did instead: he sold the shares to Chandar for their fair market value of $500,000, but she didn't pay him cash. Rather, he took back a promissory note as conditional payment for the shares. The note does not bear any interest, but provides Rajneesh with the right to demand payment gradually over the next five years. Since Rajneesh did not collect the full proceeds in the year of the sale to Chandar, he's entitled to a reserve, or deduction, for the portion of the gain not yet collected. In actual fact, our tax law requires the gain to be included in income over a period of no more than five years. So, Rajneesh had to report one-fifth of the gain in the year of sale. He'll report the balance of the gain over the next four years. Rajneesh can simply forgive the promissory note at the time of his death in his will, and Chandar will not have paid cash at any time to Rajneesh. In effect, this was a gift to Chandar.*

Did you catch that? A capital gains reserve will allow you to report a capital gain in income over a period as long as five years where you haven't collected the proceeds of disposition yet. If you're going to involve a promissory note in a sale transaction as Rajneesh did in my example, be sure to read CCRA's Interpretation Bulletin

Action Step

Speak to a tax pro if you're planning to transfer to your children the shares of a small business corporation, shares of a family farm corporation, an interest in a family farm partnership, land used in farming, or depreciable property used in farming. In these situations, the capital gains reserve can work to spread your tax hit over a period as long as ten years. This is more generous than even the five-year capital gains reserve available on the transfer of other property.

IT-436R since the note will have to be worded properly to allow for a reserve!

Want my advice? Visit a tax pro if you're thinking of claiming a capital gains reserve as I've outlined here. Your i's must be dotted and your t's crossed in order to make this work properly.

TO MAKE A LONG STORY SHORT:

- A capital gains reserve is simply a deduction that you may be entitled to if you sell property and collect the proceeds of disposition in a future year or over a number of years.
- The reserve will allow you to spread any capital gains over a period as long as five years (ten years in the case of certain business and farm property).
- It may be possible to structure a transfer to your heirs to take advantage of this reserve.

WINNING THE ESTATE PLANNING GAME

Giving assets away during your lifetime can be a very effective method of reducing taxes and probate fees on death. In this chapter, I've detailed for you the challenges you might face when gifting assets, and some very practical solutions to making the gifts properly. By now, you know the routine: turn to the *Estate Planning Tip Sheet* at the front of the book and review the tips I gave you in this chapter.

For each tip, ask yourself the question: "Does this apply to me?" Then check the appropriate answer: "Yes," "No," or "Not sure." This tip sheet will form the basis for your complete estate plan once you've read the entire book. Time for Chapter 6, where I'll talk about the use of life insurance.

ENSURING FIRST PLACE: UNDERSTANDING THE LIFE INSURANCE MAZE

When exercise and healthy eating does no good, insurance does help.

6

In August 1996, the London, England, insurance brokerage, Goodfellow Rebecca Ingrams Pearson, announced that it would begin to offer insurance policies to cover people worried about alien abduction. A premium of about $155 a year would pay about $160,000 to an abductee (provided the abductor was not from Earth) and double that if the insured is impregnated during the abduction. Since alien powers are unknown, men can also purchase the impregnation rider. Goodfellow director Simon Burgess said, "I personally would not buy this policy." The fact is, however, that several clients felt that this type of insurance would help them to sleep better at night. After all, isn't this what insurance is really all about—not alien abduction, but simply sleeping better at night?

Reasons to Insure

Whether you're insuring to provide for dependants, to cover an expected tax bill on death, to shelter investment income, for business reasons, or to provide for your family in the event of alien abduction, one thing is for sure: your life insurance is there to allow you to sleep better at night. In any event, before buying life insurance, make sure you understand why you're buying it.

Tim's Tip 43: Identify the reasons you are buying life insurance before handing over any premiums.

Why are you buying life insurance? It's an important question. Don't get me wrong, I believe that life insurance is an extremely valuable item in the estate planning toolbox. I wouldn't be caught dead without it—and I won't; I've purchased enough. I know exactly why I've purchased life insurance, however. You should identify this reason for yourself. Only once you've grasped the reason for your insurance can you identify how much is enough, and which type to buy. There are really five broad reasons to buy life insurance.

1. Providing for dependants.

The first question to ask is whether or not your death would cause financial hardship for others. If so, you need life insurance. You see, the most valuable asset you own is your ability to generate income. When that asset disappears on your death, you might leave your spouse, children, or even parents in a tough spot financially. You might even have an obligation to provide a certain sum of money to your children or an ex-spouse under a separation or divorce agreement. Ask yourself the following questions:

- Can your spouse, children, and other dependants survive on the income they earn alone?
- Would the loss of your income have little or no impact on your dependants?
- Could your spouse work full- or part-time after your death and earn enough to comfortably meet the needs of your dependants?
- Will there be enough money to pay for the education of your children if you die suddenly tomorrow?

If you answered "No" to any of the questions above, you have a need for life insurance, specifically for the purpose of providing for your dependants. How much is the right amount of life insurance? I'll talk about this in Tip 45, later in this chapter.

2. Covering final disbursements.

Dying can be expensive. Think carefully about the types of expenditures that your executor is going to have to make on your behalf. The dollars can add up. In addition to the usual expenses that will arise on your death, there's the issue of the debts you leave behind. You'll do your heirs a favour by providing enough insurance to cover not only your final expenses, but also the income taxes and other debts outstanding at the time of your death. Consider the following items that you'll want to pay off after your death:

DISBURSMENTS AFTER DEATH	
• funeral and related costs	• income taxes owing after death
• legal and accounting fees	• probate fees
• executor fees	• U.S. estate taxes
• mortgages outstanding	• other:
• credit card balances	• other:
• lines of credit and other loans	• other:

If you start putting dollar figures to these expenditures, you'll see how they can add up.

3. Providing equitable or larger bequests.

If you're like many Canadians, you may have some children with greater financial need than the others. In fact, maybe you've given away portions of your estate already, in an effort to help certain kids. If it's your intention to leave all of your kids with the same inheritance, regardless of whether they receive it today or on your death, you may want to buy life insurance to replace some of the assets you've already given away so that there's enough to treat all of the kids equally. Consider another situation where you want to leave a large asset, say the cottage, to one child since he or she uses it most. If you want to leave the other kids inheritances of equal value, it may be necessary to buy life insurance to provide the cash to do this. Maybe you simply have a desire to leave a lot more to your kids—or to charity—than you could without life insurance. The bottom line? Life insurance can fill a void if you're hoping to leave larger bequests, or simply want to be equitable in leaving assets to your heirs.

Did You Know?

Any proceeds paid under a life insurance policy on your death will be paid completely tax-free to the beneficiaries of the policy. This tax-free payment extends not only to the face value of the policy (the death benefit), but the investment component (often called the cash surrender value) as well. You can generally make withdrawals from the cash surrender value of the policy, but there may be a tax hit when doing this.

4. Sheltering investment income from tax.

Believe it or not, I've got a few clients who have more money than they'll ever be able to spend in a lifetime. These are precisely the type of people whom you would think have absolutely no need for life insurance. While it's true that they may not buy life insurance for the reasons I've already talked about, many are turning to life insurance strictly as a tax shelter! You see, a universal life insurance policy can act much like an RRSP in that the investment component of the policy can grow on a tax-sheltered basis. The likeness to an RRSP ends there. The policy can offer other benefits that an RRSP cannot: the death benefit (the face value of the policy) plus the accumulated investments in the policy are paid out completely tax-free to the beneficiaries on your death.

5. Insuring the health of your business.

If you're a business owner, there may be a number of good reasons to buy life insurance—and all have to do with providing for the continued health and management of the business. Specifically, if you're a business owner you should consider buying life insurance to:

- provide cash for a surviving partner to buy out your share of the business from your estate or heirs
- provide cash to the business in the event of the death of a key person, whose death could bring hardship on the business
- pay off any debts of the business on your death
- repay the business for any significant expenditures incurred (such as pension contributions made for your benefit).

In most cases, the insurance that you buy for business purposes will best be purchased by the business, as opposed to by you personally—particularly when you operate your business through a corporation that is taxed at the low rate of approximately 20 percent (varies by province) on active business income.

Rob and William are equal shareholders in an active business. They have purchased "criss-cross" insurance on each other's lives so that, if one of them dies, the other will have enough cash to buy the shares of the deceased shareholder. This will leave the surviving shareholder with 100 percent of the company. The company is paying for the policies out of its earnings. The company has been named as beneficiary of the policies. When one of the shareholders dies, the insurance proceeds will be paid into the company, and then can be paid to the surviving shareholder on a tax-free basis out of the "capital dividend account" of the company. The premiums are not tax deductible to the company, but it still makes sense for the company to pay for the insurance rather than for Rob and William to pay for the policies personally.

There are a couple of lessons to be learned from Rob and William's story. First, criss-cross insurance (where each shareholder will receive a cash payment on the death of the other shareholder) is a common strategy to provide for the succession of a business (see Chapter 8 for more on succession planning).

Second, every corporation has something called the "capital dividend account" where certain tax-free proceeds (such as life insurance proceeds) received by the company are tracked. Tax-free dividends can then be paid to the shareholders of the company to the extent that there's a balance in the capital dividend account. So, the value of life insurance proceeds paid to a corporation can generally flow tax-free to the surviving shareholders for their use in buying the deceased shareholder's shares, or for other uses.

Action Step

When you own an active business corporation, consider having your company buy the life insurance. It's generally cheaper this way. In order to pay, say, $10,000 of premiums personally, you'd likely have to earn between $16,000 and $20,000 so that, after taxes, you're left with $10,000 to pay the insurance premiums. In the case of a small business corporation, it needs to earn just $12,500, give or take a few bucks, in order to be left with $10,000 after tax to pay the premiums.

TO MAKE A LONG STORY SHORT:

- Before paying insurance premiums, make sure you understand exactly why you're buying insurance.

- There are five general reasons to buy life insurance: providing for dependants, covering final disbursements, providing for larger or equitable bequests, sheltering investment income from tax, or insuring the health of your business.

Types of Insurance

Insurance reminds me a little of people: there are two general types. In the case of people, there are men and women. In the case of insurance, there is temporary and permanent. In the case of the opposite sex—you can't live with 'em, and you can't live without 'em. Same goes for insurance—you can't live with it (many Canadians don't like to pay premiums), and you can't live without it (just consider the reasons in Tip 43 for having insurance!).

Tim's Tip 44: Understand the two broad types of insurance, then choose the type that suits your purposes.

There are really two types of insurance: (1) temporary insurance, and (2) permanent insurance. Temporary insurance, as its name suggests, may not stay in force forever. It usually lasts for a specific period of time, or until you reach a certain age, then the coverage ends. Permanent insurance is different in that it stays in force forever, until you die. Now, this assumes that you continue to pay your premiums as required under the policy, of course. If you suddenly stop paying your premiums when you're required to pay them, even your coverage under a permanent policy can lapse! Let's look more closely at these types of policies.

Temporary Insurance

Temporary insurance often goes by another name: term insurance. Term insurance is the least expensive type of insurance. It is nothing but pure insurance since you're paying for insurance coverage only, unlike certain other policies which also have an investment component (also called the cash surrender value) to them. With term insurance your coverage will last for a term of one, five, ten, or twenty years generally. Regardless of the length of the term, your policy must be renewed at the end of each term if you want your coverage to continue. Not surprisingly, your premiums will increase each term as you get older. Term insurance is considered to be temporary since it typically expires at age 75 or 80 (most term policies are not renewable beyond this age).

If you're going to buy term insurance, make sure your policy is:

1. ***Renewable.*** This ensures that the policy can be renewed at the end of the policy term, regardless of your health.
2. ***Convertible.*** This enables you to convert your term insurance into permanent insurance at your option.
3. ***Guaranteed.*** Your policy premiums will increase each term according to a schedule guaranteed at the start, rather than being negotiable at the end of the term.

Did You Know?

In some cases, a term-to-100 policy may provide the option of receiving a cash payment at age 100—although this payment will be taxable. Benefits paid out after your death, however, are not taxable. So, if you've got a choice at age 100, you may want to pass on the payment during your lifetime if you don't need the cash. Of course, if you'd rather take the cash and travel the world at age 100, more power to you!

Permanent Insurance

Permanent insurance policies work a little differently than temporary policies. The most notable feature is that they will stay in force until your death, provided you pay your premiums. There are different types of permanent policies too. The three most common types are:

1. Term-to-100 insurance.

Wait a minute—sounds like a term insurance policy, and, as you know, term insurance is temporary insurance. Don't be fooled by the name of term-to-100 policies. These are policies that, like term insurance, generally have no investment component to them. You're buying pure insurance only. The policy is permanent, however, because it stays in force until your death. The premiums on a term-to-100 policy generally stay the same throughout your lifetime. This "level premium" is a common feature of most permanent policies. At age 100, the policy typically becomes "paid up," meaning that you won't be required to make any more premium payments.

2. Whole life insurance.

Whole life policies are also permanent policies in that they stay in force until you die. Unlike term or term-to-100 policies, whole life policies have an investment component, often referred to as the cash surrender value. The premiums on your whole life policy will remain constant over time, and will be higher than term insurance premiums in your younger years. In your younger years, you'll pay more in premiums than the true cost of insuring your life. The insurance company will use these excess premiums in the early years to build up the cash surrender value of the policy.

WHOLE LIFE INSURANCE POLICIES

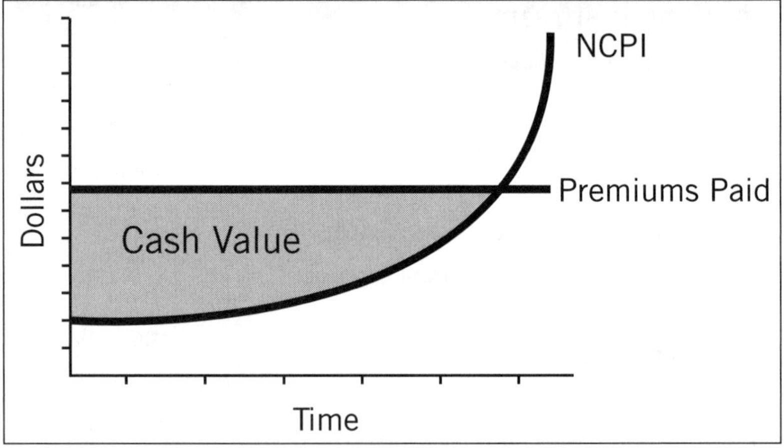

Take a look at the graph. The line labeled "NCPI" is the "net cost of pure insurance." This is what it costs to insure your life each year. As time moves on, you can see that it costs more to insure your life since you're closer to dying than you were the year before—it makes sense. The premiums paid on the policy are, however, represented by the flat line labeled "Premiums." You can see that, in the early years of the policy, you're paying more for your insurance than what it truly costs to insure your life. The excess premiums in the early years become the cash surrender value of the policy. This cash value can be used later to pay future premiums, or as security for loans. You can even borrow the cash value of your policy, although doing so is really borrowing your own money, and the loan isn't free—you'll pay interest on the loan. Further, policy loans like this are actually taxable, although you'll get a deduction when you repay the loan.

At the time of your death, the beneficiary of your policy will get not only the face value of your policy, but the accumulated cash value as well. The proceeds on insurance policies are always received tax-free by the beneficiary.

3. Universal life insurance.

Here's where permanent insurance gets exciting (as exciting as insurance can be). Universal policies are really a breed of whole life insurance that has unbundled the insurance, investment, and expense components of the policy. As a result, universal policies are extremely flexible. You have control over each of these components. The insurance component of the policy typically looks like a term insurance contract—and you can choose one-, five-, ten-, or twenty-year terms if you'd like. The investment component of the policy is flexible enough that you can actually choose where your money is invested. This is not the case with a whole life policy. You can even choose the level of premiums that you pay on the universal policy. You'll be required to pay a base premium to cover the cost of your insurance (the NCPI line in the graph above), but you'll be able to pay additional premiums above the base to be invested. You can't simply plow as much as possible into the investment component of the policy—there is a limit (known as the MTAR limit, which stands for "Maximum Tax Actuarial Reserve")—but the limit is quite generous. For every dollar of insurance that you buy, you can generally place another $3 to $4 inside the investment component of the policy. Your investment options generally include money market, fixed income, and equity investments that track specific benchmarks such as the TSE 300, S&P 500, or certain bond indexes. You can even vary the face value, or death benefit, of the policy as your needs change. I really like these policies from a tax perspective because the investment component of the policy grows tax-sheltered, and will be paid out tax-free to your beneficiaries upon your death. Today, you will find few, if any, whole life policies being sold because universal policies are so much more flexible.

Action Step

A joint first-to-die policy can make sense when you have two business owners with an agreement that, when one dies, the other will use the insurance proceeds to purchase the deceased partner's interest in the business. In this case, the insurance will be needed on the death of the first business owner, so a second-to-die policy, which would be cheaper, won't do the trick. Your financial advisor can run the numbers to determine if a joint first-to-die policy is less expensive than simply buying two policies—one on the life of each business owner.

Joint Insurance Policies

Once you've decided on a temporary or permanent policy, you've got to answer a question: whose life should be insured? You see, any time that you can purchase a policy on a joint basis (where two lives are insured), there is the possibility to cut your insurance premiums significantly. A joint second-to-die policy, for example, will pay a death benefit only upon the death of the second person whose life is insured. In this case, the policy will be cheaper because two events have to take place before the insurance company forks over the cash—both you and the other individual must die. This type of policy makes a lot of sense where spouses plan to leave all taxable assets to each other on death. In this case, there won't be a tax hit until the death of the second spouse, so a joint second-to-die policy will provide the cash to cover the tax bill precisely when it's needed.

The Best Type of Insurance

Which of the policies that I've talked about is best? It all depends on why you're buying the insurance—remember that discussion in Tip 43? Temporary insurance is best in some cases, while permanent insurance is better in other situations. Consider the table, which identifies the best type of insurance depending on your purpose for the insurance.

Temporary Insurance	Permanent Insurance
• Mortgage insurance (your mortgage won't be around forever, so insurance to cover the outstanding balance doesn't need to be either). • Key person insurance for your business (it's likely that the key person will retire before age 80, so temporary insurance should suffice). • Loan insurance (as loans are paid off, the need to insure outstanding balances will also disappear).	• Provide for dependants. (This need could be temporary as dependants become self-supporting, or as you build other assets to provide for your family in the event of your death. Few people build enough assets to completely provide for dependants, however.) • Cover final disbursements (including funeral costs, professional and executor fees, probate fees, U.S. estate taxes, and debts on death). • Cover a tax bill on death. • Fund a business succession plan. • Leave a larger or equitable bequest. • Pay off debts of a business. • Recover costs previously paid by a business.

There's no question that, particularly in your younger years when you're supporting a young family and your income is generally lower than it will be in the future, the cost of the insurance may dictate the type of insurance. It's been my experience, for example, that many young families will buy term insurance because it's cheaper, even where permanent insurance would be most appropriate. There's no question that some insurance is better than no insurance where you've got a reason to buy it.

As a general rule, if you're going to buy term insurance when you're younger to provide for your dependants in the event of your death, consider converting to a permanent policy at about age 45 if you have a need for permanent insurance. It could get much more expensive if you wait too long.

If you've decided to buy permanent insurance for any reason, choose a universal life insurance policy because of the flexibility. The only exception to this rule is where you do not plan to build up any investments inside the policy, in which case a term-to-100 policy makes sense. Give serious thought, however, to using a universal policy to build up investments, particularly where you've already put enough into your RRSP. You'll be glad to know that there are tax-efficient ways in which to access the investment component of your universal life insurance policy, which can make sense if you need the additional cash flow in retirement.

TO MAKE A LONG STORY SHORT:

- There are two general types of life insurance: temporary and permanent.
- Temporary policies are often referred to as term insurance, and permanent policies are most commonly term-to-100, whole life, or universal life policies.
- The type of insurance that you purchase should depend on the purpose for buying it.

Buying the Right Amount

Once you know why you're buying life insurance, and the type of insurance to buy, the question of how much to buy becomes much easier to answer.

Tim's Tip 45: **Determine how much insurance to purchase by first deciding the purpose and type of insurance.**

Let me walk through some examples to show you how you might best determine the amount of insurance to buy.

Providing for dependants and final expenses: *Fred and Sarah have two young children, and Fred is the breadwinner in the family. Sarah is at home with the kids for now. The couple has determined that they need insurance to provide for Sarah and the kids in the event that Fred dies. How much insurance is the right amount? Step 1 is for the couple to decide on the annual income needs of the family in the event that Fred were to die. Step 2 is to add up all of the income-producing assets that they would have on Fred's death, and to determine how much income those assets would generate each year. Step 3 is to determine whether there's a shortfall between what will be provided (from Step 2) and what is needed (from Step 1). Step 4 is to add up all of the final disbursements that should be covered by life insurance, such as funeral costs, professional and executor's fees, income taxes, and debts. Step 5 is to calculate the amount of life insurance needed, which Fred and Sarah determined from Step 3 where they calculated the shortfall in annual income and Step 4 where they calculated the final disbursements.*

Action Step

If you're the main breadwinner in the family and your spouse is at home with young children, be sure to buy some insurance on your spouse's life to help pay for childcare if he or she dies. For the record, I have two children under age 3, and I've purchased $250,000 of term insurance on my wife's life. This $250,000 would conservatively last for 12 years if I assume annual childcare costs of $25,000 indexed to inflation at three percent annually. Term insurance will do the trick since we won't need the insurance for this purpose in another 15 years—our kids will be grown.

If you turn to Appendix E at the back of the book, you'll find a worksheet that will help you to calculate the amount of insurance you'll need for the purpose of providing for your dependants. By the way, the emphasis in this example was on insurance for Fred since he's the breadwinner. What would happen, however, if Sarah were to die? Fred might have to hire a nanny or incur other childcare costs to enable him to keep working. Insurance on Sarah's life is probably a very good idea in order to cover those additional childcare costs.

Providing for succession of a business: *Joel and Don are both shareholders in a business. They started the business from scratch ten years ago, and today the company is worth $4 million ($2 million each). They have signed a shareholder agreement that requires the corporation to redeem (cash in) the shares of either shareholder should he die. How much insurance does the company need? $2 million on the life of each shareholder. This will provide enough cash to the company to redeem the shares of either shareholder if he dies in the near future. If the company continues to grow in value, however, more insurance will be needed later. A universal life policy can work well here since it's possible to increase the death benefit by simply paying greater premiums, or by drawing* *down on the investment component of the policy to cover the additional insurance.*

Deciding how much insurance to buy in a business scenario like this may require that a valuation be done on the business itself. It's important for Joel and Don to know how much their company is worth in order to buy the right amount of life insurance.

Sheltering investment income from tax: *Gordon has accumulated enough investments over the last few years that he has more than he needs to live comfortably. His primary concern is to keep the tax collector away from his investments, and to pass as much as possible to his kids on his death. Gordon is willing to set aside $25,000 annually over the next ten years to purchase a life insurance policy. He wants to maximize the investment component of the policy. His financial advisor crunched the numbers and, at his age and health, purchasing a $500,000 policy will cost him $8,000 annually in premiums, and he'll be entitled to put another $17,000 into the investment component of the policy at this level of insurance. This brings his total investment to $25,000 annually. Assuming he lives for 25 years, the life insurance benefits to be paid to his kids will amount to over $1.2 million—tax-free (which includes the $500,000 face value plus the accumulated investments). His total investment will be $250,000 over ten years, so the benefits that his kids will receive look quite attractive.*

In Gordon's example, we did things a bit differently. Since the universal life insurance policy is to be used strictly to accumulate investments and pass them tax-free to his kids on his death, Gordon started with the amount that he is willing to invest each year. This enabled his financial advisor to determine how much insurance he could buy given that Gordon wants to maximize the investment component of the policy.

Caution!

A word of warning. Some advisors might suggest a simple rule of thumb when determining the amount of insurance to buy, such as "five times your salary" (or some other multiple). Avoid rules of thumb like the plague—no rule of thumb can accurately determine your insurance requirements, and to be honest, it's not that difficult to calculate how much insurance is the right amount.

Just remember that the right amount depends on your purpose for the insurance, and the type that you buy. Appendix E at the back of the book will help if you're looking to calculate how much you'll need to provide for your dependants. In the end, if you're having difficulty with the calculation, visit a reputable financial advisor for some help.

TO MAKE A LONG STORY SHORT:

- Determining how much insurance to buy becomes easy once you know why you're buying the insurance, and the type that you should buy.
- Appendix E at the back of the book will help if you're looking to calculate the amount of insurance to provide for your dependants if you die.
- When it comes to calculating how much insurance is the right amount, avoid rules of thumb like the plague.

Insured Retirement Plans

There's nothing worse than running out of retirement income before running out of retirement. Insurance can play an important role in providing enough cash flow in retirement.

Tim's Tip 46: Consider an insured retirement plan as a top-up to your other retirement savings or pension plans.

Wouldn't it be nice if the income that you received in retirement was tax-free? Fat chance, right? Let's face it, RRSP or RRIF withdrawals and benefits paid out of registered pension plans are not exactly tax-efficient. These payments are fully taxable. In actual fact, it is possible to establish an insured retirement plan (IRP) that can provide tax-free payments in retirement.

How does an IRP work? It involves the purchase of a universal life (UL) insurance policy that will be "maximum funded" in order to build up a decent investment component in the policy. You'll recall that, with a UL policy, you can choose how much you'd like to deposit into the investment component of the policy each year—subject to certain limits (the MTAR limit under our tax law). Over a period of, say, 10 years or so, you'll be able to build a decent investment component to a UL policy. The greater the face value of the policy, the higher the MTAR limit and the more you can invest in the policy.

Once you've built up a nest egg inside the policy and you're ready for retirement, you can then approach a financial institution and borrow money on a monthly basis using the investment component of the policy as security for the loan. Each loan advance will be tax-free (since loans aren't taxable) and can be used to meet living costs in retirement. The loan can be an "interest-only" loan where you pay the interest owing each month only, or the interest can be capitalized (simply added to the growing amount of the loan).

Finally, upon your death, the face value plus the accumulated investments of the policy will be paid out tax-free and will be available to pay off the debt to the bank, with the balance going to your heirs.

Who is a good candidate for an IRP?

- those who have at least 10 years to go before retirement and whose pension plans will not provide as much income in retirement as they'd like

- those who already have enough set aside in their RRSPs to look after retirement but who may want access to an additional, tax-efficient, source of retirement income
- business owners who don't want the expense and paperwork associated with establishing a registered pension plan for themselves
- an individual who meets one of the scenarios above and is insurable.

Did You Know?

Did you know that permanent insurance policies have an adjusted cost base (ACB)? In simplistic terms, the ACB is the sum of the premiums you've paid on your policy less the net cost of pure insurance on your life. As you get older, the net cost of pure insurance on your life rises, so the ACB of your policy generally falls to the point where it is eventually nil. If you make withdrawals from the investment component of the policy, or surrender the policy, there could be some tax to pay if your ACB is less than the proceeds received.

The Risks of an IRP

Are there any risks to an IRP? Sure. Consider the following:

- Policy loans (loans from your insurance company using your policy as collateral) are taxable. As a result, a third-party financial institution is always used when borrowing as part of the IRP. The Department of Finance could shut down IRPs by changing the definition of a "policy loan" to include loans from third-party institutions. Any existing advances from the institution are likely to be grandfathered if this happens.
- The MTAR limit (which dictates the level of investments that can accumulate inside a policy) is sure to fall in the future. This won't shut down IRPs, but may make them less effective.
- The spread between the rate of return inside the policy and the interest paid to the bank could narrow. In a worst-case scenario, the financial institution could require you to pay down the loan, which might require you to surrender the policy if you haven't got other resources.

- The amount of debt to the bank on your death could be greater than the investments in the policy. The chance of this is slim to none because most financial institutions will not lend more than 50 to 75 percent of the value of the investments inside the policy.

Yes, there are risks. Are they manageable? Yes. While we can't do much to prevent the government from changing the tax law, the worst that is likely to happen is that the IRP will become less effective from the date of any change to the law, forward. Be sure to visit a reputable financial advisor if you're not sure whether an IRP is for you.

TO MAKE A LONG STORY SHORT:

- An insured retirement plan can provide tax-free cash flow in retirement and can supplement an RRSP or registered pension plan.
- The IRP works by using the investment component of a universal life insurance policy as security for a series of loan advances from a financial institution during retirement.
- There are some risks to an IRP, but they are manageable when the plan is established prudently.

Segregated Funds

Segregated funds, known as "seg funds," are a close cousin to regular mutual funds. While they're not for everyone, the do have some benefits.

Tim's Tip 47: Consider investing in seg funds when the benefits outweigh the additional fees attached to them.

In some circles, it's all the rage. No, I'm not talking about the latest toys at your kids' or grandkids' playground, or the 1970s clothing found on store shelves today. I'm not even talking about body piercing—as attractive as that sounds to an accountant. The rage I'm referring to is the proliferation of segregated funds—the mature individual's body piercing, if you like.

Seg funds are not exactly new, but they have grown in popularity. Along with the growth of seg fund assets, there has been growth in the bewilderment over exactly who should take advantage of these funds, and how these funds are taxed.

What Is a Seg Fund?

Seg funds are really mutual funds in an insurance wrapper. On the surface, a seg fund looks and acts like a mutual fund. To the untrained eye, the differences between seg funds and typical mutual funds are almost invisible. Don't be fooled, however: the differences do exist, and have a significant impact on how the tax collector views seg funds.

A seg fund is considered by CCRA (formerly Revenue Canada) to be a trust for tax purposes. When an investor purchases a seg fund, the cash is used by the seg fund trust to purchase the units of a mutual fund chosen by the investor. As a result, the investor does not own units in the mutual fund directly. Rather, it's the seg fund trust that owns the mutual fund units. The investor has not become a unit holder, but a contract holder. The contract is actually an annuity contract governed by provincial insurance law. All of this may seem confusing because advisors, seg fund investors, and mutual fund companies often refer to "units" in a seg fund. These are really notional units used simply to measure an investor's assets under the contract.

One of the greatest selling features of seg funds is the capital guarantee that is offered. Investors can sleep well at night with the assurance that their capital is protected and will be returned to them after 10 years (maturity guarantee) or on death (death guarantee)—whichever comes first. This is true, regardless of any drop in value that the investments might have suffered. Different mutual fund or insurance companies offer different capital guarantees. Guarantees typically range from 75 to 100 percent of the original capital.

There are other benefits to seg funds too. Because these funds are governed by provincial insurance legislation, the assets are typically protected from creditors, which can be great news, especially for business owners. In addition, most seg funds offer the opportunity to lock in any gains in value. That's right, if your funds appreciate in value from, say, \$100,000 to \$150,000, you can lock in the profits provided that you start the 10-year clock (over which period your capital is guaranteed) all over again. Finally, seg funds can pass directly to your beneficiaries and will bypass probate, avoiding probate fees.

Who Should Buy Seg Funds?

There is some question as to who should make use of seg funds. In actual fact, the use of seg funds can be as creative as your imagination. Consider this list of five uses for seg funds:

1. ***Seniors with an objective to preserve capital.*** The capital guarantee offered by seg funds is the most significant selling feature. Those in the "preservation of capital" mode will find seg funds particularly attractive thanks to the guarantees that are available.
2. ***Investors new to the world of mutual funds.*** Some investors have lived their lives holding interest-bearing, conservative investments. Seg funds offer the opportunity for these people to make the move to equity mutual funds without the worry of losing their capital. Once they see the benefits available through long-term equity investment returns, they may be committed to mutual fund investing forever.
3. ***Professionals and business owners looking for protection.*** Seg funds offer something that mutual funds generally can't offer: creditor protection. Because seg funds are governed under provincial insurance legislation, the assets are usually protected from creditors. There may be some exceptions; for example, when assets are channeled to seg funds in anticipation of attacks from

creditors, or where the seg funds are held inside a self-directed RRSP or RRIF.

4. ***Investors who are borrowing to invest.*** Borrowing to invest, when done prudently, can help you to build wealth over the long term. If you're familiar with the strategy, you'll understand how badly off you can be when you've borrowed to invest and your investments drop in value. Seg funds offer some protection here over the long term, thanks to the capital guarantee.
5. ***Investors donating to charity.*** It's possible for investors to donate investments to charity and to receive donation credits as they would with any cash donation. It may be attractive to donate seg funds to a charity because of the capital guarantee. Most charities lack the investment savvy or know-how to manage investments properly and, even where this expertise is available, any charity will appreciate a guaranteed value on a donated investment.
6. ***Investors developing an estate plan.*** By now, you're aware that a seg fund is really an insurance contract. Like most insurance contracts, a beneficiary is named on the seg fund contract when it is established. The assets of the seg fund will pass to the beneficiary outside of the investor's estate on his or her death. The result? Probate fees are avoided. There aren't many investment products that can provide this benefit.

How Are Seg Funds Taxed?

There are a few things to talk about when we talk about the taxation of seg funds. First, I'll talk about the death guarantee, then I'll look at leaving these funds to your spouse on death.

Death Guarantee

The first point to note is that there are three parties to any seg fund contract: the owner of the contract (the investor), the annuitant (the person whose life is used in calculating the maturity and death guarantees), and the beneficiary (the person who will receive the seg fund assets on death of the owner). These roles are important, as you'll see in a minute.

On death of the owner or the annuitant (and they can be different people), the owner of the seg funds is deemed to have disposed of the funds at their fair market value, and capital gains triggered could result in a tax hit. What about losses? If, for example, you purchased $10,000 of seg funds and died after the funds had dropped in value to $9,000, the deemed disposition on death may trigger a $1,000 capital loss on your death. Hold on, though. Where you've got a 100-percent guarantee on your capital, the insurance company will kick in an additional $1,000 to top up the value of your seg funds. This top-up will be taxed as a capital gain. The bottom line? The capital loss from the deemed disposition and the taxable top-up will offset each other, and the net tax consequence is nil.

Rollover to Spouse

If you were to die owning regular mutual funds that had appreciated in value, you could defer the tax hit on death by leaving the funds to your spouse (see Tip 30). This is not necessarily so with a seg fund. Surprised? The tax impact will depend on whether or not the annuitant is still alive at the time that the owner of the seg funds dies.

Where the owner is not the annuitant, and the owner dies, the contract is not terminated—it continues. The transfer of ownership is then treated as any other disposition on death. In this case, if the

Caution!

There's a common myth going around that seg funds are not subject to income tax in the year of death since they are really an insurance product. Not true. Seg funds, like all property, are deemed to have been sold at fair market value on the date of the death of the owner or the annuitant. This could trigger a tax hit. The danger of buying into this myth is that you could end up with less than expected in the year of your death, which could have an impact on who gets what in your will.

contract is transferred to a surviving spouse, tax on the seg funds will be deferred.

Consider a situation, however, where the seg fund owner is also the annuitant. You see, a seg fund contract is generally terminated on the death of the annuitant, the interest in the seg fund is extinguished, and the beneficiary receives a cash payment as a death benefit. If the owner and the annuitant happen to be the same person, then the contract terminates on his or her death, and there is a deemed disposition at fair market value. There is no contract left to roll over to your spouse—so there is no deferral of tax.

Here are a couple of tips when it comes to estate planning and your seg funds:

- Consider using a "successor annuitant" on a seg fund contract. This way, the contract is not terminated on the death of the owner since another annuitant is immediately named.
- Consider changing the annuitant on your existing seg funds if you have that ability.

The Reset Feature

Seg funds offer an attractive option for investors to "lock in" any accrued capital gains. This is known as the "reset feature." Resetting the guaranteed capital amount at a new, higher, value can be an attractive option despite the fact that resetting will start the 10-year maturity clock over again. The best part of this is that there are no tax implications to locking in accrued gains with the reset feature.

TO MAKE A LONG STORY SHORT:

- Seg funds are really mutual funds in an insurance wrapper.
- The key benefits include: a capital guarantee, creditor protection, the ability to lock in accrued gains, and protection from probate fees.
- There is a fee associated with these benefits.

- Seg funds will not automatically transfer tax-free to your spouse on death; care should be taken when naming the annuitant to ensure that this rollover takes place.

WINNING THE ESTATE PLANNING GAME

I know that life insurance can be an intimidating subject—especially since life insurance is not easy to understand. I hope that you feel more informed on this topic now. It's time to visit the *Estate Planning Tip Sheet* to recap the tips that I provided in this chapter. For each tip, answer the question: "Does this apply to me?" Answer "Yes," "No," or "Not Sure" for each tip. Then, move on to Chapter 7—it's time to talk about trusts.

AN ALLY IN THE RACE: MAKING THE MOST OF TRUSTS

Love all, trust a few, and entrust your assets to even fewer.

7

Cary is a good friend. I was over at his place last fall for the start of the hockey season. The first Leafs game of the year was being televised, and we weren't about to miss it. Cary's wife, Melissa, was upstairs working in the home office. Cary was standing with his hand on the television knob as he shouted up to his wife: "Melissa, do you have anything to say before the hockey season starts?"

So it is with Cary, hockey season, and me. Fortunately, my wife, Carolyn, is a hockey fan. In fact, my brother-in-law played pro hockey back in the early eighties as part of the Islanders organization when they won those back-to-back Stanley Cups.

Melissa knew that any important discussions to be had in the fall had to take place before hockey season. "Cary, before you turn on that TV, where are we spending Christmas this year, what would you like for your birthday (Cary's birthday is in November—three days before mine), and what about the family trust?" Melissa queried.

"Well," Cary replied, "I'm okay to spend Christmas at your parents' place, I'd like a new Palm Pilot for my birthday, and let's ask Tim whether he thinks a family trust makes sense."

"Done," Melissa responded.

"Can I turn the game on now, honey?" Cary asked.

"Sure," Melissa replied.

After the first period, I sat down with Cary and Melissa and talked to them about the benefits of trusts—and there can be many. Let's talk about trusts as an estate planning tool.

This Thing Called a Trust

When I first heard about trusts many years ago, I assumed, like many Canadians, that these were:

- an *unethical aggressive* tax planning tool
- solely for the rich
- something done after death
- complicated
- rigid, not flexible
- expensive to set up
- expensive to maintain.

Well, now that I'm a little older and allegedly a little wiser, I know that the characteristics listed above are *not* those of a trust. I know that a trust is a very useful tool to use in designing an estate plan!

Caution!

If you transfer income-producing assets to a trust, you'll have to beware the attribution rules in our tax law, which will require you to pay the tax on income of the trust, in some cases, rather than the beneficiaries.

I could spend 30 pages talking about the attribution rules, but I won't do that here. I will say, however, that the attribution rules can be a particular problem when it's an inter vivos trust and the beneficiaries are minor children or your spouse. I cover this issue in Chapter 2 of my book, *Winning the Tax Game*.

Tim's Tip 48: **Recognize that a trust is not an entity—it's a relationship!**

Unlike a corporation, a trust is not a separate entity under common law. No public registration of a trust is required. A trust is best described as a *relationship*. It's a relationship between three parties: the settlor, trustee, and beneficiary. To create a trust, the *settlor* must *settle*, or transfer property to, the trust. The *trustee* is the person who legally owns the property, but not for his or her own benefit. Rather, the trustee owns the property and holds it for the benefit of the *beneficiary*. Of course, there can be more than one settlor, trustee, or beneficiary in any trust relationship. The settlor provides the trustee with instructions on how to carry out his or her responsibilities. The beneficiaries will be entitled to the income earned in the trust (income beneficiaries) and/or the property itself that is held in the trust (capital beneficiaries).

Benefits of Trusts

Most people assume that trusts are set up primarily for tax planning benefits. In fact, a trust has plenty of advantages—some of which are tax-related, and some which have little to do with tax planning. Here's a list of a dozen tax and non-tax benefits of trusts:

1. ***Income splitting with family.*** It's possible to use a trust to split income with family members. You see, the beneficiaries of a

trust—and not you—will pay the tax on the income of the trust where that income is paid out to the beneficiaries or made payable to them each year. Alternatively, the trust rather than your beneficiaries can pay the tax, which makes much sense in the case of testamentary trusts (trusts created after your death) which are taxed at graduated tax rates just like any individual. I'll talk more about this later.

2. ***Multiplying tax exemptions.*** Certain tax exemptions can be claimed to offset the income of a trust, provided that the beneficiaries are entitled to claim those exemptions. I'm thinking specifically of the principal residence exemption (which allows a home to be sold tax-free), and the enhanced capital gains exemption (which shelters the first $500,000 of capital gains on certain private company shares or farm property).
3. ***Minimizing probate fees.*** Since you don't own the assets that are held in a trust at the time of your death, these assets fall outside of your estate, and you'll avoid provincial probate fees on the assets (see Chapter 10 for more on probate fees).
4. ***Avoid a disposition on death.*** You'll recall from our talk in Tip 17 that you're deemed to have sold all that you own immediately prior to your death. This can trigger significant taxable capital gains, and a tax hit bigger than the gross domestic product of Madagascar. Any assets that you place in a trust before your death will not be deemed sold at the time of your death (since you don't legally own the assets anymore) so you'll avoid a tax hit on those assets at your death.
5. ***Accomplish an estate freeze.*** I talked about estate freezes in Tip 25. A trust can be used to accomplish an estate freeze. How? By transferring certain assets to a trust during your lifetime, the future growth of the assets will accrue to the beneficiaries of the trust and will not be taxed in your hands. In many cases, a corporation is used to accomplish a freeze instead because transferring assets to a trust can itself trigger taxes (this can be

avoided by a corporation). Nevertheless, trusts can be effective for freezes in certain situations.

6. ***Protection of assets.*** A trust can offer you protection from creditors or ex-spouses. Remember—once assets are in a trust, they are no longer yours. As a result, creditors and ex-spouses cannot generally access the assets. If, however, you transfer assets to a trust knowing that creditors or an ex-spouse will soon be knocking at your door, the transfer to the trust may be invalidated under law. A trust set up to protect assets from creditors is often referred to as an *asset protection trust.*
7. ***Management of assets.*** Maybe you'd like to transfer the ownership of certain assets to your heirs, but you prefer that your heirs not manage those assets. Maybe your heirs are too young, irresponsible, or simply unable to handle the assets. A trust can solve your problem because the benefits of ownership can pass to your heirs while the management of the assets rests with the trustee.
8. ***Protecting privacy.*** A will is generally subject to probate, and it becomes a public document. Therefore, all of the assets of the estate and who inherited what becomes public knowledge. However, when assets are in a trust, they pass to the beneficiaries of the trust (who may be the same as the heirs noted in your will) in accordance with the trust agreement—not by the will. The bottom line? No public disclosure!
9. ***Avoiding compulsory succession schemes.*** Your will can be contested if a disgruntled person feels short-changed by you. In a worst-case scenario, your will could be varied (changed) to suit the needs of others. A trust will generally protect against this if it's set up properly.
10. ***Providing for disabled family members.*** If you're looking after a family member who has a mental disability, how will you manage to take care of the person once you're gone? A trust is commonly used. You can place assets in the trust, which will

provide an income to your disabled family member, and the trustee will look after disbursing the funds for the benefit of that family member.

11. ***Replacing a will or power of attorney.*** Any assets held in trust at the time of your death will be dealt with in accordance with the trust agreement—not your will. This can mean a quicker and more efficient transfer of assets to your heirs since a will must generally go through probate, while a trust does not. Similarly, a power of attorney over property is intended to provide another person with control over your assets in the event that you can't make money-related decisions for yourself. A trust can accomplish the same thing. Your trustee would be responsible for making decisions, or carrying out your wishes, in accordance with the trust agreement that you set up.
12. ***Giving to charity.*** You can actually make a donation to charity today, receive a donation tax credit for it, and still make use of the assets you've donated during your lifetime. A charitable remainder trust (CRT) can be set up for this purpose. I'll talk more about CRTs in Chapter 9, when I discuss planned giving.

Did You Know?

The residency of a trust is important—just as it is for any individual. If a trust is resident in Canada, it will face income tax in Canada each year on its income, unless that income is allocated to a beneficiary to be taxed in his or her hands. A trust is generally resident where the majority of its trustees reside. If, for example, two out of three trustees live in British Columbia, then the trust will be resident there and will be subject to both federal and B.C. income taxes.

Since we're talking about estate planning here, can you identify which of the benefits of trusts listed above are really estate planning benefits? If you answered *every one of them*, you'd be right. In one way or another, each of the benefits of trusts that I've identified can play a role in your estate planning. Refer to the list again and identify which of these benefits you might be able to take advantage of. If, at the end of this chapter, you're not sure which of the benefits listed might apply to you, take the list to a tax pro and discuss it. You'll end up with a good understanding of how you might best use trusts in your estate planning.

Types of Trusts

There are two basic types of trusts: inter vivos and testamentary trusts. An inter vivos (Latin for "among the living") trust is simply a trust that is created during your lifetime if you're the settlor. The taxation year for an inter vivos trust falls on December 31—just as it is with you and me. The first taxation year of an inter vivos trust begins on the day the trust is settled. Therefore, unless the trust is settled on January 1, the first taxation "year" of an inter vivos trust will be a "short" year.

As the name suggests, a testamentary trust is created at the time of an individual's death. The "testator" (the deceased) is the settlor. The details of the trust and the instructions to the trustees are generally laid out in the deceased's will. The trustee of a testamentary trust is free to choose any tax year-end date that he or she wants, provided that it doesn't extend beyond the day before the first anniversary of the settlor's death. So, if you die on July 1 in a given year and you've established a testamentary trust in your will, your executor can choose a year-end as late as June 30 of the following year.

Discretionary Trusts

The settlor will provide instructions to the trustees on how the trust and its assets are to be managed. The trustees may be given great flexibility in running the trust and in managing the assets of the trust. Where this is the case, the trustees have much discretion, and the trust is considered to be a *discretionary trust*.

Alternatively, the settlor may leave specific rules that must be followed, in which case you'd call it a *non-discretionary trust*. For example, each beneficiary's entitlement to the trust income and assets may be a fixed percentage, and under no circumstances can this be altered.

Most trusts established today provide the trustees with a generous level of flexibility. To be honest, I prefer discretionary trusts in most cases. Why? They simply allow for a greater opportunity to save taxes. Further, if you establish a trust at the time of your death with the intention of ruling the financial planning of your heirs from the grave, you could cause significant stress and anxiety for those beneficiaries you leave behind.

Did You Know?

Beginning in 2001, same-sex couples who have been living together for at least one year will be treated under our tax law in the same way that opposite-sex common-law couples have been for the last few years. Effectively, the tax treatment afforded spouses will also apply to same-sex partners in 2001. These same-sex couples will also be able to elect to have this treatment apply for the years 1998 through 2000 as well, but making this election should not be automatic! You could be worse off, depending on your situation.

Spousal (Partner) Trusts

A spousal trust—sometimes referred to as a *partner trust* (since the definition of "spouse" under our taw law is changing to include more than just legally married couples)—is simply a trust that you establish exclusively for the benefit of your spouse while he or she is still alive. In fact, our tax law says that a spousal trust is a trust under which your spouse is the only one entitled to the income of the trust while he or she is alive. Further, no one other than your spouse is entitled to the capital (the assets) of the trust during your spouse's lifetime. What are the benefits of a spousal trust? You'll enjoy the dozen benefits I listed above. In addition, any property transferred to a spousal trust will avoid the usual deemed disposition at fair market value upon the transfer. Rather, any property transferred to a spousal trust is transferred at your adjusted cost base, so there's no tax to pay on the transfer! On your spouse's death, there will be a deemed disposition of the property in the trust at its fair market value at that time, and the trust may have to pay some tax.

Alter Ego and Joint Spousal (Partner) Trusts

In 2000, new rules were finalized to permit the creation of *alter ego* and *joint spousal (partner)* trusts. In a nutshell, you can transfer assets with accrued gains to these trusts *without triggering the accrued gain!* These trusts are similar to spousal trusts in this respect. The trust must meet the definition of being either an "alter ego trust" or a "joint spousal (partner) trust," and there are a number of benefits to these trusts—which I'll talk more about in Tip 54.

Winding Up a Trust

The ending of a trust is referred to as a "winding-up" of the trust. This takes place on the date specified in the trust agreement (for inter vivos trusts) or the will (for testamentary trusts). Rather than a specific date being set, the time of the wind-up may be when an event occurs—say when the last beneficiary reaches age 25, for example. Upon winding up the trust, the assets of the trust are transferred to the beneficiaries of the trust. Income tax is not generally triggered here as the trust is considered to have disposed of the trust assets for proceeds equal to the tax cost (the adjusted cost base). No capital gain will generally arise. The beneficiary "inherits" the adjusted cost base of the assets received.

In many cases, the settlor will not specify a wind-up date. The task of deciding on a date is often passed on to the trustees. Where this is the case, the trustees will be given the discretion to decide on when it's best for the trust to end.

TO MAKE A LONG STORY SHORT:

- A trust is a relationship between three parties: settlor, trustee, and beneficiary.
- There are many tax and non-tax benefits to setting up trusts.
- Trusts can be discretionary, in which case the trustee is provided with much flexibility in managing the trust assets, or non-discretionary.
- A trust may be wound up on a date specified by the settlor, upon the occurrence of some event identified by the settlor, or at a time left to the discretion of the trustee.

Tim's Tip 49: **Choose the right trustee for an inter vivos or testamentary trust.**

I discussed in Chapter 2 that choosing the right executor in your will is vital to ensure that your estate affairs are properly taken care of and your assets pass to your desired beneficiaries in an efficient and prompt matter. Many of the qualities that you should seek in an executor should also be sought in a trustee—regardless of whether you set up an inter vivós trust (a trust set up during your lifetime), or a testamentary trust (created after your death). The trustee of a testamentary trust does not have to be your executor—but he or she can be!

As with an executor, a trustee can be held personally liable for any errors made if his or her duties are not performed with proper care. It's important that the trustees whom you select be willing to do the job and be capable of handing the complexity of the trust, its assets, and any family and business issues that surround the responsibilities.

Qualities of a Trustee

The trustee(s) you choose should possess certain qualities or characteristics. Consider these:

- **Availability.** Do they have the time? Will they be available to manage the trust for its duration? If not, consider someone else.

- **Expertise.** Do they have financial acumen and good business sense? If not, another choice may be better.
- **Impartiality.** Will they make decisions on an impartial basis in the case of a discretionary trust? This is important.
- **Sensitivity.** Are they sensitive to family issues and understand the relationships in the family? I hope so.
- **Willingness.** As I pointed out, it's critical that the trustees be willing to act in that capacity—it's a big responsibility.

Trustees cannot delegate responsibilities. They can, however, seek assistance from others with experience in the needed areas—investments, accounting, tax, law, etc. If you're not confident in anyone you know who might act as a trustee, or you can't think of anyone appropriate, you can hire a professional trustee—such as an accountant, lawyer, or trust company. Sure there will be fees, but you can at least be assured that you have hired someone with experience in this area. Refer back to Tip 9, where I talked about personal versus professional executors; the same guidelines apply here for trustees.

TO MAKE A LONG STORY SHORT:

- Selecting the trustees for a trust is an important part of the estate planning exercise.
- Many of the same qualities that you look for in choosing an executor for your will should be evident in those chosen as your trustees.
- If you don't know of an individual who could serve as a trustee, a professional trustee can always be hired.

Tim's Tip 50: **Arrange for the terms of your trust to be drafted by a lawyer—not your brother-in-law.**

A trust has to be set up correctly in order to ensure that your estate planning objectives are met. In order for a legal trust to be created, three certainties must be met:

1. ***Certainty of intention.*** It must be clear that you intended to establish a trust relationship. A properly drafted trust agreement will specifically address this intention.
2. ***Certainty of subject matter.*** The property to be held in trust must be identified clearly. A proper trust agreement will identify this property.
3. ***Certainty of objects.*** It must be clear who the beneficiaries are. Naming beneficiaries can be as detailed as naming them one by one in the trust agreement, or naming a class of beneficiaries such as "the children of John Doe."

In addition to addressing the three certainties, the powers of the trustees must be detailed. What decisions do the trustees have discretion over? Will the trust be wound up on a certain date or after a certain event occurs? Where a trust agreement is silent or is not clear on an issue, provincial trust law will step in and dictate what is to happen—and this

Action Step

In the case of an *inter vivos* trust, the trust agreement is generally a document separate from any other, signed by the settlor and trustee(s). In the case of a *testamentary* trust, the terms of the trust agreement are generally built into your will. A trust agreement, whether it's a separate document or encompasses part of your will, does not have to be long and drawn out. Make sure that a lawyer who is experienced with trusts drafts your trust agreement, or revises your will to include a trust.

law is not very flexible. The moral of the story? Spend the money and have a proper trust agreement prepared.

An experienced lawyer will make the terms of the trust as brief as necessary while still accomplishing your objectives. Your brother-in-law, on the other hand, may not have a clue as to how to really prepare a trust agreement (unless he's an experienced lawyer, of course!). Make sure that the lawyer you deal with has had experience drafting trust agreements, because there are plenty of i's to dot and t's to cross. In addition, you should have the trust agreement reviewed by an accountant who specializes in tax (since most lawyers don't specialize in this area) to make sure that it's okay from a tax perspective.

TO MAKE A LONG STORY SHORT

- A proper trust agreement will address the three certainties that must be met to establish a legal trust, and will address a number of other issues.
- Trust agreements can be separate documents (for inter vivos trusts) or form part of your will (for testamentary trusts).
- A lawyer experienced in drafting trust agreements should be used, and an accountant specializing in tax should review the agreement if your lawyer doesn't specialize in tax.

Taxation of Trusts

Hey, if you're going to take advantage of a trust in your estate planning, you should have a good idea of how trusts are taxed. Let's take a look at the basics now.

Tim's Tip 51: Understand how inter vivos and testamentary trusts are taxed.

A trust is considered to be a separate taxpayer—just like you and I are. In fact, a trust is treated as an individual under our tax law (even though it's not an entity under common law, but a relationship). A trust pays tax on its taxable income, just like you and I do. A trust does differ from other individuals in two key ways:

- trusts are not permitted to claim any personal tax credits
- trusts are allowed a deduction in calculating taxable income for income that is allocated to the beneficiaries (the beneficiaries pay the tax on the income in this case).

Allocations to Beneficiaries

A trust will not pay tax on any income that has been allocated to one or more beneficiaries. By "allocated," I mean that:

- the income of the trust has been *paid* out to the beneficiaries, or
- the income of the trust has been made *payable* to the beneficiaries.

You see, amounts that are not paid out of a trust can still be taxed in the hands of the beneficiaries if the income of the trust is legally payable to the beneficiaries at the end of the tax year of the trust. In this way, it's possible for the income of the trust to accumulate in the trust, allowing it to compound more quickly. When income of the trust is paid or payable to the beneficiaries, the trust gets a deduction for this amount, and the beneficiaries get T3 slips reporting the income. The beneficiaries will have to report the income on their personal tax returns, and pay the tax.

When income is allocated out to a beneficiary, it retains the character of the income that was actually earned by the trust. For example, if the trust received dividends from a Canadian corporation and allocated the income to the beneficiary, the beneficiary would report the income as Canadian dividends. Likewise, interest income and capital gains retain their character as well.

If a trust happens to pay tax on its income, rather than allocating the income to be taxed in the hands of a beneficiary, the income generally becomes part of the "capital" of the trust after the taxes have been paid. The distinction between capital and income is important because the capital of a trust can usually be distributed tax-free to the beneficiaries at any time. This treatment is logical: since the income has already been taxed in the trust, it should not be taxed again in the beneficiaries' hands.

Action Step

If a beneficiary of a testamentary trust has no other taxable income, at least $7,500 of the trust's income should be allocated to the beneficiary annually. The beneficiary's basic personal tax credit will offset the personal income tax that arises on this amount of taxable income, and the income is then effectively tax-free! If left in the trust, income of $7,500 would result in about $1,600 in taxes. This is because a trust is not entitled to the basic personal credit that other individuals are.

Tax Rates for Trusts

What rate of tax will a trust have to pay? It depends on whether you're talking about an inter vivos or testamentary trust. A testamentary trust is subject to tax at the same graduated tax brackets and rates as any individual on its taxable income. This means that the first $30,000 or so of income in a testamentary trust will be subject to the lowest marginal tax rates federally. A testamentary trust, like an individual, is also subject to provincial income taxes and surtaxes.

Inter vivos trusts, on the other hand, face different rates of tax. All of the taxable income of an inter vivos trust is taxed at the top federal rate of 29 percent. Of course, provincial income tax (again, at the top rate!) and surtaxes also apply.

Obviously, if a beneficiary of an inter vivos trust is not yet in the highest tax bracket, he would pay tax at a lower rate than the inter vivos trust, which pays tax at the top federal rate of 29 percent. As a result, it would be prudent to have the trust income taxed in the beneficiary's hands rather than in the inter vivos trust. An individual enters the top tax bracket of 29 percent once his taxable income exceeds approximately $60,000 (this is to be increased to $100,000 based on proposals in the October 18, 2000 federal mini-budget). Where an individual's taxable income is less than this amount, the trustees should be made aware of this so that allocations to the beneficiaries can be made if desired.

Both testamentary and inter vivos trusts are entitled to the dividend tax credit on Canadian dividends, and pay tax on just 50 percent of capital gains (note: the 50-percent inclusion rate for capital gains was proposed in the October 18, 2000 federal mini-budget. Prior to this budget, it was set at 66.67 percent).

TO MAKE A LONG STORY SHORT

- A trust is taxed in the same manner as an individual. A trust is not, however, permitted personal tax credits, but is permitted a deduction for amounts allocated to beneficiaries and taxed in their hands.
- A testamentary trust is entitled to the same graduated tax rates as any individual, while inter vivos trusts are taxed at the highest rate going.

Tim's Tip 52: **Be aware of the 21-year rule, which could trigger a huge tax hit down the road!**

Talk about a bummer. On the twenty-first anniversary of a trust's creation, the trust is deemed to have sold all of its assets for proceeds equal to fair market value at that time. In addition, this deemed disposition will take place every twenty-one years after that. Consequently, accrued capital gains in the trust are triggered every twenty-one years (as well as any *recapture* where the trust owns depreciable assets, such as a building; a discussion of recapture is beyond the scope of this book).

You can imagine the potential tax hit that could arise on the twenty-first anniversary of the trust. We're talking about capital gains that might have accrued for a full generation! There are exceptions to the 21-year rule in the case of a *spousal (partner) trust, alter ego trust, or a joint spousal (partner) trust.* Accrued gains in these types of trusts will not be subject to tax until you die or your spouse does, as the case may be, or when the trust sells the assets—whichever comes first.

Action Step

A trust files an annual return referred to as Form T3—"Trust Income Tax and Information Return." It is the trustees' responsibility to ensure that the T3 is prepared and filed on time. One of the trustees must sign the return. The T3 return must be filed with CCRA within 90 days of the taxation year-end of the trust. Where the trust has a December 31 year-end, March 31 is the due date (90 days after December 31)—unless it's a leap year, when the deadline is March 30. Penalties and interest can be assessed if you're late, so file on time!

Avoiding the 21-year Rule

How do you avoid the 21-year rule? Your options are slim. While the 21-year rule cannot be avoided altogether, there are a couple of ways to minimize the impact of the rule. If a trust, on its twenty-first anniversary, has no assets with accrued capital gains or potential recapture, the deemed disposition will have no impact. So how can you ensure that the trust does not have assets with large accrued capital gains or potential recapture on its twenty-first anniversary? You've got two key options:

1. ***Realize gains before the twenty-first anniversary.*** If you trigger capital gains earlier than the twenty-first anniversary, then the 21-year rule won't hurt as much. This will mean paying tax earlier than the twenty-first year, but it may be possible to trigger some gains over time while the beneficiaries are younger and in a low tax bracket. It could be that the

beneficiaries will pay little or no tax at all on the gains. Where triggering gains early will result in significant taxes to pay, this idea may not make sense.

2. ***Distribute trust assets prior to the 21-year anniversary.*** If you distribute any assets with accrued capital gains or potential recapture to the trust's capital beneficiaries prior to the twenty-first anniversary, you'll avoid the deemed disposition in the trust. Remember that the distribution of trust assets to beneficiaries can generally occur without triggering any tax. The beneficiary simply assumes the adjusted cost base of the trust. This option is often your best bet to minimize the impact of the 21-year rule. The downside *(why does there always have to be a downside?)* is that the asset is no longer under the control of the trustee—the beneficiary now has ownership.

TO MAKE A LONG STORY SHORT:

- A trust is deemed to dispose of its assets at market value on each twenty-first anniversary, likely triggering taxable capital gains and recapture.
- Minimize the impact of the 21-year rule by triggering gains earlier than—or distributing property of the trust prior to—the twenty-first anniversary.

Using Inter Vivos Trusts

Creating a trust during your lifetime can provide a number of estate planning benefits. Don't believe me? Read on—then consider how you might utilize an inter vivos trust in your situation. Don't get me wrong. An inter vivos trust is not for everyone, but where your situation warrants it, the benefits can be great.

Tim's Tip 53: Take advantage of an inter vivos trust to reduce taxes on death and protect your estate.

Remember back to Tip 48, where I listed a dozen benefits to trusts. You might not be able to take advantage of all of those benefits, but some or many could apply. The best way to understand how a trust might benefit you is to consider an example.

Let me share with you the story of Cary and Melissa, whom I introduced in the opening paragraphs of this chapter. After discussing their situation, I recommended a trust, and you'll see from their example how they've benefited.

Cary is 35 years old, and his wife, Melissa, is 32. They have a young child—Stephen, aged 6—who has a mental disability. Cary has decided to set up a trust for Stephen in order to accomplish a few things. Cary is the settlor and settled the trust by transferring $10,000 to the trust. He plans to transfer an additional $5,000 each year to the trust in order to build up enough assets in the trust that Stephen will always be provided for. Cary has named Melissa and a trusted accountant as trustees. The trust will likely generate close to $1,000 of income in its first year, and this amount will grow annually as more money is placed in the trust.

What have Cary and Melissa accomplished by setting up an inter vivos trust for Stephen? Consider all that they have accomplished:

1. ***Income splitting.*** The income of the trust will be taxed in Stephen's hands, not Cary's. Since Stephen has no other income, the trustees can allocate up to approximately $7,500 of taxable income to him annually, and no tax will be owing on the amount. The trustees have invested the money in the trust to generate capital gains primarily (not interest or dividend income). A full

$15,000 in capital gains can be realized annually before Stephen pays any tax ($15,000 of capital gains will result in $7,500 of taxable income at the 50-percent inclusion rate). Capital gains will not be attributed back and taxed in Cary's hands, whereas interest and dividends would be.

2. ***Minimizing probate fees.*** If Cary were to die tomorrow, probate fees would apply to any assets in his estate. The assets held in the trust are not considered to be part of his estate, so he'll avoid probate fees on these assets.
3. ***Avoiding disposition on death.*** Since the assets in the trust are owned by the trustees for the benefit of Stephen, Cary will not face a deemed disposition of those assets on his death. This will save him taxes.
4. ***Managing assets.*** Cary wants to set aside money for Stephen, but he recognizes that Stephen can't handle the money on his own, so the trustees will look after this. The trust agreement says that, on the death of any trustee, Cary will name a new trustee. If Cary is not alive at that time, the surviving trustee will name another trustee of his or her choice.
5. ***Providing for Stephen.*** Stephen will not have to worry about financial support once his parents are gone. Cary is putting money into the trust annually, and Cary has purchased a life insurance policy, the proceeds of which will also be placed in a trust for Stephen on Cary's death.

Did You Know?

After the settlor of an inter vivos trust has prepared the trust agreement and has contributed the property (the settlement) to the trust, his or her work is generally finished! The settlor may no longer have any responsibilities related to the trust. If desired, the settlor can retain the right to replace trustees. If you want to be involved in the trust as a trustee or beneficiary, it may be better to have a friend or other family member settle the trust. This way, you'll avoid the attribution rule found in subsection 75(2) of our tax law.

How about another example? Consider Grant's story.

Grant is a widower, aged 70. He rents an apartment in downtown Oakville, Ontario. Grant has a pension that adequately provides for his needs, and he owns $150,000 of GICs and a cottage worth $220,000 that originally cost him $100,000 (his adjusted cost base). He'll never need the $150,000 in GICs and has decided to invest the money for growth over the next few years, then to pass it to his only daughter, Kayla, upon his death. Kayla will also inherit the cottage. Grant is somewhat concerned about Kayla's marriage. He doesn't want her husband to walk away with half of anything if the marriage fails. By the way, Kayla is in the lowest tax bracket, while Grant is in the highest.

Suppose for a minute that Grant dies at age 75. His cottage is still worth $220,000 at that time, and the $150,000, which he moved from GICs to equity mutual funds, has grown to be worth $275,000 at the time of his death. What happens to his estate? Here's what happens:

- the accrued gain on the cottage of $120,000 ($220,000 less the adjusted cost base of $100,000) is triggered and a tax bill of $30,000 is due
- the accrued gain on the investments of $125,000 ($275,000 less the adjusted cost base of $150,000) is triggered and a tax bill of $31,250 is due
- probate fees of $6,925 are due to the province of Ontario on his estate
- total taxes and probate fees owing on Grant's death equal $68,175.

Was this tax and probate cost absolutely necessary? Absolutely not. You see, if Grant had taken advantage of an inter vivos trust, he could have saved these costs on death, and could have left Kayla with much more, in addition to accomplishing other objectives. Let me show you how.

Suppose that Grant establishes an inter vivos trust this year. His GICs mature and he transfers his $150,000 to the trust to be invested. He also transfers his cottage to the trust. While Grant will be deemed to have sold the cottage at fair market value when transferring the property to the trust, he can shelter the gain from tax by using his principal residence exemption. (Note: visit a tax pro before you try the same thing, in order to determine whether you'll be able to use your principal residence exemption as Grant did!) Grant names his daughter, Kayla, as the sole beneficiary of the trust. Kayla is also a trustee, along with Grant's lawyer. Now, suppose Grant dies at age 75. The cottage is still worth $220,000, and the investment portfolio in the trust is worth the same $275,000 we assumed before. What happens on Grant's death? Here's what happens:

1. ***Avoids deemed disposition on death.*** Grant avoids the deemed disposition of the cottage on death since the trust now owns the cottage. The result? No tax to pay on the cottage. Grant also avoids income tax on the investment portfolio since the trust—not Grant—owns the assets.
2. ***Avoids probate fees.*** There are no probate fees to pay since, again, Grant does not own the assets.
3. ***Multiplies tax exemptions.*** Grant is potentially able to multiply use of the principal residence exemption by utilizing Kayla's exemption (in the event that Kayla and her husband don't already own a home, or Kayla separates from her husband, in which case she'll be entitled to her own exemption).

Did You Know?

The legal fees to set up a trust can range from $2,000 to $3,000 on average. Ask your lawyer for a quote. In addition, there are tax filings for the trust each year. You might be able to handle these filings on your own if you're the type who is comfortable doing your own tax return. Otherwise, it could cost $500 to $1,500 annually on average to have the return prepared by an accountant. These fees are pretty small when you consider some of the benefits of setting up a trust.

4. ***Accomplishes an estate freeze.*** Grant accomplished an estate freeze with the trust. That is, all future growth after transferring the assets to the trust was not taxed in his hands upon his death—but will eventually be taxed in Kayla's.
5. ***Income splitting with Kayla.*** Kayla will pay the tax annually on any income earned by the trust, and on any capital gains when assets of the trust are sold. There is no attribution of income back to Grant since Kayla is an adult. Since she's in a lower tax bracket than Grant is, less tax is paid.
6. ***Protection of assets.*** Grant ensured that the assets left to Kayla will be protected against claims by her husband if they separate or divorce. The trust agreement ensures this.

TO MAKE A LONG STORY SHORT:

- Inter vivos trusts can offer significant benefits in estate planning, including: income splitting, multiplying tax exemptions, minimizing probate fees, avoiding a deemed disposition on death, accomplishing an estate freeze, protecting assets, managing assets, and providing for family members, among other benefits.
- The costs of setting up a trust are often much smaller than the potential benefits.

Tim's Tip 54: **Consider establishing an alter ego or joint spousal trust for a number of benefits.**

Every once in a while (not very often, mind you) the Department of Finance sees fit to introduce new tax provisions that offer some sort of planning opportunities for Canadians. In 2000, two new types of trusts were introduced: alter ego and joint spousal (partner) trusts.

Alter Ego Trusts

An alter-ego trust can be set up by an individual, provided that he or she has reached age 65. The terms of the trust must provide that the individual establishing the trust (the settlor) alone is entitled to all of the income of the trust earned before his or her death. In addition, the trust must provide that no one other than the individual is entitled, before his or her death, to the capital of the trust. In other words, the individual becomes both the settlor and beneficiary. The individual can also be a trustee.

The good news is that there is no deemed disposition at fair market value when you transfer assets to an alter ego trust. Rather, the assets are transferred at your adjusted cost base, so there is no tax to pay on the transfer. On your death, however, there is a deemed disposition of the assets in the trust, and you'll pay the tax personally in your year of death on any accrued gains—just as if you had owned the assets directly.

At the time that the trust agreement is prepared, contingent beneficiaries (your heirs) would be named who would receive the income and/or capital of the trust after you die. An alter-ego trust is an inter vivos trust, so it's subject to the high rates of tax that I spoke about in Tip 51. It cannot be converted to a testamentary trust on your death.

There's no legal requirement for the settlor of the trust and the trustee to be different people. In fact, the settlor can also be a beneficiary. Wearing the settlor's hat and that of a trustee or beneficiary could, however, have adverse tax consequences! You see, subsection 75(2) of our tax law could cause you to pay tax on all of the trust's income, if you've transferred property to the trust and maintain control over the trust property as a trustee, or where the property can revert back to you later as a beneficiary. Visit a tax pro to be sure that your trust is established properly!

Caution!

Caution!

Neither alter ego nor joint spousal trusts are good for income splitting. The reason? All income of these trusts will be taxed in your hands (and your spouse's hands in the case of a joint spousal trust). In addition, you wouldn't use these trusts to accomplish an estate freeze since, again, all future growth of the assets in the trust will eventually be taxed in your hands, either when you sell the assets, or on your death.

Joint Spousal (Partner) Trust

Joint spousal (partner) trusts are much like alter ego trusts—but for two people. As the name implies, this is an inter vivos trust where both spouses can benefit during their lifetime. No one else can be entitled to any of the income or capital. The individual(s) making a transfer to the trust must be at least 65 at the time. The deemed disposition rules will apply at the death of the second spouse.

What are alter ego and joint spousal trusts good for? These are best if you're simply looking to:

- minimize probate fees on death
- protect your privacy
- avoid compulsory succession schemes
- replace your will, or
- replace your power of attorney.

Refer to Tip 48 for more on these benefits.

TO MAKE A LONG STORY SHORT:

- Alter ego and joint spousal (partner) trusts work much like other trusts, except that there is no deemed disposition upon transferring assets to these trusts, and taxes will be due personally on any income of the trust, or upon your death.
- Only those aged 65 or older can set up these trusts.
- These trusts can help you to avoid probate fees, and they offer a few other benefits.

Using Testamentary Trusts

Now that you have a grasp on how an inter vivos trust might be used, let's talk about testamentary trusts. If you're leaving income-producing assets behind on your death, these trusts can be more valuable than gold.

Tim's Tip 55: Take advantage of a testamentary trust to provide your heirs with tax savings and asset protection.

I've read a lot of wills. If you and your spouse are like most Canadians, I can probably tell you what your wills say. They likely provide that:

- on the death of the first spouse, the assets owned by the first spouse are to be passed to the surviving spouse
- on the surviving spouse's death, the assets are to be passed to the children of the two spouses.

So what's wrong with this? Well, nothing, except there can be a *better* way—a way in which the intentions of all are maintained but the income tax is reduced! Rather than your spouse and then your kids directly inheriting your estate, why not leave the assets in testamentary trusts, where your spouse and kids are the beneficiaries of these trusts set up just for them? The result? Tax savings!

Remember that a trust is a separate taxpayer, and testamentary trusts are taxed at graduated tax rates. By leaving income-producing assets to a testamentary trust rather than directly to your heirs, the trust can pay the tax on any income generated on that inheritance. Your heirs could save as much as $11,000 annually in taxes, depending on their province and income level. Consider the example of Clara and Milt.

Action Step

When you and your spouse visit a lawyer to have your wills prepared or revised, don't simply accept "mirror image wills" from your lawyer. These are wills that are generally "cookie cutter" in nature, where all of your assets are left to your spouse on death, and vice versa, then left to your kids on the death of the surviving spouse. Consider instead whether establishing testamentary trusts in your wills can make more sense. They may cost a little more than the boiler-plate wills often prepared by lawyers, but they can be more effective at reducing taxes when you're gone!

Clara's spouse, Milt, recently died. At the time of his death, Milt owned 1,000 shares in a Canadian public company. The adjusted cost base of these shares was $100,000, and the value on Milt's death of these shares was $250,000. Milt's will stated that all of his assets were bequeathed to Clara. Due to the spousal rollover rules (see Tip 30), Milt's $150,000 accrued gain was not triggered on his death. Clara inherited the shares as well as the $100,000 adjusted cost base. The shares pay $10,000 in dividends each year. Since Clara now owns the shares, she'll receive the dividends and pay tax on them. If her taxable income from other sources (say, from a pension and other investment income) is already $60,000 (to be increased to $100,000), the $10,000 will be taxed in Clara's hands at the top tax rate and she'll pay about $3,300 in income tax annually on the dividends.

What could Milt have done differently to save Clara tax after his death? Right: he could have set up a testamentary trust in his will. If the $250,000 of stocks had been left in a trust for Clara, what would be the tax result annually? The $10,000 in dividends could be taxed in the trust rather than in Clara's hands. If the trust has no other source of income, the tax to the trust would be about $500—much less than the $3,300 that Clara would pay herself.

Spousal Trust Rollover

If you happen to leave your assets to a trust for your spouse, it's quite easy to structure the terms of the testamentary trust so that it's defined to be a spousal trust. The benefit of a spousal trust is that any assets that you transfer to the trust will enjoy the same tax-free rollover as you'd get if you had left the assets directly to your spouse. In my example above, Milt left his stocks directly to Clara, so there was no tax to pay on the transfer to her after his death. If he had instead left the shares to a spousal trust for Clara's benefit, not only would Clara enjoy the tax savings I mentioned above, but there would also be a tax-free rollover of those shares to the trust on Milt's death. Follow me?

A spousal trust exists to hold assets for the *exclusive use* of your spouse. While your spouse is alive, he or she must have sole right to the income earned in the trust and the assets themselves. (If these conditions don't exist, then a spousal trust does not exist and the spousal rollover rules will not apply.)

The spousal trust inherits the adjusted cost base of the assets from you on your death, just as if your spouse had received the assets directly. If any of the assets with accrued capital gains in the spousal trust are sold, a taxable capital gain will be realized. On the death of your surviving spouse the accrued gains on the remaining assets are triggered and will be taxed in the spousal trust.

Back to our example of Milt and Clara. After the trust has paid its tax, it could pay out its after-tax funds of $9,500 ($10,000 in dividends received less the $500 that the trust paid in income taxes) to Clara on a tax-free basis. In the absence of a testamentary spousal trust, Clara would have kept just $6,700 in her pocket ($10,000 in dividends less $3,300 in taxes). Once income has been taxed in a trust, it is generally considered to be tax-paid capital and can typically be distributed to the trust beneficiaries on a tax-free basis.

A spousal trust also has these advantages:

- it is a way to preserve assets of the deceased to the death of the surviving spouse

- in the event that your surviving spouse remarries (or cohabitates), you can ensure that your children from your marriage will eventually receive the assets—not the new spouse or his or her kids
- depending on the income level of your surviving spouse, the spousal trust may work to avoid your spouse having his or her Old Age Security benefits "clawed back"
- on your death, your assets will generally be subject to probate fees. These fees will apply again on those same assets when your spouse dies. This second hit of probate fees can be avoided when the assets are held in a testamentary trust rather than in your spouse's hands directly.

Caution!

Using multiple testamentary trusts after your death can multiply the tax savings, but where the beneficiaries of the trusts are identical, the tax collector could combine the trusts into one for tax purposes, wiping out some of the income-splitting benefits. Ensure that your trusts have different investment philosophies, trustees and beneficiaries. The moral of the story? Don't get greedy. Here is one of the tax planning mottoes that I live by: pigs get fat, hogs get slaughtered.

Trusts for the Kids

In my example of Milt and Clara, Milt left his assets to a testamentary trust for Clara—his wife. If Milt had left those assets to his children, a testamentary trust could have been used in the same way. Rather than leaving certain assets directly to his kids, he could leave them to a trust for the kids. In fact, he could set up a separate trust in his will for each of his kids. This will multiply the tax savings. Keep in mind, however, that if you leave assets to a trust for your kids, you won't get the same tax-free rollover that you would get if it were a spousal trust. In Milt's example, his stocks had accrued gains of $150,000, which would have been taxable on his death had he left those shares to his kids or to a trust for his kids.

Insurance Trusts

Whom have you have named as the beneficiary of your life insurance? Your spouse? A child or grandchild? Regardless of whom you intend to receive the life insurance proceeds, give thought to leaving these proceeds to a testamentary trust. There are four potential benefits to setting up a testamentary trust to receive insurance proceeds on your death:

1. ***Income splitting.*** You can achieve a splitting of income as the income earned on the insurance proceeds is taxed annually in the trust—not in the beneficiary's hands. As I noted above, the tax savings can be as high as $11,000 annually.
2. ***Control over proceeds can be maintained.*** Again, where you feel that the beneficiary does not have the skills to properly manage the insurance proceeds, a trustee can assume this role.
3. ***Minimize probate fees.*** Where the insurance proceeds flow directly to the insurance trust and not to your estate, probate with respect to the value of the insurance proceeds can be avoided.
4. ***Fund support obligations.*** An insurance trust can also be set up to fund spousal and child support obligations that continue after your death. The benefit of a trust here is that you can be assured that the funds will be used for the intended purpose.

Cottage Trusts

A testamentary cottage trust is often used when a family cottage is to be shared by an individual's children after his or her death. Rather than bequeathing the cottage to one of a number of children that cherish their cottage memories, the cottage is essentially bequeathed to them all. The use of a testamentary trust will not result in any tax savings on your death, as the deemed disposition rules still come into play. Having the trust will, however, let trustees work with your children to minimize their squabbles and make sure that the financial and maintenance obligations of the cottage are shared appropriately.

Dual Trusts

Here's a strategy that can work very well when you've got some assets that have appreciated in value and others that have not. Consider setting up a spousal testamentary trust in your will to receive any property that has appreciated in value. You'll defer income tax on these assets on death by transferring them to a spousal trust. As for the assets that have not appreciated in value, these can be left to a family testamentary trust under which your spouse and kids are beneficiaries. Your spouse can still be entitled to the income of this family trust during his or her lifetime. There won't be any tax to pay when placing these assets in the family trust, since the assets have not appreciated in value. The benefit of the family trust is that the assets of the trust will not be deemed to have been sold on the death of the surviving spouse (as the assets of the spousal trust will). Rather, the assets of the family trust can generally pass tax-free to the kids on the death of the surviving spouse.

TO MAKE A LONG STORY SHORT:

- A testamentary trust is taxed at graduated tax rates, and can therefore offer income-splitting opportunities for your heirs.
- The annual tax savings could be as high as $11,000 per trust, depending on your province and the income level of your beneficiaries.
- Testamentary trusts can be particularly effective in holding income-producing assets, insurance proceeds, or a cottage.
- Dual trusts (a spousal and family trust) on death can offer income splitting and tax savings on the death of the surviving spouse.

WINNING THE ESTATE PLANNING GAME

By now, you should have a decent understanding of how trusts might be used as part of your overall estate plan. Still confused? Consider a visit to a tax pro who can clear some of the muddy waters. Now, flip back to the *Estate Planning Tip Sheet* at the front of the book. For each tip, ask yourself the question: "Does this apply to me?" Then check the appropriate answer: "Yes," "No," or "Not sure." This sheet will form the base for a proper estate plan. Let's move on to Chapter 8, where we'll look at business succession planning.

PASSING THE BATON: SOLVING THE BUSINESS SUCCESSION PUZZLE

Keep thy shop, and thy shop will keep thee.

8

What type of business do you own? I've seen all kinds. Consider Wesley Nunley, 73, who recently declared that the $10,000 concrete slab that he built on his property near Dallas was open for business as "UFO Landing Base 1." He said that it has been a dream of his for decades to have aliens land on his property, even though the landing pad is located in a quarry and is surrounded by mud much of the year. Nunley's best friend told the *Dallas Morning News* that Nunley was "a little off."

Consider also Mr. Vidal Herrera's business. Using a van painted with "1-800-AUTOPSY," Herrera acts as a freelance coroner in Los Angeles County, where budget cuts have reduced the size and efficiency of the county coroner's office. He offers services ranging from routine autopsy to the delivery of brains and other body parts to organ banks. Said Herrera, "The death business is recession-proof."

The fact is, even these business owners will one day have to decide how the succession of their businesses will be handled—particularly Mr. Nunley with the concrete slab, since he's already aged 73! Let me help you with this succession issue.

Your Succession Options

If you're the owner of a business, you may have some difficult planning ahead of you. The question of what to do with your business upon your retirement or death is not easy to answer. You'd better do some thinking on this issue today, because it'll take some careful planning to ensure that your family and the business are looked after once you're out of the picture.

Tim's Tip 56: Recognize the options that you have regarding the succession of your business.

Generally, there are five options when it comes to the succession of your business, either during your lifetime or on death. You'll need to decide which makes the most sense in your situation. Here are the five options that I'm talking about:

- transferring the business to family members
- selling the business to key employees
- selling the business to outside parties
- taking the business public
- winding up the business.

Transfers to Family

One of the things that I really enjoy about my work is watching family businesses move from one generation to the next. I guess it's a special sight to see because it's so rare these days. Why is it so rare? There are a number of factors that determine whether it makes sense to pass the business to your spouse, children, or another family member, and too often, these factors just don't point to succession within the family. I've broken these factors down into a set of questions. If you can answer YES to the following questions, transferring the business to your family is probably your best option.

1. ***Can your business survive without you?*** Some business owners *are* the business. Where you've introduced your family to the operations of the business over time, however, chances are that things may run smoothly once you're gone.
2. ***Is the business your retirement plan?*** If the business is your most significant asset, your spouse may need to rely on it for income once you're gone. Perhaps the business can be sold for enough money to secure your spouse's future, but in many cases the business may be worth more to your family than what an outsider will pay for it. In this case, it may be best to keep it in the family.
3. ***Does your family have the ability to run the business?*** If you've built up a successful business, you probably have a certain aptitude for the goods or

Action Step

I know this may sound radical, but if the relationship between two or more of your kids is strained, and they are working in the family business, consider arranging for family therapy. If issues can be resolved and tensions relieved, the potential for an effective transfer of the business to your kids will be much greater. Even where one of the children may not take the idea of therapy seriously, make sure that the others do get some help.

services that you're providing. The question is—does anyone in your family have the same ability? If so, you've overcome a significant hurdle.

4. ***Is your family willing to take over the business?*** Next to having the ability to run the business, it's very important that someone in the family have the willingness to take it over. Getting your kids involved in the business early in life and making it fun for them may predispose them to taking it over later.
5. ***Is it clear which family members should take over the business?*** Often, there will be one child who is involved more than the others in the family business. If you've got more than one family member who is interested in the business, it will be very important for them to be able to work in harmony together as joint owners, if you choose this route.
6. ***Will you compensate those who don't inherit the business?*** If it's clear that certain family members should not be involved in the business once you're gone, perhaps because they haven't been involved to date, you'd be wise to ensure that they will still inherit something else from you—to be fair. Often, life insurance proceeds will be left to the other family members who didn't inherit the business.

Chances are that you weren't able to answer YES to every question that I've posed. That's okay, provided that you answered most with a YES. If any answers were MAYBE, consider taking steps now to change those answers to a YES, because the more certainty that surrounds the succession of the business, the better.

Transferring the business to your family can be done in a number of ways. Most commonly, businesses are passed on by way of an estate freeze. Why? Because it makes so much sense from a tax perspective. With an estate freeze, you're able to issue new shares in the business, for a nominal amount, to the family members of your choice—or to a trust for the benefit of your family members.

If you're not entirely sure today who should inherit the business, issuing new shares to a trust makes great sense. You can then decide at a later date which of the beneficiaries of the trust should receive the shares of the business. You can even decide to sell the shares held in the trust to a third party later without any problem. An estate freeze may also allow you to lock in the benefits available from the $500,000 enhanced capital gains exemption—potentially entitling you to tax-free capital gains on your business's shares. I talked about estate freezes in detail in Tip 25.

Selling to Key Employees

No one knows your business better than those who have worked in the business for a period of time. There may be key employees without whom you couldn't operate the business. Selling the business to these employees can be done quite easily. You may want to offer the business at a very reasonable price since the employees are going to have to ultimately finance the purchase with earnings from the business.

Want an example of how this type of sale might take place? Consider Susan's story.

S*usan is a business owner. Her company, Design Inc., specializes in graphic design for large corporations. The business has recently been valued at $1 million, and Susan's adjusted cost base is nominal at just $100. Susan is looking to retire soon. She would like to sell the business to Michael, her most trusted employee, who knows the business and its clients like the back of his hand. Here's how they will accomplish the sale: Michael will borrow $500,000 from the bank to purchase 50 percent of Susan's shares from her. Susan will receive the $500,000 tax-free since she will shelter the capital gain with her enhanced capital gains exemption. They will each then own 50 percent of the company. Susan will gradually remove herself from the business by redeeming (selling back to the company) the balance of the shares* *that she owns. She'll do this after she retires to provide a source of income in retirement. Each dollar that she receives on these redemptions will be taxable as a deemed dividend.*

So far, so good—right? You might be wondering how in the world Michael can afford to borrow $500,000 from the bank to buy half of Susan's shares. Even more perplexing—how will Michael pay the loan back? In this case, the company could purchase a life insurance policy on Susan's life. The policy would be pledged as collateral for Michael's loan from the bank.

On Susan's death, the life insurance proceeds would be paid out tax-free to the company, and then as a tax-free dividend to Michael. You see, life insurance proceeds, net of the adjusted cost base of the policy, flow into the "capital dividend account" (see Tip 43, point 5) of the company, where amounts can be paid as tax-free dividends to the shareholders. When Michael receives the insurance proceeds, he'll use the funds to pay back the bank. Get the picture?

Selling to a Third Party

Selling the business to someone outside of your family or the business (to a competitor, for example) might make the most sense when your family or employees lack the ability or interest to take it over. If you're going to choose this option, keep the following tips in mind:

Action Step

If you're planning to sell your business to an employee, or to anyone else for that matter, and the business has grown significantly in value, there are ways to bring down the value of your business prior to a sale, to reduce your capital gain. One method is to have a holding company take ownership of your operating company, and to pay tax-free dividends from the operating company to the holding company. This will keep the value of the operating company down. Visit a tax pro, however, to talk about the issue of "safe income" before trying this.

1. ***Don't wait until you're dead and gone to make the sale.*** There are two key reasons for this. (1) You'll be passing a significant burden to your executor, who may be under pressure to sell the business as quickly as possible so that your heirs will receive their share of the proceeds sooner rather than later, and who may not understand the business as well as you do, making its sale more difficult. (2) Your estate will likely have to accept a lower selling price for the business since you won't be around to advise the new owner on how the business has been run day to day, and because the new owner risks losing customers without you being there to make an introduction.

Roy was a dentist who passed away recently. Upon his death, his wife had to move quickly to sell the dental practice since its value dropped daily as patients found out that he had died and left the practice to find new dentists. Had he taken steps to bring a younger dentist to the practice earlier, the practice would not have lost as many clients, and there would have been a purchaser ready to take over. The moral of the story? Arrange a sale before you're gone.

---

2. ***Consider selling shares rather than assets.*** It will be in your best interest in most cases to sell the shares of your company, where you're incorporated, rather than the assets. The reason is simple: your shares may qualify for the $500,000 enhanced capital gains exemption, potentially making the sale, or a portion of it, tax-free. A sale of assets won't qualify for the exemption. In addition, selling the shares passes any unexpected liabilities and all administrative headaches to the new owner. If you sell the assets but keep the shares, you'll still have to make annual filings to CCRA each year for the corporation. It's just as easy to set up an entirely new corporation after selling the old one, if you're intent on having a corporation available to you. There's one situation where you might consider a sale of assets to be better than a sale

of shares: when the selling price is higher for the assets than for the shares. The price will have to be higher in this event to compensate you for any lost tax advantages. In any event, you'd be wise to have a professional valuator, or an accountant with valuation experience, perform a review of the business to tell you its true worth.

3. ***Take payment over time.*** If you do sell your business, consider taking payment over a five-year period where you're selling at a profit. The tax collector will allow you to report the capital gain on the sale over a five-year period (maximum) where the proceeds are collected by you over time. That sure is better than paying tax on the gain all in one year. The exception to this, of course, is where you're using the $500,000 capital gains exemption and, as a result, you won't be paying tax anyway. In this case, you'd be better off to report the gain right away—to use up the exemption before the government decides to take it away. Don't like the idea of taking payment over time? Try charging interest on the outstanding balance each year to make the idea more palatable. Even better, build the interest into the selling price so that it's taxed as a capital gain, rather than interest income. After all, capital gains are taxed at a lower rate than interest.

If you're going to sell your business and take payment over time, you should have a very good sense that the new owners will be able to operate your business in a profitable manner. You see, if the new owners can't make a go of it, then you may be unable to collect the cash proceeds that you negotiated at the time of the sale. You may be able to gain some comfort about taking payment over time if certain assets of the business (a building or equipment, for example) are pledged as security for the loan that you've made.

Caution!

Taking the Business Public

Taking your business public may work if the business is well-established, has a history of profitability (I know, I know, some high-tech companies have been far from profitable), or has a unique product or service, the demand for which could explode in the near future. Taking your business public is referred to as an "initial public offering" (IPO), and typically involves bringing in beefed-up management and giving up control over your business. One nice thing about owning shares in a public company is that your succession plan becomes simple: pass ownership to a large group of people and liquidate your shares by trading them on the open market as you have a need for cash.

Winding Up the Business

The fifth option that you have is to wind up the business. This can be done during your lifetime, or by your executor after your death. Winding up the business is the option of last resort because you'll likely walk away with (or your estate will receive) less money through this option than through the others. In addition, there are still things to be done if you're going to wind up the business. Here's a list:

- notify your customers or clients, and suppliers
- notify your landlord, where applicable, and consider waiting until your lease is up to avoid unnecessary penalties
- sell or dispose of any unwanted business assets, including your customer or client list
- de-register for GST, PST, and provincial payroll taxes
- prepare all final tax and other government filings
- consider your obligation and ability to pay retiring allowances or severance payments to employees, if any
- visit your lawyer to discuss any final obligations to creditors and employees
- for corporations, consider delaying the wind-up until the company has paid off balances owing to you, and sufficient dividends have

been paid to clear out the company's capital dividend account and refundable dividend tax on-hand account
- consider dissolving the corporation where one exists.

As you can see, closing up shop may take a little work, but it is certainly a valid option.

TO MAKE A LONG STORY SHORT:

- Planning today for the succession of your business is critical. Succession can take place during your lifetime, or after your death.
- The most common succession options are: transferring the business to family members, selling to key employees, selling to outside parties, going public, or winding up the business.

Buy–Sell Agreements

Do you own your business with one or more other shareholders? If so, you should have a shareholders' agreement in place! Unfortunately, I see too many businesses that have overlooked this agreement. Shareholders' agreements often deal primarily with the issue of how a business is bought and sold upon the death of an owner, so the term "buy–sell agreement" is often used to refer to the shareholders' agreement.

Tim's Tip 57: Consider the use of life insurance to fund a properly drafted buy–sell agreement.

A properly drafted and funded buy–sell agreement can be a very effective succession tool. A buy–sell agreement should detail the terms under which a surviving shareholder, or the company itself, is to purchase the shares of a deceased shareholder. The agreement will, among other things, specify a price at which the surviving shareholder or the company is to buy the deceased shareholder's

Caution!

Where a shareholders' agreement contains buy–sell provisions so that the surviving shareholders take over ownership of the business upon the death of another shareholder, make sure that your will is consistent with the wording of that agreement. You see, if your will provides that your spouse or children are to inherit your shares upon your death, but the shareholders' agreement provides a buy–sell arrangement, the shareholders' agreement will override the will, and your estate distribution may not be as you thought.

shares, or it will detail a formula for calculating a price. Where the price is built into the agreement itself, periodic revisions to the price are common as the value of the business changes. The revised price can be made part of the buy–sell agreement through an addendum to the agreement.

If you've got a properly drafted buy–sell agreement in place, there is still one important question to answer: where is the surviving shareholder, or the company, going to get the cash to buy the shares of the deceased shareholder? If the agreement requires the surviving shareholder to buy the deceased's shares from his estate, he may have to borrow the money to buy the deceased's shares. What if he can't borrow that much money? If the agreement requires the company itself to purchase the shares of the deceased shareholder, where will the company get the cash? From its operations? From the bank?

You need to realize here that the amount of money necessary to buy the shares of the deceased shareholder can be staggering in many cases. It's not uncommon for a business to have a valuation of $2 million or more. If we're talking about a business worth $2 million owned by two shareholders, then the surviving shareholder will have to come up with $1 million in cash to pay for the shares of the deceased shareholder if one of them dies. I don't know about you, but I haven't got $1 million in cash lying around. Most business owners don't either.

The solution? Life insurance can make the most sense. Consider six common types of funding methods using life insurance:

1. ***Corporate-owned insurance.*** The company can purchase insurance on the lives of all shareholders so that, upon the death of any one of them, the company receives insurance proceeds tax-free. The cash can then be used to redeem (purchase from the estate or the surviving spouse) the shares of the deceased. (See Tip 43, point 5 for an example of corporate-owned insurance funding a buy–sell agreement.)
2. ***Criss-cross insurance.*** Each shareholder can purchase insurance on the life of the other shareholder. If one shareholder dies, the other will receive insurance proceeds tax-free, which can then be used to acquire the shares of the deceased from his estate or beneficiaries.
3. ***Split-dollar insurance.*** This is an arrangement where the company will own the cash value of the insurance policy while the shareholders will each own the face value component of the policy. The company will pay part, if not all, of the premiums and the shareholders will pay the balance. On the death of a shareholder, the face value is paid to the surviving shareholder while the cash value is paid to the company. The funds can then be used to purchase the shares from the deceased's estate or beneficiaries.
4. ***Key person insurance.*** If your business might suffer from the death of a key person, you should buy insurance on that person's life to provide the company with a needed boost at a critical time. The death of a key person can lead to loss of customers, direction, skills, and borrowing capacity, among other things.
5. ***Cost recovery insurance.*** A company may spend significant dollars during the retirement years of a key person just by funding retirement benefits. Insurance could be purchased on the life of that key person so that, on his death, the company is reimbursed for the costs previously incurred.
6. ***Debt insurance.*** If the company has debts—perhaps a line of credit—it can make sense to insure the lives of owners for the

amount of the debt. This way, if an owner dies, the business becomes debt-free at a time when it might be able to use the financial help.

TO MAKE A LONG STORY SHORT:

- A properly drafted and funded buy–sell agreement is a very important succession tool when you're one of two or more shareholders in a business.
- Life insurance should be considered to fund the purchase of the deceased's shares by a surviving shareholder or the company.

Action Step

Here's your game plan: you want to reduce the tax hit as much as possible in the course of passing your business to others and, to the extent that you can't avoid a tax hit, attempt to defer that tax hit for as long as possible. That's right, the strategy is to reduce taxes first, and then to defer whatever taxes must necessarily apply. How? Through the tools in the succession toolbox, including: an estate freeze, the capital gains exemption, a capital gain rollover, a spousal rollover, family farm provisions, and the capital gains reserve.

Minimizing the Tax Hit

When planning for the succession of your business, you'll be surrounded by tax issues. The good news? There are methods available to keep the tax collector at bay.

Tim's Tip 58: Understand the tax issues surrounding the succession of your business.

Whether you're passing your business to family members or selling it to outside parties, you should take the time to look through the "tax toolbox" to see what measures can be taken to reduce a tax hit when the business finally changes hands. Here are the most common tools available.

The Estate Freeze

An estate freeze will allow you to take the value of your business today, and capture or "freeze" that value in a single class of shares that you will own. Then, new shares in the company will be issued for a nominal amount (say, $100) to your successors where you can identify them, or to a trust when you're not yet sure who will ultimately take over the business. The future growth of the business will accrue to the new shares issued to the successors or the trust, as the case may be. Now, consider the story of Burt and his son, Randy. Burt did things the wrong way.

Burt started a construction business many years ago, and he owns 100 percent of the company. Today, the company is worth $3 million, but Burt's adjusted cost base is just $1. Burt wants his son, Randy, to take over the business one day. Burt decided to have the company issue new shares to Randy out of its treasury for a nominal amount. Burt had the company issue enough shares to Randy to dilute Burt's ownership percentage to just 60 percent. Randy will now own 40 percent. Burt didn't think there would be any tax implications to this move. He was wrong. The tax collector argued that even though Burt did not sell any of his shares to Randy, he effectively disposed of 40 percent of his ownership interest in the company, resulting in a taxable capital gain of $1.2 million ($3 million gain × 40 percent). The taxman used the court case The Queen v. Albert Kieboom *(1992) to justify this treatment.*

Ouch. Can you imagine being liable for tax on a $1.2 million capital gain—with no cash to pay for it? Burt could have accomplished the very same thing without having to trigger any tax at all. He could have completed an estate freeze. Here's how this transaction should have looked:

Burt owns 100 percent of the construction company that he started many years ago, which is now worth $3 million. He wants his son, Randy, to own 40 percent of the business—and to eventually take over the whole enchilada. Burt completed a freeze to accomplish this. Here's how: Burt exchanged his common shares worth $3 million for new special shares that are also worth $3 million, but which are frozen in value. That is, he "captured" the full value of the company in a new class of special shares (typically, these are preferred shares). The company then issued new common shares to both Burt and Randy. Randy received 40 percent of the new common shares, while Burt took the remaining 60 percent. Randy will now enjoy 40 percent of all future growth in the company.

In this situation, there are no adverse tax consequences to Burt. Randy now owns 40 percent of the future growth of the business. Burt can redeem (sell back to the company) his common shares and special frozen shares over time if he wants. This will provide income to Burt in retirement, and will, over time, pass voting control of the company to Randy. I've talked about estate freezes already in Tip 25, so refer there for more information.

Enhanced Capital Gains Exemption

If you own shares in a "qualified small business corporation" (QSBC) or qualified farm property, you may be entitled to shelter up to $500,000 of capital gains on those assets from tax. As part of any proper succession plan, it makes sense to utilize this exemption.

There are two scenarios in which you'll be able to use the exemption. The first is where you sell your QSBC shares or farm property to an outside party. In this case, the first $500,000 of capital gains will be sheltered from tax. The second case is where you take steps to "crystallize" $500,000 worth of gains on the shares or property without actually selling them to someone else. By "crystallizing," I mean that you'll be able to use the exemption today to increase the adjusted cost base of your QSBC shares or farm property by the $500,000 exemption (or part thereof). This way, when you eventually sell the shares or farm property, or upon your death, the taxable capital gain triggered will be lower (a higher adjusted cost base results in a lower taxable gain).

Will virtually any shares qualify for the $500,000 exemption? Not really. The following tests must be met:

- substantially all (90 percent or more) of the assets of the company must be used in an active business carried on primarily in Canada (or be shares or debt of a company that meets this test)
- you, or a person related to you, must have owned the shares for at least two years
- throughout the two-year period, 50 percent or more of the assets of the business must have been used in an active business carried on primarily in Canada (or be shares or debt of a company meeting the 90-percent test above).

You should be aware that, where you operate your business as a proprietorship, you may still be able to take advantage of the exemption by first transferring your business assets to a corporation (which can be done on a tax-free basis). You can generally skip the two-year holding requirement if your proprietorship has been up and running for more

Did You Know?

If your company doesn't currently meet the tests to qualify for the enhanced capital gains exemption, it may be possible to "purify" the company so that the shares of the company will become "qualified small business corporation shares." This usually entails removing assets from the company that are not considered active business assets, such as excess cash. Simply paying off debts of the company, or paying dividends, can remove excess cash. Other culprit assets could be removed through a "butterfly" reorganization which involves "spinning off" certain assets to a new company.

than two years and you transfer the assets to a corporation to take advantage of the exemption.

What if your company is going public? In this case, it's possible to elect to utilize the capital gains exemption without having to actually sell your shares. Once the company goes public, the shares won't qualify for the exemption any longer, so you'll want to take advantage of this election where possible.

There are a couple of things that could cause a problem for you if you're hoping to utilize the enhanced capital gains exemption:

- if you've ever claimed an allowable business investment loss (ABIL), you'll be denied the ability to claim the capital gains exemption to the extent you've claimed an ABIL against ordinary income
- if your investment expenses (interest income, limited partnership losses, etc.) have exceeded your investment income since 1988, you'll have a positive CNIL balance. This is a bad thing! CNIL stands for "cumulative net investment loss" and this balance will reduce, dollar for dollar, the amount of the exemption that you're able to claim.

How can you utilize your capital gains exemption? Assuming you're not selling your shares or farm property to someone else, the most common technique to crystallize gains using the exemption is to complete an estate freeze. Want an example? Refer to Tip 25 for the example of Jack, who took advantage of his $500,000 enhanced capital gains exemption.

Capital Gain Rollover

Thanks to the 2000 federal budget, it may be possible to dispose of your shares in your small private company and to defer the tax on any gain by reinvesting the proceeds in the shares of another small-business corporation. A number of conditions must be met in order to qualify for this capital gain rollover, including these:

- you must acquire newly issued common shares from the treasury of the new small business

- you must be an individual (not a trust)
- only dispositions after February 27, 2000 qualify
- there's a cap of $500,000 (by reference to your adjusted cost base) on the number of shares on which you can defer your gain
- the carrying value of the assets of the company you're investing in cannot exceed $2.5 million immediately before the investment is made and $10 million immediately after.

The federal mini-budget of October 18, 2000 proposes to increase the cap from $500,000 to $2 million, the $10 million limit to $50 million, and to eliminate the $2.5 million threshold.

This rollover can provide a simple solution to the business owner looking to exit one business but enter another. Talk to a tax pro for more details if you think you qualify.

Rollover to Spouse

There's probably no simpler business succession plan than to simply leave your shares in your company to your spouse on your death. As you'll recall, any assets left to your spouse on death will enjoy a tax-free rollover. That is, there will be no tax on your death, and your surviving spouse will simply step into your shoes and will have the same adjusted cost base you've had. Only upon the death of your spouse, or upon a sale of the shares by your spouse, will tax be levied.

This tactic may not, however, solve the problem of who is going to run the business once you're gone if your spouse is not interested or capable. It may be wise for your spouse to hire outside help to manage the business, or to promote key employees to keep the business humming along in a profitable manner.

Family Farms

Normally, a transfer of business assets or shares from you to another family member (except your spouse) is treated as a disposition at fair market value. Farming businesses are, however, entitled to some tax breaks that other businesses are not. Specifically, property that is used

Action Step

If you transfer your business to family members during your lifetime, there's always the chance that they could mismanage the business and cause it to fail. This could be disastrous where you're relying on the business to provide retirement income. To protect yourself, consider transferring valuable assets such as land, building, and equipment out of the company to you personally. You can then lease these assets back to the business. This way, if the business fails, you'll have assets that can be liquidated to provide retirement income.

in an active farming business can be transferred to your spouse, child, grandchild, or great-grandchild at your adjusted cost base. The result? No capital gains are triggered on the transfer. The heir of the property will inherit your adjusted cost base so that tax may be paid eventually on the gain.

In addition to this intergenerational tax-free transfer of farm property, you'll be able to shelter up to $500,000 of capital gains on the disposition of qualified farm property using the enhanced capital gains exemption that I spoke about earlier. Property used in an active farming business and farm quotas can qualify for the exemption.

Capital Gains Reserve

There is a general capital gains reserve that's available when you've sold something at a gain and have not yet collected the entire proceeds of disposition from the buyer. The rules work so that you're able to spread the capital gain out over a period as long as five years. The news is even better in the case of shares in a small-business corporation or certain farm property. In this case, the capital gain can be spread out over a period as long as 10 years when the sale is to a child, grandchild, or great-grandchild. I don't see this reserve claimed very often—only because transfers to a child are usually made by way of a freeze in which your child does not actually pay fair market value for the business. If you think that a sale to your child is appropriate, however, this reserve could defer tax for quite a while!

TO MAKE A LONG STORY SHORT:

- There are a number of tax breaks that could apply in a business succession situation. The most common technique is an estate freeze.
- Other "tools in the toolbox" include: the enhanced capital gains exemption, the capital gain rollover, a spousal rollover, exemptions for family farms, and the capital gains reserve.

WINNING THE ESTATE PLANNING GAME

Deciding what to do with your business when you retire or when you die is not an easy task. The tools introduced in this chapter should, however, provide you with some help in knowing how to minimize taxes on the transfer of your business, and how to defer those taxes that are inevitable. Now, give your estate planning a push in the right direction by referring to the *Estate Planning Tip Sheet* at the front of the book. For each tip, ask yourself the question: "Does this apply to me?" Then check the appropriate answer: "Yes," "No," or "Not sure." You've heard this before, but the tip sheet will form the basis for your complete estate plan once you've read the entire book. Let's move on to Chapter 9, where we'll talk about planned giving.

HELPING OTHERS IN THE RACE: PLANNED CHARITABLE GIVING

Be a joyful giver; keep on giving until you have to laugh about it.

9

Sunday school teacher: "Now, Jimmy, I want you to memorize today's verse, 'It is more blessed to give than to receive.'"
Jimmy: "Yes'm. My father says he always lives by those words in his work."
Teacher: "Oh, that's wonderful! And what does your father do for a living?"
Jimmy: "He's a prize fighter, ma'am."

My guess is that you're not a prize fighter. But if you're like many, giving still brings more joy than receiving (although I learned early on that receiving isn't too bad either). Making charitable gifts is something that you can do during your lifetime or after, and your gift can be in cash, or in kind. Gifts in kind include any assets of value, such as stocks, bonds, mutual funds, real estate, artwork, and more. You can even give of your time if you haven't got other resources, although you won't get tax relief for time donated. One thing is for sure: if you're going to make donations to charity, you might as well make the most of the tax breaks—even if this isn't your primary motivation.

Tax Benefits of Giving

For many people, giving to charity is as important as contributing to their RRSPs, or saving for a child's education. In fact, in 1998, 5.4 million Canadians reported charitable donations on their income tax returns, up 2.1 percent from 1997. As well, Canadians are choosing to donate more. In 1998, donations increased from $4.3 billion to $4.6 billion—an increase of 7.7 percent. While the tax benefits of giving may not be the entire reason for these increases, they have no doubt played a role since the tax benefits have improved over the last few years.

Tim's Tip 59: Understand the tax relief that is available when you give, but make sure that your primary motivation is a desire to help.

Individuals who donate to charity receive a donation tax credit that reduces both their federal and their provincial income tax. How much tax relief can you expect? The amount of the credit is calculated as 17 percent of the first $200 donated (likely to be reduced to 16 percent based on proposed changes in the federal mini-budget of October 18, 2000), and 29 percent of any donations in excess of $200 made

Did You Know?

In 2000, about half of the provinces moved to a tax-on-income system from a tax system where taxes were levied as a percentage of federal taxes. Most of the remaining provinces will be moving to this tax-on-income system in 2001. The result? Most provinces will now have to publish annually the tax relief that they're willing to provide for charitable donations. You can expect, however, that the tax relief will come close to about one-half of the relief offered by the federal government.

during the year. Although this is a federal tax credit, provincial tax savings will result too.

This year, Tibor made a $1,000 donation to his favourite charity, as well as making other donations amounting to $200. Tibor can expect to save $290 in federal taxes on the $1,000 donation. In addition, his province will kick in an additional credit worth about another $160, for total tax relief of approximately $450—or 45 percent of his $1,000 gift.

The tax savings in Tibor's case represents the tax relief that the average Canadian is likely to enjoy. If you're in the top marginal tax bracket, you may save a little more because you'll save provincial surtaxes too. The most that you'll save from a donation is, on average, 48 percent of the amount donated.

You should recognize one important fact from this example: you'll never get back tax relief amounting to more than you donated. Some people mistakenly think that if they give away certain assets on death, they'll reduce the tax that they have to pay and their heirs will be better off. Not true. For every dollar given away, your estate may save 48 cents in tax, but the other 52 cents of the dollar is gone from your estate. Your heirs will be worse off than if you had left them with everything. The bottom line? Make sure that you're motivated to give for reasons beyond the tax relief. That is, you should have genuinely charitable intentions. If you're only doing it for the tax relief, you'd be better off financially not to give.

Limits of Charitable Giving

Individual taxpayers can claim donations of up to 75 percent of their net income annually, plus 25 percent of the taxable capital gains from donations of any property that has appreciated in value. Further, up to 100 percent of net income can be donated in the year of death. If you make a donation during your lifetime and the donation exceeds the allowable limit, the excess can be carried forward and claimed in any of the subsequent five years. If donations made in the year of your death exceed 100 percent of your income, the excess can be carried back and applied to the year prior to death—up to 100 percent of your income in that year as well. This means that a significant donation made on your death could actually eliminate all of the tax that would otherwise be owing in the year of your death, and could further recover some of the taxes paid in the year prior to death.

TO MAKE A LONG STORY SHORT:

- Charitable donations will provide you with a donation credit that will save taxes of up to 48 percent of the donated amount.
- You can donate up to 75 percent of your income each year, and up to 100 percent of income in the year of your death.
- Excess donations during your lifetime can be carried forward up to five years, and in the year of death can be carried back to the year prior to death.

Tim's Tip 60: **Structure gifts after your death properly in your will, or you may lose the donation credit in your final year.**

If you've decided to make a gift to your favourite charity after your death through your will, make sure you do it right! You see, your aim should be to structure the gift so that you're entitled to a donation tax credit on your final tax return. After all, you'll likely need the tax

Action Step

Make sure that your will clearly names the charities to which you'd like to donate after your death, and provides either a specific amount or a specific property to donate, or details a formula that does not leave the amount of the donation to be determined by the executor. If you fail to do this, you may not be entitled to claim a donation tax credit for donations made by your executor after your death. You'll want to avoid this problem like the plague.

relief in your final year. If you don't structure the gift properly in your will, you may not be entitled to the tax relief that you're expecting. The fact is that the donation credit might end up instead in the hands of your estate, not in your hands on your final tax return.

It's the view of the tax collector that you'll be entitled to a tax credit on your final tax return for donations made after your death only where the following conditions are met:

- it's clear that you intended to make gifts to specific qualified donees, who are named in the will
- the amount of the donation to be made to each charity is stipulated as a specific amount, a specific property, or a percentage of the residue of your estate
- your will clearly specifies what is to be paid from your estate in determining the amount of any residue
- your will does not provide for discretionary encroachments on capital
- a "gift" must actually be made.

One thing is clear here: where the executor of your estate has the discretion to decide which charities should receive gifts, or the dollar amount of the gifts, the gifts would generally be considered to have been made by the estate rather than by you in the year of your death. This is CCRA's view at the moment, as expressed in a technical interpretation dated December 1, 1999.

TO MAKE A LONG STORY SHORT:

- You're generally entitled to claim a donation credit on your final tax return for donations made after your death.
- You could be denied a claim for the donation on your final tax return where the tax collector deems the gift to have been made by your estate, and not by you at the time of your death.
- Take steps to properly word the gift in your will and avoid this unexpected tax treatment.

Assets to Donate

Gifts to charity can take on many forms. Donations of certain assets will provide greater tax relief than others, and some provide no tax relief at all. Let's look at the highlights.

Tim's Tip 61: Recognize the various assets that can be given, then choose the ones that are best for you.

The most common types of assets donated to charity include: gifts of cash, gifts in kind, gifts of securities, gifts of life insurance, gifts of certified cultural property, and gifts of time. Let's look at each of these now.

Gifts of Cash

To be honest, most charities like cash gifts best. Cash is simple to deal with. The amount of the donation is clear and can't be disputed, and cash can be used quickly without having to be stored, liquidated, or kept in a brokerage account. You may not always have cash available to donate, however. If you're expecting some cash to come your way in the near future—perhaps next year—but you'd like to claim a donation credit this year, there's a strategy you can try. Consider Fred's example.

Fred is a self-employed entrepreneur. He wants to make a $10,000 donation to charity before the end of this year to claim the tax relief this year, but doesn't have the cash on hand at the moment. He plans to pay himself a dividend of $10,000 from his company to cover the donation, but he'd prefer not to pay tax on the dividend this year. Fred has a strategy. He borrows $10,000 in December of this year and donates the cash to charity. In January of next year, he pays himself a dividend from his company of $10,000. He then uses the cash dividend to pay off the advance from the bank.

Action Step

If you're short on cash to make a donation, consider this idea. Make a contribution to your RRSP (borrow if you have to), and then claim the RRSP contribution on your tax return. Take the tax savings generated by the RRSP contribution (which usually comes back as a refund when you file your tax return) and contribute those savings to charity. Alternatively, use your tax refund resulting from an investment in labour-sponsored funds or flow-through shares to make a donation to charity.

Did you catch the benefits to Fred? He borrows $10,000 and donates it to charity this year, so he saves about $4,800 in taxes this year. He then receives a dividend one month later, which he'll pay tax on, but the tax won't be due until next year since the dividend is received in the next calendar year. The dividend, by the way, will cost Fred about $3,300 in taxes. Fred only paid interest on the borrowed money for one month.

Okay, so you're not a business owner. It doesn't matter. If you're expecting any cash payment to arrive at your doorstep next year, but you want to make a donation this year to claim the tax relief sooner, consider borrowing to make the cash donation.

Gifts in Kind

Instead of donating cash to a charity, you might choose to make a gift of tangible property. No, the charity probably doesn't want those old sweat socks—you know, the ones with the holes—or the fuzzy dice you've had hanging in your car window for the last 10 years. Where you've got something of value, however, you can help the charity and receive tax relief at the same time.

Donations other than cash are referred to as "gifts in kind." These gifts might include investments, real estate, artwork, vehicles, or clothing, just to name a few. These types of donations are eligible for the same donation credit outlined above. The amount of the donation is based on the fair market value of the asset at the time that it's donated. In some cases, an independent appraisal may be needed to determine the value of the gift.

Keep in mind that when you make a gift in kind, you're actually disposing of an asset, and you'll have to report that disposition on your tax return. What are your proceeds of disposition? Well, a special rule in our tax law will allow you to elect an amount to be your proceeds of disposition. The amount elected can be between your adjusted cost base and the fair market value of the asset donated. The amount elected serves as your proceeds of disposition, but also as the amount of the donation on which your tax credit is calculated. In the past, this election was used to avoid a huge taxable capital gain when donating to charity an asset that had appreciated significantly in value. This was often necessary because it used to be that you could only donate up to 20 percent of your income to charity in a given year, so the tax relief from the donation credit was often too small to offset the large capital gain triggered.

Today, it's rare to see this election used since the available donation credit generally offsets any taxable capital gains that might arise on the gift. So, you can expect to report a disposition at fair market value in most cases today, and then claim a donation credit to offset the tax on the gain.

Gifts of Securities

A donation of securities is also considered a gift in kind; however, special tax treatment applies to gifts of publicly traded securities. Changes introduced in the 1997 federal budget make it more attractive for investors to donate publicly traded securities rather than the cash equivalent. Those who donate these securities (and mutual funds are included) need to report only one-half of the taxable capital gain that would otherwise result from the disposition of the security. This means they pay only half of the tax that they would otherwise have owed had they sold the shares and donated the proceeds.

Mike holds 100 units of a Canadian equity fund, which he bought for $1,000 and which are now worth $10,000. Mike's marginal tax rate is 50 percent and he has already given $200 to charity in the year. Mike wants to know if he should sell the units in the fund and donate the cash proceeds, or donate the mutual fund units directly instead.

DONATING CASH VS. SECURITIES

	Donate Cash	Donate Securities
Proceeds of disposition	$10,000	$10,000
Adjusted cost base	$ 1,000	$ 1,000
Capital gain	$ 9,000	$ 9,000
Taxable capital gain (Note 1)	$ 4,500	$ 2,250
Tax owing	$ 2,250	$ 1,125
Donation tax credit	$ 4,800	$ 4,800
Taxes owing	$ 2,250	$ 1,125
Net benefit of donation	$ 2,550	$ 3,675

Note 1: The taxable capital gain is 50% of the capital gain, and one-half of this amount when securities are donated directly.

The above example shows that Mike will save an additional $1,125 in taxes if he donates the units of his mutual fund directly. This savings amounts to one-half of the tax otherwise owing. The special rule that allows a reduction in taxes when donating securities will be around until the end of 2001, after which time the government will decide whether or not to extend the measure indefinitely.

Gifts of Life Insurance

There are three ways in which to help charities with gifts of life insurance, and the 2000 federal budget changed the way in which most Canadians should approach this type of donation. Let's look at the three methods of donating life insurance.

1. ***Designate a charity as the beneficiary of the policy.*** In this case, you would retain ownership of the policy, but the charity collects the insurance proceeds on your death. Before the 2000 federal budget, the death benefit paid to the charity would not have qualified as a donation for purposes of claiming a tax credit in the year of your death. The 2000 budget changed this. Now, for deaths occurring after 1998, designating your favourite charity as beneficiary of your policy will qualify you for a donation credit on your final income tax return.
2. ***Transfer ownership of the policy to the charity.*** This involves an actual disposition of your policy by making the charity the owner, and naming the charity as the beneficiary at the same time. Under this scenario, a donation credit is available for any cash surrender value that exists at the time that the policy is transferred, plus a credit for any premiums paid by you after the date of transfer. You won't be entitled to a donation credit at the time of your death for the death benefit paid to the charity, since you are no longer the owner of the policy. Be aware that, in this situation, there's a disposition at fair market value on the transfer of the policy. That is, there may be a tax liability if the cash surrender value exceeds the adjusted cost base of the policy, although the donation credit will generally outweigh the tax hit.

Action Step

If you're going to designate your estate as the beneficiary of your life insurance policy and then leave instructions in your will for a donation of the proceeds to be made to charity, be aware that your heirs could contest your will if they feel like they've been short-changed on the inheritance that they've received. This could leave the charity with absolutely nothing if your will is varied by the courts. Be sure always to consider the needs of your heirs before leaving large sums to charity.

3. ***Name your estate as the beneficiary.*** This method involves naming your estate as beneficiary and simply leaving instructions in your will that the death benefit be given to charity. In this scenario, the insurance premiums paid would not be eligible for a donation credit. The death benefit would qualify as a testamentary donation, however, and you'd be able to claim a donation credit on your final tax return.

Which of these methods makes most sense? I like the first idea—naming the charity as beneficiary of the policy. In this case, you'll get the tax relief on death that will be so helpful to reduce your tax burden on death, and you'll avoid probate fees at the same time. Idea 2 above works well if you'd like the donation credit today, but the total tax relief will not likely be as great as it would be under Idea 1. Idea 3 does not make sense any longer since Idea 1 accomplishes the same thing, but you'll face probate fees under Idea 3 that you won't under Idea 1.

Gifts of Cultural Property

Our tax law provides special tax relief for gifts of *certified cultural property*. If you happen to own this type of property and you donate it to a designated cultural institution, you'll be entitled to a tax credit for the fair market value of the property, but unlike other gifts in kind, you won't face any taxable capital gains on the disposition of the property. In fact, where the property is worth less than what you paid, you'll be able to claim a capital loss under the normal rules around capital losses. For a property to qualify, a certificate must be issued by the Canadian Cultural Property Export Review Board.

Here's some advice. If you own property that may be certified cultural property, make sure that you have it certified before your death if possible. Because of the tax benefits of this type of property, you may want to donate this property to charity rather than gifting something else at the time of your death. This will cut the amount of tax owing in your year of death. Don't leave this for your executor to figure out, however: he or she will have enough to do already without having to obtain certification from the appropriate authority.

Action Step

If you're already in the highest tax bracket, it won't generally make sense to take a taxable payment for your services to a charity and then donate the cash back to the charity. The reason? The income will be taxed at about 48 percent, and the donation credit will, at best, offset most of the tax on that income. At worst, the tax credit won't quite cover the tax you'll pay. Where you're in the lowest tax bracket (earning under $30,000 in the year), however, the idea can make good sense.

Gifts of Time

A gift eligible for a tax credit must involve property. Sorry, contributions of services (time, skills and effort) are not considered to be property and won't qualify you for tax relief. There's nothing to stop a charity from paying for services and later accepting the return of all or a portion of the payment as a gift from you—provided it's donated voluntarily.

Under this type of arrangement, you must of course report the taxable income received from the charity, either as remuneration (in which case the charity may be obliged to issue a T4 slip) or as business income.

TO MAKE A LONG STORY SHORT:

- There are many different assets to consider giving to charity, although charities would generally prefer cash.
- Gifts in kind and gifts of life insurance can be excellent alternatives to giving cash.
- Gifts of publicly traded securities and certified cultural property offer special tax relief.

Vehicles for Donating

What do I mean by "vehicles" for donating? No, I'm not talking about donating your car or that mini-van you've been driving around. Rather, I'm talking about tools for making donations. This is different than talking about which specific assets to donate, which is what I dealt with in the last section.

Tim's Tip 62: Recognize the various vehicles through which gifts can be made.

There are really three different vehicles for donating that I'd like to talk about here: charitable remainder trusts, charitable annuities, and private foundations.

Charitable Remainder Trusts

A charitable remainder trust (CRT) is an irrevocable trust set up by you in which a charity is named the capital beneficiary and you're the income beneficiary. That is, the charity will be entitled to the assets, or capital, of the trust once you're gone, but you'll be entitled to any income earned in the trust during your lifetime.

As the donor, you'll make a donation to the trust that is irrevocable—there's no turning back once you've made the gift. A variety of assets can be donated, including mutual funds, real estate, securities and anything else of value. A donation credit can be claimed in the year in which the assets are donated to the trust.

Unlike a gift in kind, however, the amount that is eligible for the donation credit is not the fair value of the assets at the time that they're transferred to the CRT. Instead, the value of the credit must be determined by an actuarial calculation based on your age and interest rates. Since you retain some interest in the property transferred, the calculation is devised so that the older you are, the greater the tax credit. By about age 80, you can expect to receive a donation credit for about 80 percent of the value of the donation made. On average, just 50 percent of the value of the property donated will be claimed as a donation.

Did You Know?

You can set up a charitable remainder trust that will pay out income to you and your spouse during your lifetimes, rather than basing the income payments on your life alone. This will, however, reduce the amount of the donation tax credit that you'll receive in the year of the donation to the trust, since the time period until the charity receives the capital from the trust will be extended.

A CRT makes sense for people who still want to enjoy the right to use their property or to receive any income earned from the property. Like most good things, CRTs have costs associated with them. In particular, transferring property to a CRT may give rise to a taxable capital gain if the property has appreciated in value since it was purchased. The good news is that the donation credit will likely reduce, if not offset, the tax liability resulting from the gain. There are also initial costs to set up the trust, as well as fees for the annual tax returns required. Be sure to weigh these costs against the tax savings before setting up a CRT.

Charitable Annuities

You may have a desire to donate to charity today, but don't want to give up the cash flow that is generated on your money. There may be a solution. Your favourite charity could receive a donation from you now while you continue to receive the cash flow you're looking for. The tool? A charitable annuity.

Under a charitable annuity, you'll give a set amount of money to the charity and take back a life annuity. The amount of the annuity payments is fixed up front. The donation credit is calculated on the basis of your life expectancy. (Canada Customs and Revenue Agency has published a mortality table for this use. See Interpretation Bulletin IT-111R2.)

If the cash gift made by you is expected to exceed the total amount of cash paid out to you during your lifetime under the annuity, the excess is treated as a donation at the time the gift is made. The charity will not generally take on the risk that you'll live too long and thereby collect more than you donated initially. This risk is passed to an insurer who will make the annuity payments for the charity.

Hal established a charitable annuity with a charity that he wanted to help. He paid $60,000 to the charity. Hal will be receiving payments of $5,000 annually, and based on his age (81 years) and the mortality table provided by the tax collector, he is expected to live for another nine years. As a result, he is expected to collect a total of $45,000 in payments under the annuity during his lifetime ($5,000 annually for nine years). Since his original payment to the charity was $60,000, Hal is entitled to a donation credit of $15,000 ($60,000 less the $45,000 in expected payments) in the year he established the charitable annuity.

The nice thing about the cash flow that you'll receive under a charitable annuity is that it is 100 percent tax-free since it's considered to be a return of your original capital.

Private Foundations

I know that setting up a private foundation sounds like a step that only the super-rich would take. You might be surprised that a private foundation is not just for the super-wealthy, although in order to consider a private foundation you should have at least $250,000 that you'd like to earmark for charity. A private foundation must be registered with CCRA before you'll be entitled to any donation credits for making contributions to the foundation. Information Circular IC-80-10R can be found on CCRA's Web site (**www.ccra-adrc.gc.ca**); it details the requirements that you've got to meet in order to set up a private charitable foundation. In a nutshell, the requirements for a private foundation are that in any tax year:

- it must be constituted and operated exclusively for charitable purposes
- it must not carry on any business
- it must not acquire control of any corporation
- it must not have incurred any debts, other than debts for current operating expenses, debts incurred in connection with the purchase and sale of investments or debts incurred in the course of administering charitable activities
- it must annually expend its "disbursement quota" (an amount that is determined by a complex formula, but which is generally 80 percent of the prior years' donations received) on charitable activities.

If you're going to establish a private foundation, there are special rules relating to donations of shares or debt of private corporations. Generally, the private foundation will have to dispose of these assets within five years of receiving them as gifts, otherwise your donation credit will be denied, and will only be permitted once the assets have been disposed of. The rules are simplified here, and you'll need to visit a tax pro if you're considering these types of gifts to a private foundation.

Caution!

What are the real benefits of a private foundation? Consider these two benefits:

- **Privacy over gifts to outside charities.** This privacy may arise since it will be the private foundation, and not you personally, which makes the gift. Of course, if the foundation is named after your family, privacy may not be available.
- **Control over the timing of gifts.** You can make a gift to the foundation today without having to decide today which outside charitable cause will ultimately receive your donation. You'll still get the tax credit for donating to your foundation.

TO MAKE A LONG STORY SHORT:

- There are three key vehicles that you should consider when making charitable gifts: a charitable remainder trust, charitable annuities, and a private foundation.

- Charitable remainder trusts and charitable annuities will provide you with continued cash flow from the assets donated during your lifetime.

WINNING THE ESTATE PLANNING GAME

If you've got charitable intentions, you will now understand how to make the most of your charitable dollars. It's not that tax relief is your primary motivation, but you might as well get the most tax relief for your gifts as possible. Turn now to the *Estate Planning Tip Sheet* at the front of the book. You know the routine. For each tip, ask yourself the question: "Does this apply to me?" Then check the appropriate answer: "Yes," "No," or "Not sure." Each "Yes" or "Not Sure" answer may form part of your overall estate plan. Now, let's move to Chapter 10 and talk about probate fees.

BAD NEWS AT THE FINISH LINE: HANDLING PROBATE FEES

A tax by any other name is still a tax—and worthy of avoiding.

10

It has become a national pastime for Canadians to sweat and complain over probate fees. Let's take a look at exactly what probate fees are, and how to minimize their impact.

Defining Probate

It's time to consider what probate fees actually are. Make no mistake, they sure look a lot like taxes.

Tim's Tip 63: Understand the probate process and what it means to receive "letters probate."

Before we talk at all about the fees associated with probating a will, it's a good idea to understand how the probate process works, and why it exists. Probate is simply a process by which your provincial court puts its stamp of approval on your will. That is, the probate process involves an independent review of your will by your provincial court to ensure that it complies with all of the appropriate legal requirements. Once the court is satisfied that your will is valid, "letters probate" will be issued to confirm the validity of the will, and these letters probate will be attached to the will.

Why bother with the probate process? The fact is that most financial institutions or others with custody of your assets at the time of your death will not simply transfer the assets to your executor so that he or she can distribute them in accordance with your will. Take your bank accounts or mutual funds as an example. Don't count on your bank or the mutual fund company to allow your executor to withdraw all of the cash in your bank account or redeem your mutual fund units without some verification that your will is valid and that the executor has the right, therefore, to administer the assets. Letters probate will provide assurance to any third parties that your will is valid.

Until these custodians receive a probated copy of your will, most will refuse to transfer any assets to the custody of your executor. In the meantime, the assets will remain in your name and will not be available to your

Did You Know?

If you happen to die without a will, your estate will still have to go through the probate process because the custodians of your assets will want assurance that the administrator of your estate who is appointed by the courts has the authority to deal with the assets of your estate. In this case, "letters of administration" are granted by the court, rather than "letters probate."

executor to pay off debts or otherwise distribute to your heirs. When the custodians of your assets are satisfied that your will is valid, they will transfer your assets to the name of your estate (i.e. the assets will go from being in the name of "John Doe," to "The Estate of the Late John Doe."

What is subject to probate? All assets forming your estate will be subject to probate. In fact, probate fees charged by the courts for granting letters probate are based on the total value of your estate at the time of your death. Your liabilities at the time of death will not be applied to reduce the amount of your estate that is subject to probate fees. The one key exception is debt encumbering real estate—which I'll talk about in the next tip.

If you're a resident of Quebec, you'll be glad to know that probate is not generally a requirement in your province.

TO MAKE A LONG STORY SHORT:

- Probate is the process of receiving a stamp of approval from your provincial court that says your will is valid.
- Most financial institutions and other custodians will not release your assets to your executor until the will has been probated.
- The value of all assets making up your estate at the time of your death will be subject to probate.

Avoiding Probate Fees

I think I'd rather eat asparagus than pay probate fees. You should know that asparagus gives me a rash; that should tell you just how little I think of probate fees. Most Canadians—asparagus lovers or not—agree that avoiding probate fees is a worthwhile pursuit. The key is to make sure you don't shoot yourself in the foot in the process of planning to avoid these fees.

Tim's Tip 64: **Recognize that probate fees are simply another type of tax, and can be minimized with proper planning.**

If you ask the provincial government, they'll tell you that probate fees aren't a tax, but when something looks, feels, and smells this much like a tax—it's a tax. You see, probate fees are not simply a fixed fee, rather, they are charged by your provincial court and are calculated as a percentage of the assets making up your estate. In actual fact, it costs your province the same, administratively, to probate a large estate as it does a small one—so it's not clear why probate fees are charged on an increasing scale based on the estate assets. Looks like a tax to me.

The Supreme Court agrees. In 1998 that court ruled, in the *Eurig* case, that probate fees are actually a tax—and an indirect tax at that—which is beyond the jurisdiction of a province to impose under the Canadian Constitution. Many people thought that the 1998 ruling would spell the end of probate fees. It didn't. Most provinces simply introduced legislation retroactively as required to make probate fees enforceable. Sorry about that.

How much will probate fees set your estate back? Take a look at Appendix D at the back of this book. You'll find a list of the provinces and the probate fees charged by each. You'll find that, generally, probate fees range from 0.5 percent to 1.5 percent of the value of the assets in your estate on your death.

Probate fees can be a nuisance at best, and downright expensive at worst. So, let me share with you nine different ways to reduce the impact of those fees. Before introducing these strategies to you, I should mention that some of these ideas come with their own costs. For example, giving your assets to your kids before you die will certainly avoid probate fees, but you might incur some income tax on the gift. The question is, which will cost you less? The answer: each idea has to be evaluated in light of your personal circumstances.

Now, here are those nine ideas that I promised.

1. ***Arrange joint ownership.*** When you register ownership of any assets in joint tenancy with another person, with right of survivorship, those assets will transfer to the other person upon your death, bypassing your estate and thereby avoiding probate fees. *Potential drawbacks*: (1) you give up control over the asset; (2) there could be income tax implications when transferring all or part of an asset to another person since the transfer is considered to be a sale at fair market value; and (3) the other owner's share of the assets could be subject to attack by his or her creditors, if any.

2. ***Designate beneficiaries.*** When you designate a beneficiary under the terms of your RRSP, RRIF, pension plan, or life insurance policy, those assets will pass directly to the beneficiary without passing through your estate, and you'll avoid probate. *Potential drawback*: some financial institutions (insurance companies excluded) may still require your will to be probated in order to pass your RRSP or RRIF to your beneficiaries. Check with them to see if they'll be satisfied without probate.

3. ***Gift assets before death.*** If you transfer any assets to your beneficiaries while you're still alive, those assets will never make it to your estate after your death, and you'll avoid probate fees in the process. *Potential drawbacks*: (1) when you give an asset to a beneficiary, the tax collector will consider you to have sold it at fair market

Action Step

A great time to think about planning for probate is when you're completing an estate freeze at the same time (see Tip 25). You see, completing an estate freeze often involves setting up a private company. The shares of any private company can pass to the next generation free of probate if multiple wills are used (based on court case precedent set in Ontario): one will for probatable assets, and one for non-probatable assets such as the private company shares.

value, which could result in a tax bill. This generally holds true for any assets that have appreciated in value since you bought them. (2) You'll also give up control over the assets given away; and (3) those assets could be subject to attack by creditors of your heirs.

4. ***Transfer assets to a trust.*** Much like gifting your assets to another person, you'll be able to transfer any assets to a trust before you die, thus bypassing your estate and avoiding probate fees. You might also consider having your estate transfer assets to a spousal trust today, or once you're gone, to avoid probate fees being charged on the same assets a second time once your spouse dies.
   Potential drawback: transferring assets to a trust while you're alive will be considered a sale at fair market value of those assets, and could mean some income tax where those assets have appreciated in value. This is not a problem with a spousal trust, alter ego trust, or joint spousal trust.
5. ***Utilize an alter ego trust.*** Alter ego trusts are a new type of trust under our tax law, and can be set up by those aged 65 or over. When you transfer property to an alter ego trust, there will be no taxable disposition for tax purposes as is usually the case! Under the terms of the trust, you alone will have the right to all the income of the trust, and no other person will have access to the income or capital of the trust during your lifetime. You'll be taxed on the income of the trust annually. On your death, the property of the trust will be deemed sold—just as if you continued to hold the assets directly. The good news? The assets of the trust will pass to your heirs in accordance with the trust document and will not form part of your estate, so probate fees are avoided.
   Potential drawback: the annual costs of maintaining the trust might exceed the probate fees saved unless you've got a large estate.
6. ***Hold assets in a different province.*** Certain provinces enjoy lower probate fees (Alberta comes to mind). If some of your assets were located in a province with lower probate fees, you'd enjoy those savings upon your death. Moving assets to another province can be

done by setting up a corporation in that other province and transferring assets to that company. The shares in the new corporation will pass through a will in that new jurisdiction at lower probate rates. *Potential drawback*: there will be costs to setting up and maintaining the corporation.

7. ***Multiple wills.*** You can minimize probate fees by passing certain assets that are not subject to probate through one will, and those assets that must be probated through another. This strategy has proven successful in Ontario where, in *Granovsky v. The Queen (1998)*, the taxpayer successfully used two wills in the same jurisdiction (Ontario) to avoid probate on certain assets (private company shares and debt owed by private companies) that had no third-party custodian to be concerned about probate. *Potential drawback*: you'll have to be sure that the second will does not revoke the first, otherwise some of your assets will be distributed according to the intestacy laws of your province. I'd recommend getting legal advice before trying this idea.
8. ***Convert personal debt into a mortgage.*** The value of any personal real estate that passes through your will is subject to probate fees. The value subject to probate will, however, be reduced by any personal mortgages on the property. So, where you've got personal debt (a line of credit for example), convert the debt to a personal mortgage on your real estate, and reduce the value of your assets subject to probate fees! *Potential drawbacks*: (1) you'll need equity in your real estate to arrange a

Caution!

If you own life insurance on your own life, pay careful attention who you've designated as beneficiaries. You see, if you name your estate as the beneficiary of your life insurance policy, any benefits paid out to your estate on your death will be subject to probate fees. By simply naming specific individuals, charities, or a corporation as beneficiary, you'll manage to avoid probate on those proceeds.

personal mortgage, and (2) your real estate is at risk if you fail to make the mortgage payments. These two drawbacks will not be serious concerns to many people.

9. ***Buy life insurance to cover the probate fees.*** Of course, if you prefer not to implement any of the above strategies to minimize probate fees, you could simply buy enough life insurance to cover the probate fees that will arise on your death. This will preserve the value of your estate for your heirs.
   Potential drawback: depending on your age and health, life insurance could be expensive or unobtainable.

TO MAKE A LONG STORY SHORT:

- The impact of probate fees can be avoided in one or more of nine ways.
- Each strategy has its own potential drawbacks, so understand these before choosing your course of action.

WINNING THE ESTATE PLANNING GAME

This has been a short discussion on probate fees. Actually, there's not much more to say about the issue than what I've covered here. Nevertheless, you'll agree that there are a number of ideas to consider when planning to reduce probate fees. Now, turn to the *Estate Planning Tip Sheet* at the front of the book. You know the rest of this story. Review the tips that I've given you in this chapter. For each tip, ask yourself the question: "Does this apply to me?" Then check the appropriate answer: "Yes," "No," or "Not sure." This tip sheet will form the basis for your complete estate plan once you've read the entire book. Time to look at certain U.S. tax issues in Chapter 11.

RACING DOWN SOUTH: CANADIANS WITH U.S. CONNECTIONS

My family is quite tall, but no one has longer arms than Uncle Sam.

11

"Another bite like that, young man," a mother told her young son, "and you'll have to leave this table." The little boy's reply: "Another bite like that and I'll be finished."

The Canadian tax bite is big enough. Add to it one more bite—this time by the United States—and you could be left with very little on your plate! Besides, paying taxes in the United States and in Canada will only complicate your affairs.

To be honest, those with U.S. connections don't usually end up paying more tax than they would have paid to the Canadian government alone, but the tax will often be split between the two countries. In a worst-case scenario, you could end up paying double tax; that is, paying tax twice on the same income—once in each country. Pay close attention here, however, and your estate will be protected from the long arm of Uncle Sam.

Paying Tax Down South

Are you liable to pay tax down south each year? Will you be liable to pay U.S. estate taxes on your death? Good questions. Let's look at the answers.

Tim's Tip 65: Understand who is liable to pay tax in the U.S., and plan for those taxes if you're in this boat.

You live in Canada, so you're immune to taxes levied by the Internal Revenue Service (IRS) in the U.S. Right? Wrong! There are many situations in which Canadian residents are liable for tax in the U.S., and these taxes could be owing during your lifetime, or on death. Want the lowdown? Here are the rules about who might owe tax down south.

U.S. Citizens and Residents

If you happen to live in the U.S. full-time, or you're a citizen of the U.S. (regardless of where in the world you live) you've got to pay U.S. tax each year on your worldwide income. In addition, on your death you'll pay U.S. estate tax on the value of your worldwide estate. I've met many Canadian residents who also happen to be U.S. citizens who have not been filing U.S. tax returns. Bad move.

You could face penalties for not filing, and the IRS and the CCRA (formerly Revenue Canada) have an information-sharing agreement in addition to an agreement to assist each other in collecting taxes.

Did You Know?

In many cases, filing a U.S. tax return will not result in much, if any, tax in the U.S. for those who are citizens of the U.S. Why? Because of the foreign earned income exclusion, which is a deduction available to offset the first US$76,000 of "earned income" for employment or services provided outside of the U.S. By the way, the US$76,000 exclusion is scheduled to rise to US$80,000 for 2002 and later years.

Non-resident Aliens

A non-resident of the U.S. is simply someone who lives outside of the U.S. and, contrary to popular belief, an "alien" really has nothing to do with coming from another planet. An "alien," for U.S. tax purposes, is simply someone who is not a U.S. citizen. So, a "non-resident alien" (NRA) is someone who is not a U.S. citizen and who lives outside of the U.S. Most Canadians will fall into this boat.

NRAs can also be liable for tax in the U.S. in a number of situations. Try these on for size.

Employment Income

If you live in Canada but spend some of your working days in the U.S., you'll pay tax in the U.S. on your employment income earned there unless:

1. your total employment income earned in the U.S. is under US $10,000, or
2. you meet all of the following tests:
   (a) you are physically present in the U.S. for less than 183 days in the calendar year
   (b) you are paid by a non-U.S. company
   (c) your employer is not reimbursed by a related U.S. company.

How do you calculate your employment income earned in the U.S. in a given year? It's easy. A normal year consists of 240 workdays, so calculate the number of workdays that you were in the U.S. and prorate your salary accordingly.

Ned works for a Vancouver-based software developer, but was sent by his company to work in the U.S. for two weeks (10 working days) this year. Ned earns CDN$80,000 annually. Since a normal year consists of 240 working days, and Ned worked 10 of those days in the U.S., then Ned's U.S.-source employment income will be CDN$3,333 $\left(\frac{10}{240} \times \$80{,}000\right)$. *This is well under the US$10,000 threshold, and so Ned is exempt, under test (1) above, from U.S. tax on his U.S.-source employment income.*

Business Income

If you're running a business that operates in the U.S., you could be liable for tax south of the border. You see, the U.S. will tax you on any U.S.-source income that is "effectively connected with a U.S. trade or business." Consulting work is considered to be "effectively connected" and "U.S.-source" if the services are rendered by someone who is physically present in the U.S. Don't worry about U.S. tax if your client or customer is in the U.S. but you perform the work in Canada. If you ship goods to the U.S. and legal title transfers there, you'll be liable for U.S. tax (and you potentially may have U.S. state income and sales tax issues to consider).

There could be relief for you under the Canada–U.S. tax treaty if you think you're otherwise caught under the U.S. tax rules as I've outlined them above for business income. As an NRA, you'll be exempt from U.S. tax under the treaty as long as you don't have a "permanent establishment" (PE) located in the U.S. What's a PE? It includes an office, place of management, factory, or workshop. In fact, a PE can also include an employee working in the U.S. Most full-time employees resident in the U.S. will count as a PE. If you're exempt under the treaty from tax in the U.S. on your business income, you've still got to file a U.S. tax return to claim that exemption under the treaty.

Don't forget to consider the states in which you operate. You may be liable for state tax as well. As for U.S. social security taxes, NRAs are not subject to these taxes on business income.

Action Step

While you won't generally save taxes by investing some of your money south of the border (or anywhere else offshore for that matter), consider the other benefits, such as diversification or the expectation of greater returns. Again, don't count on tax savings. In each case, whenever tax is paid on your investment income in the U.S., you'll generally be entitled to claim a foreign tax credit in Canada for those U.S. taxes paid.

Investment Income

If you're hoping to invest some of your money south of the border and actually save taxes—don't hold your breath. As a resident of Canada, you'll pay tax at Canadian rates, regardless of where in the world your money is invested.

Consider the various types of investment income, and how the U.S. will tax these.

1. ***Interest income.*** If you earn interest income on U.S. bonds or other investments, a 10-percent withholding tax will apply. The usual rate under U.S. tax law is 30 percent, but our tax treaty with the U.S. reduces the rate to 10 percent. The company paying the interest to you is required to withhold and remit this tax to the IRS. There's an exception here for interest earned on deposits in U.S. banks (no withholding tax will apply in this case).
2. ***Dividend income.*** A 15-percent withholding tax will apply to dividends earned on U.S. stocks. Again, the rate is usually 30 percent, but our treaty with the U.S. reduces that rate to 15 percent. Keep in mind that U.S. dividends are taxed in Canada at the same marginal tax rates as interest income since there is no dividend tax credit available to reduce the tax on foreign dividends. This makes Canadian dividends more attractive.

3. ***Capital gains.*** You'll be glad to know that a sale of U.S. stocks or bonds that generates a capital gain will not be taxed south of the border under our treaty with the U.S. as long as you're resident in Canada. Real estate located in the U.S. and business assets located in a permanent establishment in the U.S. are different stories. Any gains on the sale of these assets will be taxed by the IRS.
4. ***Rental income.*** If you own a U.S. property, such as a condo or home, and you rent the property, you'll be taxed in the U.S. Now, you've got two choices in how you'll be taxed:
   (a) The renter can withhold 30 percent of the gross rents (ouch!) and remit it to the IRS to satisfy your tax bill, or
   (b) You can file a U.S. tax return each year and report your rental income and expenses, paying tax only on the net income. This is called the "net rental income method."

In almost every case, you'll be better off choosing the net rental income method. The reason? After deducting mortgage interest, property taxes, condo and similar fees, and depreciation (which is mandatory in the U.S.), you'll likely pay less tax than the 30-percent withholding on the gross rents. If you're an NRA, you'll have to file Form 1040NR by June 15 each year (for the previous year's rental activities) if you're using the net rental income method.

Retirement Income

If you've contributed in the past to any type of U.S. retirement plan, such as a 401(k) plan, IRA, or Keogh plan, you're going to pay a 15-percent withholding tax to the IRS on periodic withdrawals. Lump sum withdrawals will generally cost you more in tax (you'll pay tax at regular U.S. tax rates, subject to some complicated averaging rules). In Canada, these withdrawals will be taxable as any withdrawal from, say, an RRSP or other registered pension plan. You'll be entitled to a foreign tax credit in Canada for any U.S. taxes that you pay.

There's a potential pitfall here. If you were resident in Canada back when you made your contributions to the U.S. retirement plan, you would not have received a deduction in Canada for the contributions to the U.S. plan. You will, however, pay tax on the withdrawals. This is a double tax hit. Be sure to visit a Canadian tax pro who understands U.S. tax if you are or expect to be in this boat.

One last comment here. If you've got a U.S. Individual Retirement Account (IRA) which is equivalent to Canada's RRSP, it generally makes the most sense to leave the plan intact and simply make withdrawals as you're required to under U.S. tax law. The alternative is to transfer all of the assets to your Canadian RRSP. This transfer to your RRSP can be done tax-free from a Canadian tax perspective, but you'll still pay tax in the U.S. on the full withdrawal from the IRA. Further, there are no foreign content restrictions in the IRA, and you'll have a wider variety of non-Canadian investments to choose from.

Action Step

If you're a Canadian resident (not a U.S. citizen) and have sold some U.S. real estate, file Form 1040NR to report the sale and any resulting gain or loss. Often, the sale of your U.S. property will have resulted in a 10-percent tax (on the selling price) withheld by the purchaser and remitted to the IRS. Only by filing a 1040NR tax return can you recover some of those taxes if your total tax bill is actually less than 10 percent of the selling price. If your tax bill is higher than this, you'll have to remit the difference.

Social Security Income

An NRA that receives benefits from the U.S. government in the form of U.S. social security payments will be taxed only in Canada on those payments—thanks to our tax treaty with the U.S. Further, you'll be glad to know that just 85 percent of those benefits will be taxable in Canada.

Real Estate in the U.S.

If you sell at a profit real estate that is located in the U.S., you're going to pay some tax to the IRS. I won't get into all the details here, since I've covered this thoroughly in Chapter 7 of my book, *Winning the Tax Game*. Just keep in mind that steps can be taken to minimize the tax hit, but understand that the tax hit will be there in this situation.

U.S. Estate Tax

I'm going to spend more time on this issue in Tip 66. At this point, let me just say that those domiciled in the U.S., U.S. citizens, and NRAs (most Canadians) can be liable for U.S. estate tax. NRAs will be liable for this tax if they own any "U.S. situs property" (which can include U.S. stocks in your Canadian brokerage account, among many other things).

TO MAKE A LONG STORY SHORT:

- Both U.S. residents and citizens will pay tax annually on their worldwide income in the U.S. In addition, U.S. estate taxes will apply to these individuals on death.
- Non-resident aliens (NRAs) might also have some tax to pay in the U.S. This can include annual income tax, or estate taxes on death.

Avoiding U.S. Estate and Gift Taxes

Unlike Canada, the U.S. doesn't levy a capital gains tax on death or on gifts made to others. Rather, a nasty estate or gift tax can apply to the full value of certain assets that you might own at death, or which you give away during your lifetime. If you're a U.S. citizen or are domiciled in the U.S., you could be subject to U.S. estate or gift taxes on the value of all of your assets, on death or when you give them away. In addition, even non-resident aliens (NRAs—which includes most Canadians) can be subject to these taxes.

Tim's Tip 66: **Figure out whether you'll be liable for U.S. estate tax on death, then take steps to reduce the tax hit.**

While Canada does not levy estate taxes upon death, the U.S. does. If you're a Canadian citizen residing in Canada (a non-resident alien, or NRA, under U.S. tax law) but you own U.S. property, you could be hit with a U.S. estate tax bill at the time of your death.

U.S. Domestic Law

Under U.S. tax law, NRAs will be subject to estate taxes on their U.S. assets, with a meagre credit worth US$13,000. This credit will offset the estate tax on the first US$60,000 of your U.S. assets. You might also be subject to state estate taxes, but the U.S. federal estate tax is reduced by any state estate taxes paid. Most states will limit their estate taxes to the amount of this $13,000 credit, so the total federal and state estate taxes paid will not generally be increased by the state wanting a piece of the action too.

Taxable Assets

Which of your assets will be subject to U.S. estate tax? If you're a U.S. citizen, or someone domiciled in the U.S. (note that residency in the U.S. for *income tax* purposes and domicile for *estate tax* purposes are different things), then you'll be subject to estate tax on your entire worldwide estate. As an NRA, you pay estate tax on your "U.S. situs" assets, which include:

- U.S. real estate
- tangible property located in the U.S. (furniture, art, vehicles, etc.)
- assets used in a business located in the U.S.
- shares of U.S. corporations (publicly traded or not, and regardless of where the brokerage accounts or share certificates are held, or where the shares are traded)
- debt obligations of U.S. corporations, individuals, and governments

Caution!

Some have argued that you can avoid U.S. estate tax by owning Canadian mutual funds, which, in turn, invest in U.S. securities for you. Generally, this is true, but you've got to make sure that the funds you invest in will cut the mustard. Specifically, the funds you invest in should be mutual fund or pooled fund *corporations—not trusts.* Trusts may not work since the IRS may not recognize these trusts as separate entities and may consider you to directly own the U.S. securities held in the trusts.

- interests in a partnership carrying on a business or holding the above types of property
- U.S. pension plan amounts and annuities, including IRAs.

There are some general exceptions to the list of assets that are subject to U.S. estate tax: shares of non-U.S. corporations, U.S. bank deposits, certain U.S. corporate bonds traded outside of the U.S., and certain debt obligations that qualify for the "portfolio debt" exemption (these obligations pay "portfolio interest," which is exempt from U.S. income tax because they are designed to be sold to NRAs only).

There are certain deductions that can be claimed when arriving at the total value of the estate to be taxed. The most common deductions are these:

- final expenses and liabilities, including funeral costs, estate administration fees, charitable donations, and debts owing by the estate
- amounts left to a surviving spouse if that spouse is a U.S. citizen (he or she will pay estate tax upon death)
- amounts transferred to a "qualified domestic trust" (QDOT), which I'll talk more about in a minute
- the amount of non-recourse debt secured by U.S. real estate.

After determining the taxable estate, a schedule of graduated tax rates will apply (see Appendix F).

Amount of Tax

U.S. estate taxes can be huge. Once the value of your assets subject to the tax has been added up, the tax will apply at graduated rates that begin at 18 percent on the first US$10,000 and increase to 55 percent once your estate is over US$3 million. Any credit that you're entitled to will then be applied to reduce the total amount of tax. Want some examples of the tax hit that you could face? Check out the table below. Remember, this is the estate tax bill before any credits are claimed:

Taxable Estate	Estate Taxes Before Credits	Effective Tax Rate (%)
$50,000	$10,600	21.2%
$100,000	$23,800	23.8%
$200,000	$54,800	27.4%
$500,000	$155,800	31.2%
$750,000	$248,300	33.1%
$1,000,000	$345,800	34.6%
$2,000,000	$780,800	39.0%
$3,000,000	$1,290,800	43.0%

As you can see, the amount of estate tax owing before any credits are claimed can be staggering.

Tax Credits and the Treaty

As I said, every Canadian resident can claim the $13,000 credit offered by Uncle Sam under domestic law down south. I've got even better news for you, however. The Canada–U.S. tax treaty will extend protection to NRAs beyond the small $13,000 credit under domestic law that I spoke about. In fact, the treaty offers additional relief from U.S. estate taxes in four key ways:

1. ***Small estates exemption.*** If your total worldwide estate is less than US$1.2 million, then the IRS will go easy on you. You won't be subject to tax on all of your "U.S. situs" property. Rather, you'll only have to pay the tax on your U.S. real estate (which can

include corporations that own principally U.S. real estate) and assets used in an active business in the U.S.

2. ***Unified credit.*** This is a credit that can apply against your U.S. estate taxes otherwise owing. The small $13,000 credit available under U.S. domestic law is increased under the treaty. The amount that is claimable under the treaty is US$220,550 for 2001 (which offsets the first US$675,000 of taxable estate), but is pro-rated for the percentage of your worldwide estate made up of U.S. property (see the example below). The credit is due to rise steadily to US$345,800 by 2006, which will offset the first US$1 million of taxable estate.
3. ***Marital credit.*** If you transfer your U.S. property to your spouse on death, the IRS will allow an additional "marital credit" that is equal to the unified credit from (2) above, or the amount necessary to completely offset the estate tax, whichever is less. If you're a U.S. citizen or are domiciled in the U.S., you'll be entitled to similar relief in the form of the "marital deduction."
4. ***Foreign tax credits.*** If you're required to pay U.S. estate tax on death, your executor may be able to claim a foreign tax credit on your final Canadian tax return for those taxes. Here's the deal. A foreign tax credit can be claimed for the estate tax only to the extent that you have Canadian tax owing on U.S.-source income in

A foreign tax credit is generally available for any U.S. estate taxes paid in the year of your death. The tax credit will be applied against any Canadian income taxes resulting from the deemed disposition of those U.S. assets on your death. Where those U.S. assets have not appreciated much in value, there may be little or no Canadian taxes owing on those assets on death. You would then be unable to claim much of a foreign tax credit, if any. Proper planning will allow better matching of the Canadian capital gains tax and the U.S. estate taxes owing, permitting a foreign tax credit claim.

Caution!

the year of your death. U.S.-source income can include the capital gains triggered on death as a result of the deemed disposition in Canada of those U.S. assets that resulted in U.S. estate taxes.

Donna owned a condominium in Arizona that was worth US$275,000 on the date of her death. Her total assets upon death were worth US$1 million. Donna's U.S. estate taxes were calculated to be $79,300 before any credits. The unified credit that Donna was able to claim was $60,651, calculated as follows: $\left(\frac{\$275{,}000}{\$1{,}000{,}000} \times \$220{,}550\right)$. *Donna's total estate tax bill was $18,649 ($79,300 – $60,651). If Donna had left her condo to a surviving spouse, she would also have received a marital credit equal to the unified credit, or the balance of the estate tax owing, whichever was less. In this case, the marital credit would have been worth $18,649 and would have wiped out her estate tax bill altogether. If Donna had had U.S.-source income in the year of her death, any estate taxes owing could have been applied to reduce the Canadian tax owing on that U.S.-source income in the year of her death.*

If you're like many Canadians, you'll be leaving your assets to your spouse on death. If this is the case, then you'll be entitled to the marital credit to offset any U.S. estate taxes otherwise owing in addition to the unified credit. In fact, U.S. estate taxes won't kick in thanks to the unified and marital credits until your estate reaches the following values in 2001 (which differ based on the percentage of your estate that is U.S. property):

ESTATES SUBJECT TO U.S. ESTATE TAX

	Percentage of Property that Is U.S. Property			
	25%	**50%**	**75%**	**100%**
Value of estate at which U.S. estate taxes will be owing (for 2001) assuming assets are left to a surviving spouse.	$1,465,000	$1,350,000	$1,283,000	$1,233,000

These numbers may seem high, but more and more Canadians will be caught by the U.S. estate tax net as their assets grow over time.

Sidestepping Estate Taxes

Let me share with you the top dozen strategies to reduce the hit of U.S. estate taxes:

1. ***Keep worldwide assets under US$1.2 million.*** I've already mentioned that this is called the "small estates exemption." If your total worldwide estate is under US$1.2 million, you'll face estate tax only on U.S. real estate and business assets in the U.S. This could keep your estate tax down when you've got other assets that would otherwise be subject to the estate tax.
2. ***Leave assets to your spouse.*** As I've mentioned already, leaving assets to your spouse on death will help to minimize a U.S. estate tax hit since it will entitle you to a marital credit to apply against any estate taxes owing. The marital credit will equal the value of the unified credit claimable, or the balance of the estate tax owing, whichever is less. Refer to the section entitled "Tax Credits and the Treaty" above for more information.
3. ***Split ownership with someone else.*** If you're thinking of buying a vacation property or other "U.S. situs" assets, consider buying them jointly with one or more others—perhaps family members, including your spouse. The other owner(s) will have to actually contribute financially to the purchase for the IRS to consider a portion of the property truly theirs. If you split ownership this way, only your share of the property will be included in your taxable estate on death.
4. ***Rent instead of buying.*** As a renter, you won't actually own the property that you're using when you make trips south of the border, so it makes sense that you won't face U.S. estate tax on the property at the time of your death. This idea works very well when you're heading south primarily for the lifestyle, and not because you care so much about the property as an investment.

5. ***Give assets away today.*** Giving "U.S. situs" assets away today will mean that you'll own fewer of those assets at the time of your death. The bottom line? Less estate tax to pay. You should be aware, however, that U.S. gift taxes could apply to gifts of U.S. property. Yes, even if you're an NRA (I'll talk more about U.S. gift tax in Tip 67). Don't forget that giving assets away during your lifetime could result in a deemed disposition at fair market value for Canadian tax purposes. You know what? Cash always makes a good gift. You'll avoid both U.S. gift tax and Canadian capital gains taxes on gifts of cash.
6. ***Buy life insurance to cover the tax.*** Consider buying life insurance to cover all or part of a U.S. estate tax hit that will arise on your death. If you're an NRA, life insurance proceeds will not form part of your taxable estate on death (even if it's a U.S. insurer), but will be included as part of your worldwide estate for the purpose of calculating your unified credit. U.S. citizens and those domiciled in the U.S., on the other hand, will have to include life insurance proceeds in their taxable estates.
7. ***Use a Canadian corporation for U.S. assets.*** A corporation never dies. As a result, if you hold certain "U.S. situs" property in a Canadian corporation, you could avoid U.S. estate taxes.

Action Step

If you're a U.S. citizen or resident, the value of any life insurance proceeds paid on your death could be included in the value of your estate that will be subject to U.S. estate taxes. It's possible to establish an insurance trust where the proceeds would be paid into the trust and would be excluded from your taxable estate. This could save significant estate taxes. These trusts are not as necessary for non-resident aliens since insurance proceeds, while considered part of your worldwide estate, are not considered to be part of your taxable U.S. property on death.

This strategy has a number of potential drawbacks to be aware of, however, namely:

(a) one-time set up costs and ongoing annual fees to maintain the corporation

(b) U.S. estate tax may still apply if the IRS determines that the corporation was simply acting as an agent or title-holder for you; proper legal paperwork can avoid this problem

(c) taxes on investment income earned by the corporation, and later paid out to you as dividends, could be taxed at a higher rate than if you had earned the income directly

(d) transferring to a corporation any U.S. real estate that you already own could result in taxes to pay in the U.S. The tax may be reduced where you've owned the property since a time prior to September 27, 1980. This strategy may be best for new acquisitions of U.S. real estate rather than real estate currently owned

(e) Canadian provincial capital taxes apply to corporations with assets over certain levels; this tax could apply to your corporation holding U.S. assets and must be considered a cost of the strategy

(f) if the company is going to hold a personal vacation property, you could be considered to have received a taxable benefit from the corporation, for Canadian tax purposes, when you use the property personally

(g) if the property in the corporation will be sold after your death and the cash proceeds distributed to your heirs, the total income tax cost could be higher than the estate taxes that might have otherwise applied if you had owned the property personally.

Okay, now that I've thoroughly scared you away from the tactic of using a corporation to hold your U.S. property, let me just say that it's still commonly done, not so much with real estate, but with marketable securities. The idea can make sense, but you should visit a tax pro to evaluate the idea in your circumstances.

8. ***Hold U.S. assets through a Canadian partnership.*** A Canadian partnership could be considered a corporation under U.S. law in some cases—if you elect for this treatment to apply. If you establish this type of partnership with a child, to hold your U.S. assets, here's what can happen on your death (or the death of your spouse where you've left your partnership interest to your spouse on your death). Your partnership interest and the assets of the partnership can be transferred to your child (yes, there will be a deemed disposition for Canadian tax purposes, and some potential tax to pay). In the U.S., the partnership will be treated as a corporation, so the assets of the partnership should fall outside of your estate, sidestepping U.S. estate tax. This tactic avoids many of the drawbacks of using a Canadian corporation (see point 7 above), but is going to require the involvement of a tax pro!
9. ***Obtain a non-recourse mortgage.*** Non-recourse debt secured by your U.S. real estate will be deducted from the value of the property on your death when calculating your taxable estate. Non-recourse debt entitles the lender to come after the property if you default on your payments, but not to come after your other assets where the property itself is not sufficient to cover the outstanding

If you're going to obtain non-recourse debt to reduce the taxable value of your U.S. real estate, you should ideally borrow from a lender in Canada (although it might be tough to find a non-recourse mortgage in Canada). This is because payments of interest to a U.S. lender will be subject to a withholding tax (typically 10 percent) where you're deducting the interest costs. Your interest costs will still remain deductible even if borrowing from a U.S. lender becomes necessary.

Caution!

debt. Consider arranging for this type of mortgage, even if your property is debt-free. You could invest the borrowed money, making the interest on the debt deductible (or just partially deductible if the rate on the loan exceeds the return on your investments). Keep in mind that, over time, if the property grows in value and your mortgage is paid down, your estate tax liability could grow again.

10. ***Leave assets to a QDOT.*** A "qualified domestic trust" (QDOT) is simply a trust to which you can leave your assets on death. U.S. estate tax will be deferred in this case until the death of the surviving spouse, or until distributions of capital are made from the trust. To qualify as a QDOT, the trust agreement must provide that at least one trustee be a U.S. citizen or U.S. corporation, and that no distribution of capital can be made without the U.S. trustee withholding U.S. estate taxes. A QDOT may qualify as a "spousal trust" under Canadian tax law (see Tip 48).
11. ***Consider a split interest with your child.*** It may be possible for you to split your interest in an asset with a child. This is different than joint ownership in which you each have an ownership interest during your lifetimes. Instead, you could own a *life interest* in the asset and your child could purchase a *remainder interest*. In this case, you would have a right to all the income and use of the assets during your lifetime, and your child would have a right to the assets after your death. This strategy will definitely require some professional advice from a lawyer.
12. ***Sell U.S. property before you're gone.*** The fact is that the IRS can't levy an estate tax on assets that you don't own at the time of death. So consider selling some of your U.S. assets during your lifetime. Yes, this could trigger Canadian and potentially U.S. income tax on any accrued gains, so you've got to count this cost first. Where assets have dropped in value or have not appreciated much, however, the idea can make good sense. If you're thinking of selling a vacation property that you enjoy using, consider selling

it to someone who will agree either to lease the property back to you or to allow you to rent it during certain times of the year.

TO MAKE A LONG STORY SHORT:

- U.S. estate taxes will apply to U.S. citizens and residents, but non-resident aliens (NRAs—including most Canadians) could also be liable for the tax on death.
- The tax can be substantial, but our tax treaty with the U.S. provides four basic ways to reduce the potential tax hit on death.
- Aside from the treaty, there are a dozen other strategies to consider when planning to minimize a U.S. estate tax hit.

Tim's Tip 67: **Understand how the U.S. gift tax works, and how to avoid the tax where possible.**

Think of the U.S. gift tax as the younger cousin of the U.S. estate tax. The two taxes really work together to ensure that U.S. citizens, residents, and non-resident aliens (NRAs—which includes most Canadians) who own "U.S. situs" property pay some tax when transferring assets to someone else—usually the next generation. The rules work so that the giver of a gift could be liable for tax when large gifts are made.

Mechanics of the Gift Tax

You'll be liable to pay U.S. gift taxes where you're a U.S. citizen or resident who has made a significant gift to another person, or where you're an NRA who makes a gift of "U.S. situs property." Any assets that are caught under the U.S. estate tax rules (see Tip 66) will also be caught by the gift tax rules, and U.S. gift taxes are applied using the same graduated tax rates, ranging from 18 to 55 percent, as the estate tax (see Appendix F).

Are there any exceptions to the gift tax hit that might otherwise apply? Sure. Consider the following exceptions:

- The first US$10,000 of gifts made to a particular person are exempt from the gift tax. That is, you can make gifts of more than $10,000 provided that no one person receives more than $10,000. This exclusion applies to U.S. citizens, residents, and NRAs alike.
- Where your spouse is an NRA of the U.S. (again, this includes most Canadians), you're entitled to give up to US$100,000 to your spouse each year without paying any gift tax south of the border.
- Where your spouse is a U.S. citizen, you won't face gift tax at all when making gifts of any size to your spouse. The reason? The IRS recognizes that when the recipient spouse is a U.S. citizen, estate tax will apply to the assets on that spouse's death, so taxes will eventually be collected.
- Where gift taxes apply, NRAs are permitted to shelter up to US$13,000 of gift taxes (equivalent to US$60,000 of assets given away) during their lifetime. This credit is available to shelter gifts during your lifetime, and to the extent that it's used while you're alive, the US$13,000 credit I spoke of that can reduce U.S. estate taxes is reduced (refer to Tip 66 where I talked about this credit under U.S. domestic tax law). The Canada–U.S. treaty does not provide for additional relief from U.S. gift taxes as it does for U.S. estate taxes.

Caution!

Keep in mind, if you make a gift of assets (including U.S. situs assets) to someone other than your spouse, that you'll be deemed to have sold the assets at fair market value. This could trigger income taxes in Canada. The gift could also trigger gift taxes in the U.S. The U.S. gift tax is not an income tax, and so you won't be able to claim a foreign tax credit in Canada for the U.S. gift tax paid. The result? The potential for double tax. Giving cash or non-U.S. assets may be a better idea to avoid a double-tax problem.

- Where U.S. gift taxes apply, U.S. citizens and residents (but not NRAs) are entitled to a lifetime credit of up to $220,550 (for 2001), which will shelter gift or estate taxes on up to $675,000 worth of assets. To the extent that this credit is not used to shelter gift tax during your lifetime, it can be used to shelter estate tax on death. The total credit for both gift and estate taxes will, however, not be greater than $220,550 (for 2001).

Here's a potential drawback to making gifts of U.S. property: the recipient of the gift will have a cost base in the property, for U.S. tax purposes, equal to your original cost base, plus a portion of the gift tax paid. This differs from what takes place when you make a gift after your death by way of your will. In this case, the recipient's cost base will equal the fair market value of the property on the day that you die.

Required Tax Filings

There are three situations that might require you to file an annual U.S. gift tax return:

1. ***Gifts exceed the $10,000 exclusion.*** Where you're a U.S. citizen or resident, or you're a non-resident alien (NRA) who has given U.S. assets in excess of $10,000 to any one person, you're required to file a U.S. gift tax return. You must also file if you're electing to split gifts with your spouse.
2. ***Transfers to or from foreign trusts.*** If you're a U.S. citizen or resident and you receive distributions from (or you transfer property to) a foreign trust, you've got to report this to the IRS. Penalties of up to 100 percent of the value of the property transferred can apply if you fail to report. This doesn't mean that you'll pay tax on the gift (although you might if you're the giftor and the gift exceeds the $10,000 exclusion), but you've got to report the transfers just the same.
3. ***Gifts from foreign persons.*** If you're a U.S. citizen or resident and you receive gifts or bequests that total more than US$100,000,

you've got to report the gifts to the IRS. This doesn't mean that you'll pay tax on those gifts received—it just means that you've got to report them.

Generation-skipping Taxes

You should be aware that U.S. tax law may apply an additional tax where you pass assets to your grandchildren. The idea is that Uncle Sam doesn't want you to avoid one generation of gift taxes by making the gift directly to your grandkids. The result of the generation-skipping tax is that the total tax paid will be about the same as if the assets had passed from you to your kids, and then to your grandkids. Talk to a tax pro for more information on this special tax.

Sidestepping Gift Taxes

How can you avoid the U.S. gift tax? Try these ideas on for size:

1. ***Make gifts of cash.*** There's nothing quite like gifting cash to avoid a tax hit—both in Canada and the U.S. There will be no U.S. gift taxes on gifts of cash, and no capital gains tax resulting from a deemed disposition in Canada.
2. ***Make gifts within $10,000 annually.*** It can be a great estate planning tactic to make gifts during your lifetime. You'll also manage to avoid U.S. gift tax where your gifts do not exceed US$10,000 per person annually.
3. ***Avoid gifts of U.S. property.*** If you're an NRA for U.S. purposes, avoid making gifts of "U.S. situs" property and you'll avoid the U.S. gift tax. U.S. citizens and residents won't be able to avoid the gift tax by this strategy since all gifts by these individuals could give rise to gift taxes.
4. ***Give assets to your spouse.*** You'll likely avoid U.S. gift taxes by making a gift to your spouse, since you can gift US$100,000 to your NRA spouse without triggering gift tax. If your spouse is a U.S. citizen, there are no limits on the value of the transfers that you can make and still avoid gift tax.

TO MAKE A LONG STORY SHORT:

- U.S. gift taxes will apply to gifts made by a U.S. citizen or resident, or by a non-resident alien (NRA—including most Canadians) who gifts U.S. assets.
- Credits can be claimed to offset a gift tax liability, but this will reduce the credit that is then available to offset estate taxes on death.
- There are some exceptions to the gift tax rules, including a US$10,000 annual exclusion that allows you to make as many annual $10,000 gifts as you'd like, provided that no one person receives more than $10,000 from you each year.

WINNING THE ESTATE PLANNING GAME

If you've got U.S. connections—whether you're a U.S. citizen, resident, or simply someone who owns U.S. assets—you may have to take steps to avoid U.S. estate and gift taxes, and to properly file an income tax return in the U.S. annually. This chapter has highlighted the key points that you should be aware of. Keep in mind that cross-border tax planning can be complex, and you should make a visit to a tax pro if you're not completely comfortable with your understanding of the tax issues that you face.

Now, flip back to the *Estate Planning Tip Sheet* at the front of the book. For each tip, ask yourself the question: "Does this apply to me?" Then check the appropriate answer: "Yes," "No," or "Not sure." This sheet will form the basis for a proper estate plan! Now, let's move to Chapter 12 and talk about the last big event that you'll ever attend: your own funeral.

AFTER THE RACE: PLANNING FOR YOUR FUNERAL

Thanks to the cosmeticians, I'll live long and die young.

12

A few years ago, I won a free ticket to the Superbowl through a contest at work. Unfortunately, when I arrived at the stadium I was closer to the Goodyear Blimp than to the field. About halfway through the first quarter, I noticed an empty seat 10 rows off the field, right on the 50-yard line. I made my way through the stadium, around the security guards, to the empty seat. As I sat down, I asked the gentleman sitting next to me, "Excuse me, is anyone sitting here?" "No," the man replied. "This is incredible!" I responded.

"Who in their right mind would have a seat like this at the Superbowl and not use it?" The man answered that question. "Well, actually, the seat belongs to me. I was supposed to come with my wife, but she died. This is the first Superbowl that we haven't been together since we got married in 1967." "Sorry to hear that," I said. "But still, couldn't you find someone to take the seat? A close friend, or a relative?" "No," the man replied, "they're all at the funeral."

Okay, so the story isn't quite true, but it does reflect how some view funerals: not a priority, unimportant and perhaps even a rip-off. After all, who wants to focus on the death of a loved one—and pay for it to boot? While I'm a firm believer that it makes sense to avoid overpaying for a funeral, I also think that having a funeral makes sense for a few reasons. You see, a funeral:

- acknowledges that a life has been lived
- allows mourners to remember and honour their loved one
- serves as a central gathering place for family and friends to give emotional and physical support to one another
- provides closure for the bereaved
- initiates the grieving process
- confirms the reality and finality of the death
- encourages mourners to face the pain of their loss and express their thoughts and feelings
- helps survivors to better cope with their grief and enables them to move forward with their lives.

Your Executor's Role

Let's take a look at the role of your executor in planning and carrying out your funeral.

Caution!

Your executor is not bound by your wishes where your funeral is concerned. That is, if you want *Ave Maria* played by a professional violinist at your funeral, there's nothing to stop your executor from having a rendition of *Roll Out the Barrel* played by a bagpiper instead. Chances are pretty good, however, that choosing an executor who knows you well and with whom you've had a good relationship will result in your wishes being carried out.

Tim's Tip 68: **Provide clear instructions to your executor regarding your funeral plans—today.**

It's the job of your executor to arrange for your funeral. I know that you may not want to think about your funeral today. It's critical, however, that you provide clear instructions to your executor regarding your funeral, even before you're gone. Why not simply leave these instructions in your will? Simple. Your executor may not obtain a copy of your will until after your funeral. Don't forget, your funeral is likely to take place just a few days after your death—before anyone has really had a chance to gather all pertinent information about your assets and locate the important documents, including your will.

If you're really on the ball and actually pre-plan or pre-pay for your funeral ahead of time (which I'll talk about in this chapter), then you should speak to your executor about this fact today as well. Otherwise, your executor might just plan an entire funeral totally oblivious to the fact that you have made arrangements, and might even just pay for it all over again.

As a gesture of good will, be sure to leave your family and friends with a chance to have some input into your funeral. Don't try to plan every single detail right down to who greets people at the door of the funeral home. After all, your funeral is really for your family and friends. They can decide some of these things when the time comes to announce your funeral. They'll appreciate the opportunity to provide input.

TO MAKE A LONG STORY SHORT:

- Provide written instructions to your executor today regarding your funeral, rather than leaving these instructions in your will, which may not be read until after your funeral.
- Alert your executor today if you've already made arrangements for your funeral—particularly if you've paid for it already.
- Allow your family and friends to decide on some of the details of your funeral after you're gone since the funeral is really for them.

Funeral Costs

What do you suppose it's going to cost to put on your funeral? It could range anywhere from "this-is-a-little-more-than-I-thought" expensive to "let's-mortgage the-house-to-pay-for-Dad's-casket" expensive.

Tim's Tip 69: **Understand the cost of various funeral options and don't pay more than you need to.**

In all of this, remember one thing: from a commercial point of view, a funeral is nothing more than a combination of products and services provided by a funeral director. If you were to buy any other product or service likely to cost $5,000 or more, you would shop around. The problem, of course, is that the last thing your family will have the time or desire to do once you're gone is to make calls to multiple funeral directors and haggle about the price of your funeral. You'll do them a favour by shopping around today.

Funerals don't come cheaply—regardless of whether you're looking at a burial, or cremation. Consider the following costs for a traditional funeral.

BURIAL	CREMATION
Funeral home service fees $2,550	Funeral home service fees $2,250
Casket for burial $2,200	Casket for cremation $1,475
Plot for burial $860	Cremation charges $400
Upright monument $2,400	Urn $300
Flat monument $1,400	Plot for cremation $625
Honorarium for minister $125	Upright monument $2,400
Soloist/Organist $75	Flat monument $1,400
Miscellaneous costs (flowers, obituaries, cards, etc.) $300	Honorarium for minister $125
GST for burial $526	Soloist/Organist $75
	Miscellaneous costs (flowers, obituaries, cards, etc.) $300
	GST for cremation $487
Total Average Cost $8,036	**Total Average Cost $7,437**

Interestingly, there's not a whole lot of difference in price between being boxed and buried, or boxed and burned. Many expect a cremation to be much cheaper, when actually it's not.

Keep in mind that there are really three types of funeral expenses.

1. ***Products.*** Items sold by the funeral home such as a casket, urn, and register book.
2. ***Service Charges.*** Professional services rendered by the funeral home staff, including registering your death, preparing death notices, embalming, overseeing visitation at the funeral home, services during the ceremony, and transporting your body to a cemetery or crematorium.
3. ***Disbursements.*** Ancillary products or services that the funeral home orders on your behalf, including death notices, clergy, and cemetery or crematorium fees.

Make sure that you understand what products, services, and disbursements are involved, and how much each will cost. Planning ahead—before you're gone, will ensure that your heirs won't be paying more for your funeral than they ought to.

How can you keep the cost of your funeral to a minimum, and still have your family and friends treated with dignity and respect? Consider these four options:

1. ***Your Casket.*** Rather than spending significant amounts on a lavish casket, opt for a less expensive, yet respectable looking one. You may also want to consider renting a casket instead (no, this doesn't involve digging your body up after the fact to recover a casket to be used by someone else again). Renting simply involves purchasing a container to be used for your final disposition—costing between $500 and $700. During the funeral ceremony, however, your body is placed in a much more expensive casket.
2. ***Direct Disposition.*** In most provinces, the cheapest funeral option is called a "direct disposition." It'll cost between $800 and $1,200 on average. In this case, the funeral home or transfer service will transport you from your place of death to the funeral home, and then to a cemetery or crematorium in a simple container made of particleboard or firm cardboard. The funeral home will also register the death with the provincial government and will handle all of the necessary paperwork. A nice memorial service can then be held for you at the funeral home, a place or worship, or somewhere else.

Did You Know?

CPP benefits can help to defray the cost of your funeral. If you've contributed to the Canada Pension Plan for the minimum qualifying period, your estate will receive a lump-sum payment. The government first calculates the amount that your Canada Pension Plan retirement pension is, or would have been if you had been aged 65 when death occurred. The death benefit is equal to six months' worth of this "calculated" retirement pension, up to a maximum of $2,500.

3. ***Do-it-yourself Funeral.*** The truth is, burial or cremation is not usually done without the help of a funeral home, although there is no law to stop your family or friends from doing this on their own. There are, however, some legal documents which have to be filed with the provincial government to register your death, or to arrange for cremation. Cemeteries and crematoria will require that a casket or a container be used, although any funeral home can sell these. The biggest problem with a do-it-yourself funeral is that your family will have to find a suitable vehicle to move your casket or container. Tying your container to the roof of the station wagon won't go over very well—although today's mini-vans seem to have quite a bit of room!

4. ***Buy Life Insurance.*** Another option to keep the cost of your funeral down is to buy life insurance to cover all or a portion of the expected costs. You can even name the funeral home as beneficiary of the policy to ensure that the money is used to pay for your funeral. The policy shouldn't cost much since you're only looking at purchasing coverage of $5,000 to $8,000. A life insurance broker or funeral home can help with this purchase.

Did You Know?

Earth burial is the most common type of disposition in North America today. Cremation is the other option and is a process that reduces the body to basic elements through exposure to open flame in a cremation chamber. Any funeral director can arrange for a cremation, although cremations are chosen in just 18 percent of deaths in North America.

TO MAKE A LONG STORY SHORT:

- From a commercial point of view, a funeral is nothing more than a combination of products and services provided by a funeral home. Shop around today so that your family or friends don't have to do this on short notice.

- Burials and cremations are close in price, with the average funeral costing between $7,000 and $8,000.

- Keep costs down by carefully choosing your casket, opting for a direct disposition or a do-it-yourself funeral, or buying life insurance.

Pre-planning Your Funeral

Procrastination is the art of putting off until tomorrow what you could or should be doing today, and make no mistake, procrastination can be costly, inconvenient, and simply a burden on your heirs when it comes to your funeral.

Tim's Tip 70: **Recognize the benefits of pre-planning your funeral.**

Let me say first that pre-planning your funeral doesn't have to mean pre-paying for your funeral. Pre-planning and pre-paying are two different things. Pre-planning is critical, while pre-paying may be beneficial. Why do I say that pre-planning is critical? Because the benefits are so significant. Consider the following benefits:

- Reduces stress for your heirs. Your plans will remove the burden from your heirs of organizing a complete funeral at a time when they may be emotionally drained.
- Time is on your side. Pre-planning allows you make important decisions regarding your funeral on your own time without any urgency, which will likely mean better-informed decisions.
- Protects you from inflation. If, as part of your pre-planning, you also pre-pay for your funeral, you can receive the services at today's costs. As the funeral home's prices rise, you won't have to worry about the increases.
- Reduces costs. If your heirs have to make quick decisions about your funeral with little time to shop around, it's likely that your funeral will cost more than it could have.

- Provides peace of mind. You might just sleep better at night knowing that your funeral plans are looked after and, where you've pre-paid for the funeral, that there won't be a financial burden on your heirs.
- Things are likely to be done your way. Planning your funeral ahead of time will provide some assurance that your ceremony will be carried out in the manner you would have liked.

Remember from Tip 68 that you should leave some of the details related to your funeral for your family to decide after your death. They'll appreciate this. The big stuff can be decided by you ahead of time, however. Consider the Funeral Pre-Planning Checklist in Appendix G and determine what you'll decide upon, and what you'll leave for your family to handle.

If you want my advice, let me tell you what I've done about pre-planning my funeral. I took the Funeral Pre-Planning Checklist, sat down with my closest family members, and I asked them what they'd like to decide upon as far as my funeral arrangements go. I then provided guidance on the rest by writing down my wishes using the checklist. My family will feel as though they had enough control over my funeral, but I was able to make my wishes known on the really important stuff. Try doing the same.

TO MAKE A LONG STORY SHORT:

- Pre-planning your funeral doesn't have to mean pre-paying for it, although pre-paying can make sense.
- There are many benefits to pre-planning, not the least of which are reducing stress for your heirs and minimizing the cost of your funeral.
- Look at the pre-planning checklist in Appendix G and decide which details you want to organize today, and which you'll leave to your heirs to decide.

Tim's Tip 71: Consider donating your organs and carry a signed donor card.

Part of planning ahead of time is considering whether or not you'd like to donate your organs or your entire body at the time of your death. Forget about writing these details into your will. By the time your will is read, the time frame for donating your organs or body will have passed. If you want to make this type of donation, you'll need to sign a provincial organ donor card, or the consent form on the back of your driver's licence. Then, make sure that your family knows about your intentions so they can make arrangements for a donation immediately after your death.

What can you donate? Currently, your heart, lungs, kidneys, liver, pancreas, small bowels, corneas, bones, and skin can be donated. The truth is, modern medicine has made the success rate for transplants quite high. You could be helping to save the life of another person—or even several people—by donating organs. Keep in mind that, while it would be nice to think that simply signing a donor card is a guarantee that your organs will be used, this isn't the case. You've got to be on life support, while being brain-dead, in order to donate organs.

Whom should you contact if you want more information on organ donation? Call your provincial organ donation agency. Here's a list:

British Columbia:

BC Transplant Society	(604) 877-2240

Alberta:

University of Alberta Hospital	(780) 407-8407
Foothills General Hospital	(403) 283-2243

Saskatchewan:

University Hospital	(306) 655-1000

Manitoba:

Health Sciences Centre	(204) 787-2071

Ontario:

Organ Donation Ontario	(416) 351-7328
Toronto Hospital	(416) 340-3587
University Hospital	(519) 663-3000
Ottawa Civic Hospital	(613) 761-4221
St. Joseph's Hospital	(905) 522-4941
Kingston General Hospital	(613) 548-3232

Quebec:

Quebec Transplant	(514) 286-1414
Quebec City Branch	(418) 663-5800

Nova Scotia:

Health Sciences Centre	(902) 473-5500

New Brunswick:

Organ Procurement Program	(506) 643-6848

Newfoundland:

Health Science Centre	(709) 737-6600

By the way, if you plan to donate your entire body for the purpose of education or research, be aware that not all bodies are accepted. Don't worry, it's not that your body is likely to be offensive to anyone, it's just that the school may have enough bodies already. It might also be that the cost of shipping your body a long distance to the school of your choice is not worth the school's while. The bottom line? Don't neglect to plan for a funeral simply because you expect your body to end up in a science lab. You might just end up with a funeral instead, and even if you do end up as research equipment, your family and friends will still likely want to have a memorial service for you. Your input into that service will be important.

TO MAKE A LONG STORY SHORT:

- Don't bother spelling out in your will your wish to donate organs. By the time that your will is read, it'll be too late to donate organs.
- Instead, sign a provincial organ donor card, or the consent form on the back of your driver's licence to identify your desire to donate organs.

- Discuss your intentions with your family members so that they can react quickly in the event that your organs are needed.
- Don't neglect to plan for a funeral simply because you expect your body to end up in a science lab—it might not.

Action Step

Even though you've signed an organ donor card, your family may still have to consent to a donation of your organs. That's right, you may think that your organs will be used for the benefit of others, but your family may be able to veto that intention. How can you ensure that your organs will be used if possible? Sit down and talk to your family today to let them know your wishes. This way, they're more likely to allow a donation when that time comes.

Pre-paying for Your Funeral

Paying for anything before you absolutely have to may seem to make little sense. Your funeral could be an exception. Let's talk about pre-paying for your funeral.

Tim's Tip 72: Pre-paying for your funeral could offer tax breaks among other benefits.

A few months ago, Carolyn and I were down south in Alabama, visiting her brother and his family. I answered the phone one evening when I was home alone, and the woman on the other end of the line fed me her sales pitch. "Good evening sir, I represent the Shady Acres Funeral Home, and I was wondering if I could share with you some information about our lay-away plan."

If the truth be known, every Canadian funeral home offers a similar "layaway plan." I'm talking about prepaid funeral and cemetery services. Don't expect a phone call promoting these services in Canada, however: the Funeral Act won't allow it here. You'll have to take action yourself if you're interested, and there may be some good reasons why you should be.

Prepaid funeral arrangements—known as eligible funeral arrangements (EFAs) under our tax law—can offer some surprising tax advantages in many cases. An EFA is simply an arrangement where you make payments today to cover your funeral and/or cemetery costs on death.

You see, section 148.1 of our tax law will allow you to contribute up to $15,000 in your lifetime to an EFA to cover funeral services, and another $20,000 to cover cemetery services, for a total of $35,000 in allowable contributions. Now, you won't receive a deduction for amounts contributed to an EFA, but the funds can grow on a tax-free basis in the plan. Further, when the amounts are paid to the provider of the funeral and cemetery services, there will be absolutely no tax levied on the amounts paid out of the EFA as long as the funds were used for funeral and cemetery services. With contributions as high as $35,000—the tax savings could be huge.

Did You Know?

Consider these facts: The average age of a purchaser of an Eligible Funeral Arrangement (EFA) is 77. The average length of each contract is 6 years (the contract ends on your death). What this tells me is that Canadians are not taking advantage of EFAs as early as they could be, and make no mistake, the tax benefits alone can be worth your while. Similar to other registered plans, the assets in the plan grow tax-deferred and are paid out tax-free on 'our death where the funds sed to cover your osts.

Ruth established an EFA this year at age 65 and invested $15,000 in the plan. If we assume that she earns 6 percent on that money for another 20 years, the amount available at her death at age 85 would be $48,000. The truth is, that could provide for quite a celebration on her death. If the full $48,000 were spent on funeral and cemetery services, there would be no tax at all on the accumulated *income in the EFA. That translates into $16,500 of tax savings in her case over a situation where the income earned on the $15,000 would have been taxed at her marginal tax rate of 50 percent.*

Now, suppose that your family doesn't need all of the money set aside in the EFA for your funeral. In this event, the excess money in the EFA is paid to your estate, where the accumulated income (but not your contributions) will be taxed. Regardless, that's one fantastic tax deferral.

Before you get all excited about the tax deferral opportunity here, let me say that an EFA works only where the plan is established solely for the purpose of funding funeral or cemetery services. That is, if the tax collector ever determines that your true intention was to use the plan to defer tax, it won't qualify as an EFA and you can count on paying tax annually on the income in the arrangement. The tax collector may suspect foul intentions if you happen to sock away money in an EFA and then later make withdrawals during your lifetime. If you're dead by the time the funds are paid out of the plan, however, it's safe to say that the tax collector is not likely to question your intentions and the EFA should work for you.

By the way, there are other ways to cover your funeral costs. Life insurance is the most obvious example that comes to mind. Life insurance could be a cheaper way to pay for your funeral, but its use depends on one important requirement: you must be insurable. Depending on your age, health, and other factors, you may not be able to obtain insurance, or, maybe you're just not fond of needles and blood tests (a bad excuse for bypassing insurance, by the way).

You might also consider funding your funeral out of RRSP contributions. If you're over 69, however, or are already maximizing RRSP contributions to fund your retirement, this option may not be available, or best for you.

If you want more information on EFAs, just contact your nearest funeral home.

TO MAKE A LONG STORY SHORT:

- Eligible funeral arrangements (EFAs) allow you to set aside up to $35,000 today, to cover funeral and cemetery costs after your death.
- EFAs offer a great tax deferral since the income growing on the deposit is not taxed if the funds are used for your funeral and cemetery costs.
- Even if your family doesn't use all of the money in the EFA for eligible costs, the excess is paid to your estate, where the growth (but not your contributions) will be taxed. In this event, the tax deferral is still valuable.

WINNING THE ESTATE PLANNING GAME

I know that you don't like to think about death, and planning your own funeral is about as close to death as you can get without attending your own funeral. Nevertheless, planning ahead of time is critical. Be sure to check the *Estate Planning Tip Sheet* at the front of the book and to revisit all the tips from this chapter listed there. You know the routine. For each tip, ask yourself the question: "Does this apply to me?" Then check the appropriate answer: "Yes," "No," or "Not sure." This tip sheet will form the basis for your complete estate plan once you've read the entire book. Happy planning.

APPENDIX A

Estate Planning Objectives

The table below has been designed to help you to identify your estate planning objectives. Until you really understand what you hope to accomplish, it's tough to arrive at any concrete plans. Read each of the potential objectives listed in the table. Check off on the left side of the table which objectives best describe what you hope to achieve in your estate planning. For each of these objectives, move to the right side of the table and check off whether you'd like to accomplish the objective today (during your lifetime), or on or after your death. Finally, rank each objective that you've checked off in order of importance, and note this rank in the right column below.

	My Estate Planning Objectives	Today	On/After Death	Rank
☐	Minimize income tax bill	☐	☐	
☐	Pay off all debts	☐	☐	
☐	Simplify affairs	☐	☐	
☐	Donate money to charity	☐	☐	
☐	Provide for a disabled dependant	☐	☐	
☐	Reduce tax burden for heirs	☐	☐	
☐	Pay for education of a (grand)child	☐	☐	
☐	Split estate equally among heirs	☐	☐	
☐	Split estate fairly, but not equally	☐	☐	
☐	Minimize probate fees	N/A	☐	
☐	Minimize U.S. estate taxes	N/A	☐	
☐	Other:	☐	☐	
☐	Other:	☐	☐	
☐	Other:	☐	☐	
☐	Other:	☐	☐	

Prepared by:____________________ Date:____________________

Notes:

____

____

____

APPENDIX B

Dying Without a Will: Intestacy Laws

If you die without a will, the intestacy laws of your province will determine who gets what. The table below details, by province or territory, how your estate will be distributed if you die intestate. These figures are subject to change from time to time, and may be overridden by certain elections that may be available to a surviving spouse in some provinces. I hope that your heirs will never have to face these rules. Prepare a will!

DYING WITHOUT A WILL				
	Surviving Family Members			
Province	**Spouse Only**	**Children Only**	**Spouse and Children**	**No Spouse or Children**
British Columbia	All to spouse	All to children[1]	First $65,000 to spouse; rest is split between spouse and children[3]	All to next of kin; if no next of kin, the government takes all[4]
Alberta	All to spouse	All to children[1]	First $40,000 to spouse; rest is split between spouse and children[3]	Same as above
Saskatchewan	All to spouse	All to children[1]	First $100,000 to spouse, rest is split between spouse and children[3]	Same as above
Manitoba	All to spouse	All to children[1]	All to spouse[6]	Same as above
Ontario	All to spouse	All to children[1]	First $200,000 to spouse, rest is split between spouse and children[3]	Same as above

Province	Spouse Only	Children Only	Spouse and Children	No Spouse or Children
Quebec	All to spouse[2]	All to children[1]	1/3 to spouse, 2/3 to children[5]	Same as above
New Brunswick	All to spouse	All to children[1]	Marital property to spouse, rest is split between spouse and children[3]	Same as above
Nova Scotia	All to spouse	All to children[1]	First $50,000 to spouse, rest is split between spouse and children[3]	Same as above
Prince Edward Island	All to spouse	All to children[1]	First $50,000 to spouse, rest is split between spouse and children[3]	Same as above
Newfoundland	All to spouse	All to children[1]	Estate is split between spouse and children[7]	Same as above
Northwest Territories	All to spouse	All to children[1]	First $50,000 to spouse; rest is split between spouse and children[3]	Same as above
Yukon	All to spouse	All to children[1]	Estate is split between spouse and children[7]	Same as above
Nunavut	All to spouse	All to children[1]	First $50,000 to spouse; rest is split between spouse and children[3]	Same as above

Notes:

1. If a child is deceased, his or her share goes to the children of that deceased child.

2. If there are other relatives, the spouse will get just 1/3 or 1/2 (depending on who the other relatives are) while the rest will go to parents and/or brothers and sisters.

3. The rest is split 50/50 between the spouse and child where there's just one child. If there are two or more children: 1/3 goes to the spouse, while the children inherit the rest split among them.

4. Estate is distributed to the next of kin in this order: parents, brothers/sisters, nephews/nieces, next of kin.

5. Subject to provincial legislation.

6. If all of the children are also children of the surviving spouse. If any of the children are not children of the surviving spouse, the spouse gets the greater of $50,000 or 1/2 of the estate; 1/2 of the rest goes to the spouse, and 1/2 to the children.

7. Estate is split 50/50 between the spouse and child where there's just one child. If there are two or more children: 1/3 goes to the spouse while the children inherit the rest split among them.

APPENDIX C

Revising Your Will—Is it Time?

When was the last time you revised your will? You should make it a regular habit to review your will every three years just to be sure that it doesn't need revising. This checklist will help in that review process. Read the questions in the table. If you've answered "Yes" to any questions, it could be time to revise your will. I've provided the recommended action in the table. Visit a lawyer who is experienced in the preparation of wills if you're not sure whether things need to be changed. Remember that changing your will can be as easy as simply attaching a "codicil" to your will to reflect the desired changes. Where those changes are significant, preparing an entirely new will likely makes sense.

Since you last revised your will, have you:	Potential action to take:
married?	Marriage revokes a previous will. Prepare a new will.
separated?	Separation does not revoke or change your will. You may want to make changes here.
divorced?	Divorce does not revoke all provisions of your will—just those related to your ex-spouse. You may want to make changes here.
been widowed?	The beneficiaries of your will likely include your spouse. Now that you're widowed, reconsider who will get what and make changes if necessary.
had children?	You may want to add a clause regarding guardianship of your children, or change your beneficiaries to include them.

Since you last revised your will, have you:	Potential action to take:
adopted children?	You may want to add a clause regarding guardianship of your children, or change your beneficiaries to include them.
become a grandparent?	You may want to add your grandchildren as beneficiaries.
become a mother- or father-in-law?	You may want to add a provision that all property passed to your children is excluded from their "net family property" to protect the assets in the event that your child divorces.
lost dependants?	You may want to revise whom your beneficiaries are or remove any trusts previously set up in your will for these dependants.
gained dependants?	You may want to provide for a trust to be set up in your will to meet the financial needs of your dependants.
moved to a new province or country?	Your previous will may not be valid in your new jurisdiction, or may not contemplate succession laws in that juridiction. A new will may need to be prepared.
inherited assets?	You may have additional assets now to specifically deal with in your will. Further, your expected tax bill on death might be greater now: consider life insurance to cover the tax bill.
grown your net worth significantly?	You may have additional assets now to specifically deal with in your will. Further, your expected tax bill on death might be greater now: consider life insurance to cover the tax bill.
purchased a cottage or other property?	You may want to detail how the cottage is to be handled on your death (sell it, or have shared ownership?). Consider a trust to hold the cottage after you're gone.

Since you last revised your will, have you:	Potential action to take:
purchased life insurance?	This may change who gets what. Also, consider setting up an insurance trust (see Tip 55).
started a business?	Your will should provide your executor with appropriate powers to run your business.
sold or wound up a business?	This may change who gets what. It may also mean that you've now got a lot more cash to invest, which could change your expected tax liability on death.
lent money to others?	Consider forgiving the debt in your will. There are no tax consequences to forgiving a debt at death.
developed charitable intentions?	Specifically detail in your will which charities should receive assets on your death, and how much (see Tip 60).
reconsidered your executor, guardian or trustees?	If any of these people have moved, are likely to predecease you, or are now unwilling to act in the role, consider changing these names in your will.
noticed any changes to our tax law?	Visit a tax pro to determine whether recent changes will affect your current will.
noticed any changes to family law?	Visit a lawyer to determine whether recent changes will affect your current will.

Prepared by:____________________ Date:____________________

Notes:

____

____

____

____

____

APPENDIX D

Provincial Probate Fees

Province / Territory	Probate Fees
British Columbia	Estate up to $10,000: no fees Estate $10,001 to $25,000: $208 Add $6 on each $1,000 (or part thereof) between $25,001 and $50,000 Add $14 on each $1,000 (or part thereof) over $50,000
Alberta	Estate up to $10,000: $25 Estate between $10,001 and $25,000: $100 Estate between $25,001 and $50,000: $200 Estate between $50,001 and $100,000: $400 Estate between $100,001 and $250,000: $600 Estate between $250,001 and $500,000: $1,500 Estate between $500,001 and $1,000,000: $3,000 Estate over $1,000,000: $6,000
Saskatchewan	Estate of any size: $7 on each $1,000 (or part thereof)
Manitoba	Estate up to $10,000: $50 Add $6 on each $1,000 (or part thereof) over $10,000
Ontario	Fees of $5 on each $1,000 (or part thereof) up to $50,000 Add $15 on each $1,000 (or part thereof) over $50,000
Quebec	Fees of $65 for non-notarial wills Notarial wills need not be probated, so there are no fees

Province / Territory	Probate Fees
New Brunswick	Estate up to $5,000: $25 Estate between $5,001 and $10,000: $50 Estate between $10,001 and $15,000: $75 Estate between $15,001 and $20,000: $100 Add $5 on each $1,000 (or part thereof) over $20,000
Nova Scotia	Estate up to $10,000: $75 Estate between $10,001 and $25,000: $150 Estate between $25,001 and $50,000: $250 Estate between $50,001 and $100,000: $500 Estate between $100,001 and $150,000: $600 Estate between $150,001 and $200,000: $800 Add $5 on each $1,000 (or part thereof) over $200,000
Prince Edward Island	Estate up to $10,000: $50 Estate between $10,001 and $25,000: $100 Estate between $25,001 and $50,000: $200 Estate between $50,001 and $100,000: $400 Add $4 for each $1,000 (or part thereof) over $100,000
Newfoundland	On the first $1,000 of estate: $80 Add $5 on each $1,000 (or part thereof) over $1,000, plus $75
Northwest Territories and Nunavut	Estate up to $500: $8 Estate over $500 and up to $1,000: $15 Add $3 on each $1,000 (or part thereof) over $1,000
Yukon	Estate up to $10,000: no fees Estate between $10,001 and $25,000: $140 Add $6 on each $1,000 (or part thereof) over $25,000

APPENDIX E

How Much Insurance Should You Buy?

If you've read through Chapter 6 on insurance, you'll understand that there can be many reasons for buying life insurance. Once you understand your specific reason(s) for buying insurance, you can then determine the type of insurance to buy, and how much to buy. This appendix will help to determine the amount of insurance to purchase if you have a need for insurance to provide for dependants in the event that a breadwinner dies.

How should we go about determining your life insurance needs? Simple. We'll first look at what income-producing assets you'd have if you died tomorrow, and determine how much income those assets would generate annually. We'll then compare this to how much income your dependants will require annually. If there's a shortfall, it may be necessary to buy life insurance.

Income-producing Assets of Estate

Assets:

• Cash	$__________	
• RRSPs	$__________	
• Investments	$__________	
• Life insurance owned (note 1)	$__________	
• Other	$__________	
Total income-producing assets	$__________	(1)

Liabilities:

• Final expenses (note 2)	$__________
• Mortgages (if not insured)	$__________

- Credit card balances $__________
- Lines of credit (if not insured) $__________
- Income taxes at death $__________
- Bequests to other than dependants (charities, etc.) $__________
- Other $__________

Total liabilities $__________ (2)

Income-producing net assets: (1) minus (2) $__________ (A)

Expected Income Needs of Dependants

Income needed:

Total annual income needs of dependants, before taxes $__________ (3)

Income available:

- From estate (note 3) $__________
- From CPP/QPP $__________
- From other pension $__________
- From employment $__________
- From other sources $__________

Total income available $__________ (4)

Income shortfall (surplus) (note 4) $__________ (B)

Calculating Additional Capital Required

Income shortfall:

Income shortfall (line B) (note 5) $__________ (5)

Capital required:

Additional capital required: line 5 divided by 0.07 (note 6) $__________ (C)

The additional capital required at the time of your death appears at line C. This additional capital can be provided through life insurance.

The amount at line C, therefore, represents the amount of insurance you should purchase to provide for your dependants in the event of your death.

Notes:

1. Include the death benefits on all life insurance policies owned. Don't forget to include life insurance coverage through your benefit plan at work.
2. Final expenses include funeral costs, accounting and legal fees, executor fees, and similar items.
3. To calculate the income available from your estate, simply take the figure from line A and multiply it by 0.07 (7 percent). If you believe that a rate of return greater than 7 percent is more realistic, apply a different rate. I believe, however, that 7 percent is appropriately conservative.
4. If the income needs from line 3 exceed the income available on line 4, then an income shortfall will exist. If the figure at line 3 is greater than line 4, you have a surplus and no more insurance is required to provide for your dependants. In this latter case, it is not necessary to go on to part C here.
5. If an income shortfall appears at line B (line 3 exceeds line 4), then place that figure from line B on line 5. Otherwise, place a zero on line 5.
6. Divide line 5 by 0.07 (7 percent). This provides the amount of additional capital required to provide for your dependants. If you believe that a return of greater than 7 percent can be achieved annually after your death, you may use a different rate. I believe that 7 percent is appropriately conservative.

APPENDIX F

U.S. Estate and Gift Tax Rates

Are you wondering how much U.S. estate or gift taxes you're going to pay? Here are the current rates. Refer to Chapter 11 for more details on minimizing U.S. estate or gift taxes.

U.S. ESTATE AND GIFT TAX RATES

Estate Over	But Not Over	Estate or Gift Tax +	This Percent on Excess
$ —	$ 10,000	$ —	18%
10,000	20,000	1,800	20
20,000	40,000	3,800	22
40,000	60,000	8,200	24
60,000	80,000	13,000	26
80,000	100,000	18,200	28
100,000	150,000	23,800	30
150,000	250,000	38,800	32
250,000	500,000	70,800	34
500,000	750,000	155,800	37
750,000	1,000,000	248,300	39
1,000,000	1,250,000	345,800	41
1,250,000	1,500,000	448,300	43
1,500,000	2,000,000	555,800	45
2,000,000	2,500,000	780,800	49
2,500,000	3,000,000	1,025,800	53
3,000,000	—	1,290,800	55

APPENDIX G

Funeral Pre-Planning Checklist

Do your heirs a favour—plan your funeral today! The following checklist will help you in this task. Note below those things you want to decide, and note which things you'll leave to your family to decide. Refer to Chapter 12 for a discussion of funeral planning.

FUNERAL PRE-PLANNING CHECKLIST			
Description	**Yes**	**No**	**Family to Decide**
Funeral Service (location:_______________________________)			
Memorial Service (location:_______________________________)			
Burial (location:_______________________________)			
Cremation, with ashes: (buried at:_______________________________) (scattered at:_____________________________) (other:_________________________________)			
Funeral home (location:_______________________________)			
Music (selection:______________________________) (musician:_______________________________) (vocalist:________________________________)			
Flowers (type:__________________________________)			
Donations in lieu of flowers (charity:_________________________________)			

FUNERAL PRE-PLANNING CHECKLIST

Description	Yes	No	Family to Decide
Clergy (who:____________________)			
Casket bearers (who:__________ __________ __________ __________ __________ __________)			
Eulogy/Speeches (who:____________________ ____________________ ____________________)			
Ushers (who:__________ __________ __________ __________ __________ __________)			
Open casket			
Special/scripture reading (what:____________________) (who:____________________)			
Order of service			
Casket choice (funeral home:____________________)			
Urn choice (funeral home:____________________)			
Monument (☐ upright ☐ flat ☐ none)			
Clothing to wear (description:____________________)			
Other (____________________)			
Other (____________________)			
Other (____________________)			

APPENDIX H

Personal Factfinder

There's nothing more convenient than having all of your personal information in one handy place. This Personal Factfinder can help! Complete the information here and keep a copy where your executor will know where to find it; a safety deposit box makes a good place to store this information. You may even want to provide a copy to your executor once you've completed the Factfinder. I'd recommend that you either complete the Factfinder in pencil so that you can revise it as needed, or make a photocopy of the Factfinder before filling it in so that you can revise the information later as it changes. Review the Factfinder annually to make sure it's up to date. This information can also assist any professional advisor in developing an appropriate estate plan for you.

Special thanks to Terry Ritchie of The Cross-Border Advisory Group Inc. in Calgary for developing this Factfinder.

Personal Factfinder

Date Prepared: ____________ **Date Updated:** ____________

Personal Information

Your Name: ____________________ Date of Birth: __________

Spouse Name: ____________________ Date of Birth: __________

Address: ____

City, Province: ________________ Postal Code: ______________

Home Phone: ________________ Office Phone: ______________

Fax Number: ______________ Email Address: ______________

Your Citizenship: ___________ Spouse Citizenship: ______________

Your Place of Birth: _________ Spouse Place of Birth: ______________

Your S.I.N.: ______________ Spouse S.I.N.: ______________

Your S.S.N.(US): ____________ Spouse S.S.N.(US): ______________

Health: ______________ Spouse Health: ______________

Smoke? ______________ Spouse Smoke? ______________

Your areas of concern:

1. ________________________ 2. ________________________

3. ________________________ 4. ________________________

5. ________________________ 6. ________________________

7. ________________________ 8. ________________________

9. ________________________ 10. ________________________

11. ________________________ 12. ________________________

Family Information

			Yes	No	Kids?
Child: __________	Birthdate: __________	Married:	○	○	○
Child: __________	Birthdate: __________	Married:	○	○	○
Child: __________	Birthdate: __________	Married:	○	○	○
Child: __________	Birthdate: __________	Married:	○	○	○
Child: __________	Birthdate: __________	Married:	○	○	○
Child: __________	Birthdate: __________	Married:	○	○	○

Are you currently providing for any adult children? ________________________

Any child with special health needs? ________________________

Do any of your children live outside Canada? ________________________

Additional notes or concerns: ____

____

____

____

____

____

____

____

____

____

Concerns and Objectives

	Yes	No	Uncertain
Do you have updated or current wills?	○	○	○

How old are your wills? ______________________

Location of your will? ______________________

	Yes	No	Uncertain
Have you established any trusts?	○	○	○
Are you the beneficiary of any trusts?	○	○	○
Do you have an enduring power of attorney?	○	○	○
Will you be receiving an inheritance?	○	○	○

If so, how much and to whom will the inheritance be left? ______________________

	Yes	No	Uncertain
Is estate preservation for your heirs important?	○	○	○
Do your RRSP/RRIFs/IRAs/401(k) have named beneficiaries?	○	○	○
Do your life insurance policies have named beneficiaries?	○	○	○
Do you have assets in any other country?	○	○	○
Do you own any U.S. stocks, bonds or real estate?	○	○	○

Additional notes or concerns: ____

Insurance Planning

	Yes	No	Uncertain
Do you own any life insurance?	○	○	○
Do you feel that you have enough life insurance?	○	○	○

	Yes	No
Would you like to maintain your family's standard of living in the event of your spouse's premature death?	○	○
Would you require domestic or child-care assistance raising your minor children?	○	○
Would you like to cover your children's education costs in the event of your premature death?	○	○
Do you want to continue saving for your retirement while you are raising a family?	○	○
Would you like to pay off any existing liabilities at your death?	○	○

What annual income requirement would your family need at your premature death? ______________________________

What would you estimate the annual cost of domestic or child-care help to be? ______________________________

Summary of Current Personal Insurance Policies

Company	Policy #	Issue Date	Premium	Cash Value	Death Benefit	Insured	Owner	Beneficiary	Type of Policy

For permanent insurance over 5 years old, when was the last time you requested a statement detailing all pertinent information, including cash surrender values? ________________

	Client	**Spouse**
How much group insurance do you have?	______________	______________

Business insurance details ____________________________________

____

Pledged as collateral security? ____________________________________

____

Additional notes or concerns: ____________________________________

____

____

____

____

____

____

____

____

____

Sources of Income

	Client	Spouse
Occupation	______	______
Employer	______	______
Employment Income (Before Tax)	______	______
Interest Income (Before Tax)	______	______
Investment Income (Before Tax)	______	______
Alimony Received (Before Tax)	______	______
Net Rental Income (Before Tax)	______	______
Corporate Pension Income (Before Tax)	______	______
Government Pension Income (Before Tax)	______	______
Other Sources of Income (Before Tax)	______	______

If receiving pensions, what percentage is available to the surviving spouse? ____________________

Are any pensions received adjusted for inflation, and if so by how much? ____________________

Additional notes or concerns: ____________________

____

____

____

____

____

Retirement Planning

At what age would you like to be financially independent/retired? ____________

If retired, at what age did you retire? ____________

What minimum annual income requirement will you need (after tax) ____________

	Yes	No
Do you plan to remain in Canada after you retire?	○	○

If not, which country will you move to or spend time in? ____________

	Yes	No
Do you qualify for full or partial CPP/QPP benefits?	○	○
Are you currently taking any distributions out of any U.S. Qualified Plans?	○	○

Additional notes or concerns: ____

____

____

____

____

____

____

____

____

____

Additional Information

	Yes	No
Do you own any farm property?	○	○
Are you eligible for the Small Business Capital Gains Exemption?	○	○
Do you have business partners other than your spouse?	○	○
Previously married?	○	○
Any assets held or invested offshore?	○	○
Do you have an estate planning lawyer that you are currently working with?	○	○

If so, name: ____________________ Phone number: ____________________

	Yes	No
Do you have an accountant that you are currently working with?	○	○

If so, name: ____________________ Phone number: ____________________

Additional notes or concerns: ____

____

____

____

____

____

____

____

____

____

____

Statement of Current Financial Position

Cash and Equivalents (Includes savings, chequing accounts and liquid proceeds and/or cash)

Description of Asset	Current Value —You	Current Value —Spouse	Current Value —Joint	Adjusted Cost Base
1.				
2.				
3.				
4.				
5.				
6.				

Non-Registered Assets (All taxable investment assets, including stocks, bonds, mutual funds, business values and investment real estate)

Description of Asset	Current Value —You	Current Value —Spouse	Current Value —Joint	Adjusted Cost Base
1.				
2.				
3.				
4.				
5.				
6.				
7.				
8.				
9.				
10.				
11.				
12.				

Registered and/or Qualified Plan Assets
(All RRSPs, RRIFs, IRAs, 401(k) plans and any corporate pension values available)

Description of Asset	Current Value —You	Current Value —Spouse	Current Value —Joint	Cost Amount
1.				
2.				
3.				
4.				
5.				
6.				
7.				
8.				

Real Estate (Includes value of personal residence and vacation residence only)

Description of Asset	Current Value —You	Current Value —Spouse	Current Value —Joint	Adjusted Cost Base
1. Personal residence				
2. Second home				
3. Vacation home				

Liabilities

Description Liability	Current Value—You	Current Value—Spouse	Current Value—Joint
1. Personal mortgage			
2. Second mortgage			
3. Investment loans			
4. Credit cards			
5. Personal credit lines			
6. Other:			
7. Other:			

Additional notes or concerns: ____

____

____

INDEX